"Garrett French has solidified his reputation as one of the few true, authoritative, innovative link builders in our industry. There are only a handful of marketers who have mastered and cultivated the craft of link building. Garrett is certainly one of them."

—Russ Jones, Principal Search Scientist, Moz

"Link building has always been challenging. Prior to the days of Google's Penguin algorithm, SEOs recognized that every kind of link a site could get had the potential to help improve rankings. This lead to many of us building loads of low quality links at scale. In many cases, getting a large quantity of links, even low quality ones, could really help!

When Penguin arrived in 2012, everything changed. Links are still important, but low-quality links now have the potential to actually hurt a site's rankings.

Google experimented with taking links out of the equation, but admitted that their results were much better when links were factored in. Why? Because a link is a recommendation for your website. And sites with lots of recommendations are often the best sites.

Our goal as link builders now should be to figure out what we can do to truly get people recommending our website, our business, our authors, and our content. In this book, Garrett gives us many excellent tactics to help us do just that.

Not that many years ago, it was super easy to build links that worked to improve rankings. Today, it takes skill, smart thinking, and great execution. If you want to get better at learning how to get other people to want to link to your website, read this book."

—Dr. Marie Haynes, owner of Marie Haynes Consulting Inc.

"This is the most exhaustive, detailed, and up-to-date resource on link building I have ever seen. It is packed with modern techniques, timeless principles and in-depth tool tutorials on how to actually achieve better link building results. It's not black hat. It's not snake oil. It's not made up theory—it's experience-backed knowledge by real professionals.

Whether you're an advanced link builder, or just getting started—this book will be your secret weapon for attaining real SEO success!"

—Dan Shure, owner of Evolving SEO

"This book packs a 40+year-link-building-experience punch! Strokes of genius emanate from deceivingly simple explanations and effortless workflows. Only Eric Ward and Garrett French could make the complicated world of link building look so crystal clear and manageable. This powerful edition delivers everything you need to be a successful link builder and leaves you wondering, "Wow! Why haven't I thought of that?!" over and over again."

—BRITNEY MULLER, SENIOR SEO SCIENTIST, MOZ

"Eric Ward and Garrett French have put together a solid, easy-to-read link-building primer. The book provides simple explanations and straightforward advice when it comes to building links; chapters are well outlined and flow from point to point. If you are new to link building, this book is a great resource for anyone looking for tools, tactics, and case studies to learn from."

—DEBRA MASTALER, PRESIDENT OF ALLIANCE-LINK.COM

"Eric Ward has been a thought leader in how to build links the right way since before there even was a right way. His extensive relationship-building background, mixed with challenging projects, has given him insights and methodologies that are advanced and increasingly necessary in today's internet marketing world. He has brought his many years of hard-fought experience to the pages of this book, and I heartily recommend it to anyone seeking to grow their skills."

—BRUCE CLAY, CEO OF INTERNATIONAL SEO FIRM BRUCECLAY.COM, AND AUTHOR OF
SEARCH ENGINE OPTIMIZATION ALL-IN-ONE FOR DUMMIES

"Eric Ward pioneered the practice of link building as a marketing channel and continues to be among the thought leaders of the field. His expertise and hands-on experience are virtually unmatched, and I'd recommend his book to anyone who uses links to help grow their business."

—RAND FISHKIN, FORMER CEO OF MOZ.COM

"Those who want link building done right by the best in the business flock to Eric Ward and count themselves lucky that the maestro isn't booked into the next millennium."

—JIM STERNE, TARGETING.COM, FOUNDER OF THE EMETRICS MARKETING OPTIMIZATION SUMMIT
AND FOUNDING PRESIDENT AND CURRENT CHAIRMAN OF THE DIGITAL
ANALYTICS ASSOCIATION

"An SEO classic! This link-building book by far provides the very best advice, stories, and actionable white-hat link-building tips. This is the best link-building book I have ever read!"

—Nick Stamoulis, Founder of SEO Firm BrickMarketing.com

"For anyone who's been 'hit' by Panda, Penguin, or any other algorithmic update by Google, this book is a must-read. It's time to quit looking over your shoulder and start building links that will stand the test of time. Eric has been one of the foremost thought leaders on link building since before links became a dominant ranking factor, so there's no one better to train you on seeking out and acquiring the high-quality links that will bring you visibility and mindshare that go far beyond search engine results.

—David Mihm, DavidMihm.com, Co-Founder of GetListed.org

"Eric Ward is the old school mac daddy link master."

—Lee Odden, CEO of TopRank Online Marketing,
Publisher of toprankblog.com

"Eric's skill at website promotion is legendary. We've been using his services since 1995 and on more than one occasion had to work closely with our hosting service to keep our servers up under the high traffic loads that resulted from Eric's publicity!"

—Amy Strycula, Founder of CatsPlay.com

"Eric Ward has been building links and educating people on how to do it the right way since before even search engines decided links were important. Read and learn!"

—Danny Sullivan, Founder and Editor-in-Chief of SearchEngineLand.com

"Eric Ward is hands-down the smartest thinker in the space when it comes to link building. I guarantee this book will open up any mental blocks you've had about where to get started and set you on a path to becoming a link magnet."

—Mike Grehan, Publisher of Search Engine Watch and ClickZ.com,
Producer SES International, and SEMPO Board of Directors

"If you're in SEO and take your job seriously, you know Eric and Garrett. When Eric and Garrett talk about link building, you listen. The only issue when they talk is—there's too much genius to write it all down. So, when *they* do the writing down for you, you buy the book and read it. Twice. At least. You won't regret it."

—Joost de Valk, Founder and CEO of Yoast.com

"Eric is the undisputed master of quality link building. We've worked together for years and he has frequently surprised me with new insights and little-known, and easily executed, strategies to build our customers' backlink portfolios."

—Richard Stokes, CEO of AdGooroo.com and author of *Mastering Search Advertising—How the Top 3% of Search Advertisers Dominate Google AdWords* and *Ultimate Guide to Pay-Per-Click Advertising*

Entrepreneur MAGAZINE'S

ULTIMATE
GUIDE TO
LINK
BUILDING

Second Edition

- Generate competition-proof links
- Transform SEO keywords into authority content ideas
- Find and organize thousands of new outreach opportunities

GARRETT FRENCH & ERIC WARD

Entrepreneur Press®

Entrepreneur Press, Publisher
Cover Design: Andrew Welyczko
Production and Composition: Eliot House Productions

This publication is designed to provide accurate and authoritative information in regard to the
subject matter covered. It is sold with the understanding that the publisher is not engaged in
rendering legal, accounting, or other professional services. If legal advice or other expert assistance is
required, the services of a competent professional person should be sought.

Library of Congress Cataloging-in-Publication Data
 Names: French, Garrett, author. | Ward, Eric. Ultimate guide to link building.
 Title: Ultimate guide to link building : how to build website authority, increase traffic and search
  ranking with backlinks / by Garrett French.
 Description: Second edition. | Irvine, California : Entrepreneur Press, 2020. | Series: Entrepreneur
  magazine's ultimate | Previous edition by Eric Ward and Garrett French. | Summary: "In
  this new edition of the Ultimate Guide to Link Building, link building and online marketing
  expert Garrett French shows you, step by step, how to employ a link-building campaign that
  attracts quality links, drives more traffic to your website, and earns you more sales"-- Provided
  by publisher.
 Identifiers: LCCN 2019032498 (print) | LCCN 2019032499 (ebook) | ISBN 978-1-59918-648-1
  (paperback) | ISBN 978-1-61308-409-0 (ebook)
 Subjects: LCSH: Web sites--Design. | Web site development. | Web sites--Ratings and rankings.
 Classification: LCC TK5105.888 .W3615 2020 (print) | LCC TK5105.888 (ebook) |
  DDC 006.7--dc23
 LC record available at https://lccn.loc.gov/2019032498
 LC ebook record available at https://lccn.loc.gov/2019032499

Printed in the United States of America

24 23 22 21 20   10 9 8 7 6 5 4 3 2 1

Contents

Remembering Eric Ward

I miss Eric Ward.

He died on October 16, 2017, and I still think of things to tell him, ask him, or just exclaim indignantly about. (We "old school" link builders love to get up in arms over just about everything.)

Talking with Eric was fun. He'd spring forth actionable ideas—sometimes unrelated to links at all—smashing unexpected ideas together from some sea of creativity. I'd drop my jaw, slap my forehead, and could not believe I nor anyone else had never thought of that before.

I think this ability came partly from his 20-plus years of pioneering the very practice of link building for customers like Disney and Amazon. That and he didn't use a ton of tools for guidance. He relied on ingenuity to find his way forward. Within this book, I hope you'll find some of that spark and grit—in his chapters, especially—and I hope I've channeled some of it as well.

If you have a moment and would like a sense of his fluid, holistic approach to link strategy development, please search YouTube for "Live Link Building Speed Consultations with Eric Ward & Garrett French." You could also type in this URL: https://www.youtube.com/watch?v=7FtLhX95KgY. I played that video while writing this to try and channel that excitement of his as he articulated a great idea and took a notion, then added a layer or two until it became a fully formed, actionable campaign concept.

I'm not the only one who appreciated Eric's abilities, though. I'd like to leave you with the words of an early customer whose website Eric helped launch when it was first published to the World Wide Web:

"Thanks for the great work on our launch, Eric. Your efforts and report were excellent."

—Jeff Bezos, Founder, Amazon.com

Thank you, Eric. I miss you.

—Garrett French

Acknowledgments

ERIC WARD

Thank you to my wife, Melissa, for putting up with the long hours it took to get my company off the ground in the early '90s, for waking me up at 3 A.M. when I'd fallen asleep at the keyboard in the middle of a link-building campaign, and for giving me three beautiful kids along the way. My thanks also to Mom and Dad, who are surprised I have written a book because there was scant evidence in my academic history to suggest this was a possibility. I always *was* a late bloomer. A huge thanks goes to Garrett French, my co-author, because without him, you would not be reading this right now. And finally, thanks to Rich Stokes at AdGooroo, who helped me believe I could do it.

GARRETT FRENCH

First and foremost, I must thank my wife. When I called her years ago from the office parking lot to tell her I'd been laid off, she responded: "Awesome!" She stood by me with zero doubt in the entrepreneurial years that have followed and is the world's best partner and mother.

Rich Ord, founder of iEntry, was my first business mentor. He gave me the keys to an email list of 400,000 ebusiness owners in 2001. That's where I learned about audience, content, and market conversations.

J. Donald Robinson, my grandfather, was a computer salesman back when they were mechanical. His voice lights up when we talk business and sales, and his belief in me always leaves me rejuvenated.

My industry inspirations are too many to name, but I'll give it a quick shot: Eric Ward, of course, Debra Mastaler, Wil Reynolds, Darren Shaw, Russ Jones, Andy Beal, Shari Thurow, Ammon Johns, Gianluca Fiorelli, Greg Shuey, Adam Henige, Eric Covino, Bill Slawski, Don Rhoades, Tony Spencer, Jeremy Bencken, Paul May, Paddy Moogan, Ross Hudgens, Lyndon Antcliff, Hugo Guzman, Terry Van Horne, Shaun Anderson, Patrick Gavin, Dan Thies, Tom Demers, Melanie Nathan, Ken McGaffin, Ken Lyons, Brian Chappell, Julie Joyce, Brian Gilley, and last but definitely not least, David Harry. I would like to thank Jasmine George for assisting with the second publication of this book.

Foreword

by Mike Grehan, CMO and Managing Director of Acronym

For many, it's hard to imagine a time when Google didn't exist on the web—a time before we could simply type a few words into a box on a web page and magically be presented with all manner of content related to those keywords. Essentially, that's how most websites are found on the burgeoning World Wide Web, which continues to grow exponentially each and every day.

I launched my first online business in 1995, well before Google changed the web. My background is in media and marketing. I spent ten years in broadcast media followed by ten years in marketing on both the agency side and the client side. By 1995, I'd been aware of the web for some years and certainly recognized the potential from a commercial point of view. My partner in the business knew how to code HTML and build websites, most of which consisted of a few pages of text, a couple of jpg images, and a contact form. The more websites we built, the better we got at it. But there was one vital, missing component to each of those sites, which rapidly became apparent to our customers: traffic.

Building websites wasn't the hard part of the job. Trying to figure out how to get visitors to them was. There's this famous quote, something along the lines of, "If you build it, they will come." It gets attributed to everybody from astronauts to movie characters. Regardless, whoever said that was not a web developer or an online marketer. Because build we did, and come they didn't.

That same year, 1995, a guy by the name of Jeff Bezos had this remarkably dumb idea (I thought at the time) of launching a website to sell books. Books of all things. Jeez, Jeff, there's a bookstore on every corner in the city. I can pop in, buy one, and have the first chapter finished by the end of my lunch break. And you want me to give you my credit card details online and then wait up to five days before it hits my mailbox? But more to the point, even if buying a book online was a good idea, how would Bezos get traffic? Like I say, back then, we all knew what the hard part was.

Enter Eric Ward.

Eric Ward started operating a website-awareness-building service in 1994. He went on to publish a must-read linking strategies newsletter called *LinkMoses Private* (ericward. com/lmp), but back then one of his first tasks was to contact Jerry Yang (who at the time was a graduate student at Stanford and co-founder of Yahoo!) to point out that the directory didn't have a section for web promotion. And that's what Eric did via his newly formed NetPOST and URLwire services. This was not a press release distribution service that just randomly peppered the web with the usual digital dross. This was a private email list Eric ran, made up of subscribers who were genuinely interested in hearing about new stuff on the web (a kind of early-day alerts service). And what happened when he announced a new website? It attracted links!

How could Jeff Bezos resist?

Now, I'm not going to suggest for a second that Eric Ward is responsible for the success of Amazon in becoming the world's largest online retailer (although I will personally admit to being one of the world's largest nitwits for thinking it was a dumb idea in the first place). However, I will absolutely give credit to Eric Ward for being the father of what we now know as link-building services.

Soon, his sleeves were rolled up, and he became master of the art of convincing people to link to Amazon and drive traffic. But not just Amazon, to the new customers he started acquiring on almost a daily basis. Imagine: This is a guy, in web-marketing terms, performing something akin to CPR. However, Eric wasn't the only guy with the power of links on his mind. By 1998, Larry Page, co-founder of Google, had developed an algorithm largely based on social network analysis and network theory. Basically, Google was able to analyze the complex graph structure of the web and rank documents according to relativity based on the links that pointed to them.

It was the gold rush all over again. But this time the term for gold was *backlink*!

Once the online marketing community discovered the power of links in Google's ranking algorithm, the race to the top was on. A top-ten listing at Google for a competitive keyword or phrase can drive hundreds, even thousands of visitors (or more) to any given website.

The thing is, not all links are equal. Some are more equal than others. And some are infinitely more equal. Search engines apart, one link can send more traffic than another. You'll always have good and bad links. However, inside the Google algorithm, the quality of links vastly outweighs the quantity. And if you try to artificially inflate your "link popularity"—what Google giveth, Google can also, and surely does, taketh away! I coined the term "black hat, white hat" sometime around 2002. It was based on something I noticed in cowboy movies when I was a kid. The good cowboys all wore white hats, and the bad guys wore black. I used it as an analogy for those online marketers who stuck to Google's guidelines (particularly around linking practices) and those who didn't.

The industry has become fixated on getting links, but by any means possible. And that can be a very dangerous thing. Link building has now become a combination of understanding hugely complex ranking algorithms while applying the gentle art of persuasion.

Eric Ward and I knew each other for a very long time. We've shared the stage at many conferences discussing both the art and the science of developing a long-term, quality link-building strategy. And we both agreed that if you frame this as just "getting links," then you'll probably fail in your efforts to dominate the search engine results pages (SERPs). Because the truth is, quality links are usually the byproduct of a good online marketing plan.

If you're a website owner, then no doubt your inbox has already been spammed with numerous emails from people who, as Eric would put it, offer to "link to your crap if you'll link to mine." Most likely you've had offers from foreign shores from companies offering to get you x number of links each week for $x per link. It's likely that you've even dared to venture to reply to one of these emails to see how it works. But before you even seriously consider that and before you read the rare wisdom contained in this book, I want you to do one thing. I want you to go to your own website right now, take a pen and a piece of paper, and write down ten good reasons why you should link to your own website.

Now, if you find yourself scratching your head after four or five, ask yourself this question: If I can't think of ten good reasons to link to my website, what makes me think other people would?

Seriously, I've asked everyone from owners/managers of small businesses to CMOs of major international corporations the same question and seen the same head-scratching. It's hard to say the word *search* without adding the word *social* these days. Social media sites, such as Facebook, LinkedIn, and Twitter generate links by the millions as people connect, communicate, and share. The web has changed from a web of things to a web of people. And it's all about connections, about the way we're all linked together by one thing or another.

From content development and integrated marketing techniques to purely tactical link bait, you're about to learn directly from one of the masters of online marketing. In this book, the "Moses" of link building (as Eric is fondly known in the industry) will teach you how to wisely:

- Carry out a link audit and competitor analysis
- Develop a structured, long-term link-building strategy
- Identify and approach quality, top-ranking websites with a value proposition
- Differentiate links for traffic vs. links for ranking
- Recommend the tools of the trade for ethical link-building practices
- Keep on the right side of search engine guidelines

Eric Ward was the smartest thinker in the space when it comes to link building. I guarantee this book will open up any mental blocks you've had about where to get started and set you on a path to becoming a link magnet.

Introduction

by Ken McGaffin, Head of Marketing at Majestic

I've worked with Garrett French on almost a weekly basis for many years. As you can imagine, we spend a lot of time talking about link building; and no matter what the finer points of the discussion, or what obscure aspect of the art we're talking about, I can be pretty sure that at some point Garrett will say something like, "I wonder if there's a tool to do that?" or "Hey, that would make a pretty good tool," or "How could we do that at scale?"

You see, Garrett French loves link-building tools.

He loves using them; he loves talking about them, and he loves creating them—and he has created some gems in his time.

That's good news for anyone who wants to learn about link building.

Why? Because Garrett's passion for creating tools is really a passion for solving link-building problems. And to create tools that solve link-building problems, you need to have three attributes:

1. You've got to have a deep knowledge of all the processes of link building. Not just the big picture, but the nitty-gritty details of what actually needs to be done.
2. You've got to have the creative ability to take those processes and distill them into logical steps that make things easy for other people to understand and implement.

3. You've got to know how to do it all at scale—in a way that lets agencies and individuals zip through complex processes and say, "Well, that was easy, wasn't it?"

Garrett has all three essential attributes in spades. He's one of the most practical people I know working in this space: He talks and writes about link building with great passion, with deep insight, and with a wonderful ability to communicate.

That's why I'm so excited by this collaboration with link-building legend Eric Ward. Both these guys have written stuff that makes me stop what I'm doing, make myself a brew of strong coffee, and sit down for a good read. I can't imagine a better pairing.

—Ken McGaffin

Chapter 1

A Brief Introduction to Search, Links, and Link Building

"A link is a connection from one web resource to another." This quote from the World Wide Web Consortium (W3C) makes web links sound so simple. And in some ways they are, or at least they were intended to be. But the web as a whole is huge and complex, made up of trillions of individual pages, files, and other content, while at its core the web is simple and made up of only two things: content and links.

Lots of links.

More links than any one person or search engine can count. Those links between pages and sites are the primary way web users navigate from one place to another online. A simple mouse click takes you from one site to another site, or from a search result to a specific page, or to a video, or a picture, or a song.

If you don't have a website, you probably haven't given much thought to links. But if you do have a website, be it a small blog or a huge corporate presence, then links take on a whole new meaning. In fact, links on the web will help determine the level of success your site will have on the web. In addition to the "humans" clicking on those links, every major "bot" (search engine) uses some form of link analysis when determining search results.

The purpose of this book is to simplify the complex online world of web links and help website owners create and execute link-building campaigns that attract links, increase traffic, and improve search rank.

A BRIEF HISTORY OF LINKS AND SEARCH ENGINES

As much as we take the web for granted today, it was only 28 years ago that the very first website was created. No other websites linked to it because there were no other websites.

And there were no search engines to use to find it.

The world's first website and web server, http://Info.cern.ch, launched on August 6, 1991, by the web's creator, Tim Berners-Lee, an engineer, computer scientist, and MIT professor. View the first website in Figure 1–1.

FIGURE 1–1. Info.cern.ch: The World's First-Ever Website

The site still exists today, and there are more than a half-million other websites that now link to it. A half-million links. That sounds like a lot of links, doesn't it?

Search engines like Google also exist today (see Figure 1–2 on, page 3). Hundreds of millions of sites link to Google, and billions of searches are performed there every day. Having your site appear high in a search engine's natural search results can be very profitable for most businesses. However, very few people outside of Google and Bing

FIGURE 1–2. Google's Search Box

really understand how search engines compile results, and even fewer understand how to affect those results (i.e., make a site rank higher).

There are many factors involved, and some of the most important are links from other sites to yours. The web of today is comprised of trillions of links between sites. Somehow Google and other search engines analyze these links and draw conclusions about your site based on the links that point to it.

Like a fingerprint, your links uniquely tell Google about your site. Who links to you and how they link to you is now one of the single most important factors that all search engines rely on when ranking results.

It didn't start out that way. The web's first search engine, called Wandex (see Figure 1–3), and the engines that followed (most of which are gone now), didn't analyze links at all. They only analyzed your website, the assumption being that your website would be the most accurate way to determine what your website was about.

As logical as that sounds, it didn't take long for web marketers to figure out how search engines worked and could be manipulated, and the game was on.

As the years went by, search results became less and less accurate, with those most adept at manipulating the results being the big winners, while the searcher often ended up on a page that was not very helpful.

FIGURE 1–3. The Web's First Search Engine, Called Wandex

ENTER GOOGLE . . .

Then Google came along with the idea of using the very fabric of the web itself, links between sites, as a method for determining which web pages were most relevant for any given search.

In other words, the web would collectively determine where a site should rank, based on which sites attracted links. Think of a link as a vote. And while on the web some votes matter more than others and some can actually *hurt* your search rank, it's the best analogy to use to introduce you to the concept of link building.

Put simply, you can directly impact your search rankings if you understand how and why links matter and what you have to do in order to earn them. It isn't about quantity; it's about quality. A few links from the right places are better than a ton of links from sites with no value.

Link building is both art and science. There are many ways to build links. There's what some people call the "white hat" approach, where you have a website devoted to a particular topic, and you look for and contact people who care about that topic. You let them know about your site in hopes that they'll link to your site from their site. This is a slow and methodical process, and it can produce amazing results if done correctly.

But there are other approaches, like sending a few million email messages to a list of people you don't know, with links in your email telling them about your site. This is commonly referred to as "spam."

The approach you choose for building links should be based on the content of your site, not spam. Automated link building does not result in your site earning quality links that will help your search rank.

For example, if you have an ecommerce site with generic products that can be purchased anywhere, why would anybody link to that site? There are 500 other sites where someone could buy the same product. For instance, take a look at the results for a search on "golf clubs" in Figure 1–4.

FIGURE 1–4. 3.3 Billion Results for a Google Search on the Phrase "Golf Clubs"

Why would another site link to your site instead of any of those other 500? The truth is, in this scenario, you'll have a hard time building links without paying for them. On the other hand, the more freely you create and provide unique content about subjects that you have some passion for, the more freely you will find your site able to attract and earn links. It's not as complicated as you think, really. My colleagues have often heard me say, "Every site has its own linking potential depending on its subject matter, depth of content, and intended audience."

What we mean by this is the best target sites for your site to pursue and earn links from are going to be different from those for another site. Here's a great example: If you have a site that sells archery equipment and that also has excellent archery-related content, there's a target site you would want to have a link from (see Figure 1–5). Prepare to be surprised.

Why is that site so valuable? Think of that site's intent, purpose, and author credibility. It's legitimate and trustworthy, and you can't get a link from this site just because you want one. You have to *earn* it. You have to have archery-related content of merit. You have to find the owner/author of the site, reach out to them in the proper way, and recognize that not every site will be given a link, which is one additional reason the engines trust that site. Content of merit earns these types of links.

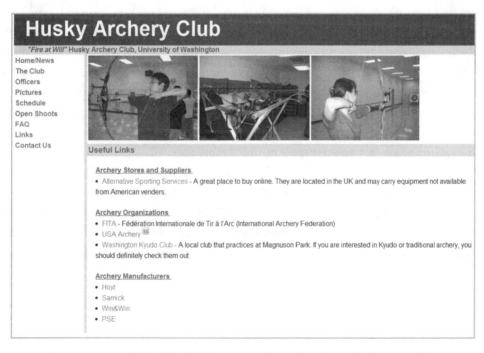

FIGURE 1–5. A Valuable Link for an Archery Products Online Retailer

FIGURE 1–6. Sometimes Link Building is Knowing When NOT to Get the Link

Now take a look at the site in Figure 1–6. Which of the two sites do you feel was created by a group with a singular interest and passion for archery? The answer is obvious when you look at a pair of sites about a very specific topic, like those featured in Figures 1–5 and 1–6, on pages 5 and 6, respectively. Unfortunately, the overwhelming majority of SEO and link-building services you can buy today are not going to help you, could hurt you (with penalties), and at best will be ignored as if they do not exist. You will have spent money for nothing.

While outright penalties and banning from the engines are rare and can be corrected over time, this is a slippery slope to be standing on while building links. It's also true that you often cannot control who links to you, so the engines must be cautious about levying a penalty until they have enough evidence. But here's a way you might want to think about it. Google employs hundreds of computer scientists and librarians, all of whom are a lot smarter than most of us are. They work every day to improve Google's ability to identify link spam, paid links, link networks, and other linking schemes. If we can spot link spam, it's only a matter of time before they will. Do you want to base your linking strategy on trying to fool a few hundred computer science Ph.D.s who are being paid to produce the most accurate search results possible?

In the next chapter, we explore how to identify and ultimately create content that makes your target audiences' lives easier (we call that "high-utility content"). Because being useful, helpful, timely, and insightful is the essence of link-worthiness.

Chapter 2

What Makes a Website Link-Worthy?

So what is the motivation for one website owner to link to another website?

The fundamental principle of the web is to allow any document to link to and to be linked from any other document. This is how Sir Tim Berners-Lee intended it when he first proposed the hypertext protocol in 1989 as a way to help researchers interlink related documents from computers all over the world.

It's interesting that nearly every commercially related web development since its founding has been in some way related to the link (that is, an attempt to find new ways for one site to be linked to another). Banner ads are, at their core, just a link from one site to another. So are text ads, whether on websites, in newsletters, or in email messages. And like buttons, badges, icons, etc., are all just another form of links. A pay-per-click (PPC) listing, a tweeted URL, or a list of search results are nothing more than links. Even that cool widget you created is a link. Anything to be clicked on that shuttles people from one place to another while online constitutes a link. In this chapter, we will discuss links and what contributes to making a website link-worthy.

USEFUL CONTENT EARNS LINKS

The development of all forms and fashion of linking types has never improved on the original, and no amount of cleverness will ever change one universal truth: The less useful your content, the less likely you are to ever receive a link to it.

If we think of the word "useful" as a continuum, then the most useful sites are those that provide rich quality content on a specific subject on which the editor or provider is an authority. Think of the U.S. Government's National Cancer Institute (what was once known as CancerNet). Located at www.cancer.gov, the site is the ultimate example of content on the right side of the continuum—tens of thousands of pages on every facet of cancer, all free, all generated by experts in the field. See Figure 2–1.

In fact, with no online marketing department, the National Cancer Institute's website has tens of thousands of links pointing to it from other sites around the world.

FIGURE 2–1. National Cancer Institute's Homepage

It's one of my standard sermons: Useful content gets linked. When CancerNet hired me for some link analysis and strategy, there wasn't a whole lot for me to do. It took me less than a month to augment and improve what was already in place—a great collection of inbound links. My impact was minimal, if any.

But the reality is we can't all be the National Cancer Institute. Most sites simply do not have the kind of content that engenders tens of thousands of links. So what do you do? What if you are simply trying to sell a few widgets and don't have any reference to quality content? If your site lands on the left side of the useful continuum, you accept that you are not going to get many links. And those links you do get, you will probably have to pay for. And those links you pay for are not likely to help your rankings and might even hurt them.

If you don't want to accept this reality and truly want to earn links to your site, you have one (and only one) other option: Make it link-worthy.

WHAT IS A LINK-WORTHY SITE?

Let's imagine you have an online magic store that caters to professional and amateur magicians. On your site, you sell tricks, supplies, hats, capes, and wands—even the saw-the-person-in-half gag.

If your content were nothing more than an online store, why would anyone link to it? You might get a few links on any magic-site web guides and link lists. But then what? If you are an online store with nothing but products as your content, then you *must* look to associate/affiliate programs as a means of generating links. Basically, you're paying for them. But maybe there is something more you can do, if you are willing to roll up your sleeves.

What if, along with your products, you create a searchable database of information on magic? What if you had complete biographies of more than 700 magicians? What if you had a section devoted to magical world records, or a glossary of magical terms, or a directory of magicians on the internet?

This would then be an excellent example of how a store site can add rich, relevant content, value, interest, and community to its website, as well as sell merchandise. Just about any writer who writes about magic and/or reviews websites would write about this site, and any magic fan with a website and a curated list of handpicked links would be likely to link to it.

The above is not just a wide-eyed, hypothetical example. It exists at http://www.MagicTricks.com (featured in Figure 2–2, on page 10).

I know from experience that it's difficult to find high-trust online venues and curator/site reviewers willing to link to sales sites. The more a site offers deep

FIGURE 2–2. Ecommerce Site with Link-Worthy Content

information on a certain subject in the form of databases, community, guides, forums, reviews, etc., the more likely editors or curators will feature it in their own content. Whether it's a business or consumer site, the more content-rich the site is, the better, especially if the site's mission is sales. A site designed to sell a product is far different from a true reference site with hundreds and hundreds of pages of free information on a particular subject.

The National Cancer Institute and MagicTricks.com could not be more different from each other, yet they do have one incredibly important thing in common: Both have topic-specific content written by passionate experts.

The best analogy I can think of to explain a sales-focused website is a public library. A library is, first and foremost, about content, although it does sell things. You can buy copies of books, order maps, buy online database search time, or rent study offices or PCs. Some libraries even have video-rental services and snack shops or restaurants.

Money definitely changes hands at a library. But nobody would confuse this commerce with a library's true mission: being content curators and helping patrons find that content. In like manner, a website also needs to be a library of information on whatever its focus might be. Add great content to your product site.

Why bother? Because useful content gets linked. Products don't. (Well, they *can*; it just requires adding useful content to them. See Chapter 18 on building links to sales.)

In the next chapter, we will explore link building campaign design. From that "campaign design" perspective, we're investigating all the stakeholders in your effort to earn links—not just your SEO team. This is a valuable chapter, even if you're building links to your own personal website projects. Knowing the "spheres" you're working with can turn up surprising ideas and directions.

Chapter 3

Link-Building Campaign Design

Quite often, link builders working outside of your organization will design campaigns based on their personal or agency strengths, tools, and processes. When the campaign ends, the links stop.

For example, in our work with clients, which typically involves expert engagement (often bloggers or other publishing experts in a space), much of the value we create is in the relationships established, not to mention the expert content we create. When we stop engaging the experts, the relationships cool off and the link momentum slows down. This is because our clients have typically not developed the infrastructure and processes to keep developing these relationships (this book is for them). For link-building agencies specializing in link buys or rentals, the decline in momentum can be even more drastic.

Designing an effective, sustainable link-building campaign (or series of campaigns) requires a delicate balance and a precise understanding of an organization's strengths and weaknesses, as well as carefully described and easy-to-measure goals. This chapter will help you to more effectively design and measure your next link-building campaign. At the very least, it will get you thinking a bit more broadly about link building!

PLANNING CAMPAIGN SCOPE: SIX FACTORS THAT IMPACT CAMPAIGN DESIGN

There are six broad factors we've discovered that impact a link-building campaign's scope. Ideally, a link builder in the campaign design phase has a suitable amount of time to think about and consider all these factors. In doing so, they will probably discover a few more factors unique to their organization's situation. The more factors you can take into consideration and design for, the more unique and effective your campaign will be.

Factor 1: What's Working Well for You Already?

We like to start client discussions with a question about what's working well already—and not just in link building! For example, we may ask how our clients currently generate their leads. Recently, it turned out that one of our clients had an email list of 10,000 subscribers that they'd built up a great relationship with over the course of the past 10 to 15 years! They estimated that at least 10 percent of their list comprised active web content publishers, which made this list the perfect place to begin designing a campaign.

On the more link-oriented side, we ran through some questions with a prospect recently to discover their linkable assets. They didn't have time or resources to create content, which is our organization's linkable asset strength. When we asked what had been working, they mentioned that they had products that they could give away for nonprofits and bloggers to use as prizes in raffles and other types of contests. This understanding then informed the link opportunities we discovered for them in that we were able to systematically discover massive numbers of prequalified prospects.

We encourage you to think about what's working well already and to keep that in mind throughout the discussion in this book. Supporting and growing from what works can be far easier and more economical than trying to create something entirely new that does not stem from currently existing strengths.

Factor 2: Your Business and Marketing Goals

Specific business and marketing goals are often missing in link-building campaign design, especially when a campaign is designed in a vacuum without input from other departments.

Because link building has the capacity to impact goals far beyond your SERP (search engine results page) rankings, we highly recommend that link builders understand and support the company's specific business and marketing goals in the campaign design phase. Not only will this ensure the link builders have a continued role in the organization, but by solving the problem of "how can link building support x," they will uncover a solution that may be unique in the market. The link-building goals section, starting on page 209, demonstrates some things link building can impact, but it's far more important to start with your organization's goals in mind.

Factor 3: Your Linkable Assets

What about your organization is linkable? This can include in-house "social media celebrities," your organization's brand, your organization's story, your free tools or widgets, your unique and helpful content, your available creative talent, actual budget and more. Further, consider that your industry's definition of "linkable" can and will differ from those of other industries. If all your competitors have free web tools, then this is no longer a strong differentiator and may not incite interest and links.

See Chapter 5 for an overview of linkable assets, from discovering them on your site and within your organization to identifying what your competitors and industry publishers have done to attract links. In Figure 3–1, the illustration demonstrates an effective example of linkable content.

Factor 4: Link Opportunities in Your Space

The link opportunities that exist from market to market can be quite different. For example, if you're targeting a consumer market, it could be that work-at-home-dad bloggers are a key segment for you. But if you sell specialty bulldozer parts, then engaging the daddy bloggers might not make as much sense.

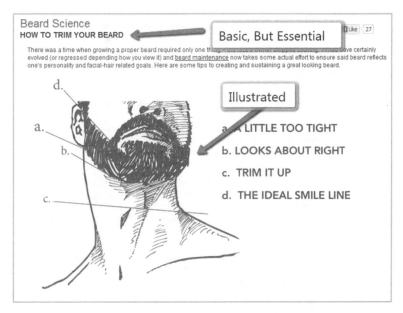

FIGURE 3–1. Illustrations Help Content Become More "Linkable"

Your market—in particular, the publishers catering to your market that you want to earn links from—determines the scope and type of opportunities available to you. Remember to always look for list results. See an example of list results in Figure 3–2. They will save you hours of searching. Further, the presence of lists indicates a robust publishing niche.

Factor 5: Departments Requiring Your Input and Influence within the Organization

As a link building agency, we find ourselves working primarily with the search engine optimization (SEO) department within an organization. Our methods typically involve content creation and industry expert engagement. This sometimes means we have to get approval from departments like PR, content strategy, social media, marketing, even the CEO before the campaign can really get rolling.

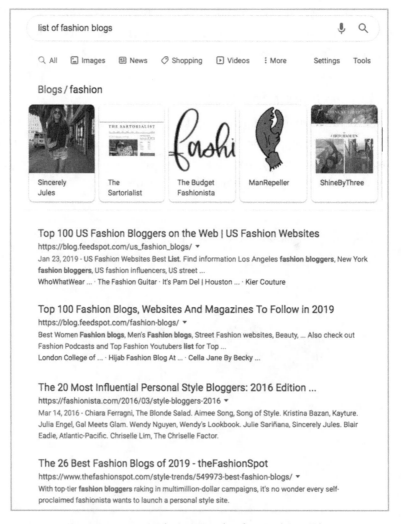

FIGURE 3–2. Typical List Results for Fashion Blogs

We typically try to identify the department that our contact is most embedded within, the department in which they have the most influence, and then we work to keep the campaign within their authority so that we can have the fastest impact. The more departments requiring input, the more work the link builder will have to do in mediating cross-departmental concerns.

However, for sustainable, ongoing link-building campaigns (and often these may *not* be called link-building campaigns internally), you will need to work the political scene within your organization and be constantly on the lookout for ways to "link-enhance" what others are already doing.

Factor 6: Your Available Resources

At the end of the day, your link-building campaign will come down to the amount of time and money you can put into it. Knowing how much time you can spend yourself, and how much work you can ask for or require of others, can help you to define the entire scope of the project. Often—and rightfully so—your available resources hinge on your abilities as a link builder, as well as your abilities in effectively communicating probable and actual returns on investment. In Chapter 4, we will look at some probable areas of link building's return.

HIRE (OR BE) A LINK STRATEGIST

If you're creating a team, the link-building campaign design phase is ideally run by what we call a "link strategist." If you're *not* building a team, you can comfortably skip this portion, though solo practitioners will ideally still have a design and strategy phase.

Link strategists love research, process, and project management. They can explore the web for hours in a fun, yet structured, way and return with a defined campaign mission, a distinct process, and a list of action tasks. Link strategists like to measure their successes (and failures), and they prefer quantitative metrics because they're scientists at heart (the mad kind). They're not afraid to try new tactics, but they're equally comfortable with scrapping an idea that doesn't work.

Each team and project will be different, but the practices and thinking outlined below can help prepare any beginner link strategist for their first link-building campaign.

1. Understand Link-Publisher Types and How to Serve Them

When we're talking about content designed for earning links, there are two distinct publisher types, each with different needs. Who will be doing the linking itself?

■ *News, blog, and community publishers.* They cover developments of potential interest to your target customers. Often, but not always, these are "in-funnel." That is, they are directly related to your marketing efforts.

■ *Links and resource page publishers.* These are people who passionately care about a topic and curate a page (or website) dedicated to sharing helpful information. Often, but not always, these are "out-of-funnel," meaning that they may not be directly speaking to audiences you're selling to.

2. Understand "Linker-Valued Audiences"

Here's the part that perhaps 99 percent of SEO strategists and at least 50 percent of active link builders miss entirely. Most believe that "linkable content" has concrete attributes, such as an ideal word count or format type (e.g., an infographic or guest post). To some extent, it does, but genuinely linkable content serves an audience that the target publisher (the linker, an actual person . . .) cares about.

Linkable content serves this linker-valued audience by catering to its distinct needs and afflictions. The linker is valuable from an SEO perspective because they serve this particular audience so concertedly (and has the link authority to prove it).

So now you know a fact that separates you from 99 percent of SEO strategists out there: You're not designing content or campaigns for the potential linkers. You're designing content for the audiences those linkers serve.

Please note that these audiences can be different from your target customers' personas. Here are a few examples of these linker-valued audiences that we're aware of and serve in our agency:

■ Senior citizens
■ People in the education space (teachers, homeschoolers)
■ People who need legal aid/legal advice (vulnerable to exploitation)
■ People who care for those who are physically vulnerable (parents, pet owners)
■ People with disabilities
■ People who care for others with medical conditions (parents of kids with addictions, relatives of people with Alzheimer's)

Now, we're not suggesting you throw away your marketing personas and shift to writing content only for seniors, nor are we suggesting that you abandon your current content marketing playbook. We are, however, suggesting that to earn links consistently, you should consider how your brand expertise could inform and empower the various audiences that the internet's vast expanse of linkers care about deeply.

3. Shifting Your Mindset from Sales Content to Linker-Valued Content

One of the most common roadblocks we see is in how SEO strategists typically think about keyword research for content creation. Though we go into this in the prospecting chapter, we'll touch on it here to better illustrate the role itself.

SEO strategists often start with keywords that are centered around sales ("running shoes," "sports cars," "hotels in London"), and these keywords lead to sales-centric content ideas. A post on "The Best Hotels in London" may be a perfect fit for your blog, but you'll have a hard time finding enough linkers who care about it to justify promotion.

However, a "Guide to the Best Wheelchair Accessible Accommodations in London" or a "Teacher's Guide to High School Class Trips to London" would be a great resource for linkers who care about people with disabilities or teachers—two linker-valued audiences. These topics solve problems for specific linker-valued audiences with distinct sets of needs that govern the utility of content.

The link strategist must help/convince the content team to direct at least a portion of their content toward a linker-valued audience. They're shifting the paradigm from "sales-oriented" content to "linker-valued" content.

Identifying Relevant Linker-Valued Topics

The first step for a link strategist in a new campaign is to find out where the company's vertical intersects with topics relevant to these linker-valued audiences. This is where they get to put on the research hat and get lost on the web for a few hours. The best way to take SEO keywords out of the "sales" space is to search your coveted terms within .gov and .edu pages to see what topics come up.

Let's use the "running shoes" example. A traditional Google search will bring up SERP after SERP of sales pages. But try ["running shoes" inurl:.gov] or ["running shoes" site:.gov]. Now the picture's a little different:

running shoes inurl gov running shoes site gov

If you have any link strategist blood in you at all, your mind's racing with unique content ideas like "How to Start a Running Program for [Audience]," "Guide to Barefoot Running for [Audience]," "How to Know If You Need Prescription Running Shoes," or "The Running Shoes Guide for People with Bone Injuries."

Searching for keywords in the government and education spaces gives the link strategist a view of the non-commercial, but keyword-relevant conversations that are happening outside of the marketplace.

Locating Linker-Valued Audiences

Topic is important, but linkable content can't happen without a specific audience to speak to. "A Guide to Barefoot Running for Seniors" is going to be a different piece from "A Guide to Barefoot Running in Seattle Parks." So remember: You're dialing in multiple facets and topics that may feel a bit mushy at first.

Typically, a piece of content created for a linker-valued audience will not appeal to your entire customer base. Is there possibly an existing subset of your customers whom linkers already serve? Or is there a cause or group of people in need that members of the company already care about, for whatever reason? This could be a good entry point into a linkable audience that makes sense for you to serve.

How do you know if a group of people qualifies as a "linker-valued" audience? You test it! Search for existing links and resource pages to test if a topic or audience has linker appeal, using a search formatted as such:

["topic/audience" inurl:links.html]

Then, review the results count:

- *50 to 200 results.* It's productive, but potentially a subtopic. You may need to brainstorm a wider or additional category.
- *200 to 1,000 results.* It's a solid topic/audience to pursue.
- *1,000-plus results.* It's an established topic/audience that could merit further refinement since there's already so much content here.

Take the following examples:

- seniors boss topic
- Seniors = Boss Topic
- running boss topic
- Running = Boss Topic
- barefoot running useable topic
- Barefoot Running = Usable Topic

Keep track of the terms you use to test. These can be used for prospecting further on. Also note that we use inurl:links.html as only a guiding proxy for potential volume of opportunity. When prospecting, which we will cover further on, we use hundreds of prospecting queries, along with authority site co-citation analysis, to thoroughly discover all the pages serving our selected audience.

4. Decide Which Audience to Address with Authority Content

Once a topic and an audience are selected, it's the job of the link strategist to work with the content team to create the best possible content for this audience. Ideally, you want to find a question that hasn't yet been fully answered or a topic area that isn't already flooded with guides, tips, and how-tos. We're looking for the information gaps that exist in this space.

This can be the most challenging aspect of a link strategist's role—finding a need an audience has and determining how to best serve it. It's also the most nebulous step to provide advice for, because it's based on intuiting what content this audience may need based on what currently exists. Unlike a business's target customers, this audience's pain may not be one that a product or service can fix. Linker-valued audiences require helpful, experience-based guidance. Further, content should generally be different when targeting resource curators vs. industry publishers, even when they're serving the same linker-valued audience. Content for resource curators will almost always be of the "Ultimate Guide" variety where you detail and describe all aspects of solving a very particular problem. Industry publishers are often interested in sharing Ultimate Guide content, but also love sharing industry news, discoveries, advances to process etc. . . .

Examples of authority content for resource curators include:

- Tips for _____
- How to _____
- Guides to _____
- Resource collection on _____
- _____ finder
- _____ calculator
- Data for _____

Examples of authority content for industry-facing publications include:

- Survey results
- Case studies
- Data analysis
- Guides to industry developments
- Expert advice and interviews
- News

Overlap happens. Sometimes you can design content that will appeal to links page curators *and* industry bloggers—just not incredibly often.

Alternately, your mission to serve linker-valued audiences could support a PR campaign. For example, a company with senior citizen customers could create a training course for seniors caring for partners with Alzheimer's disease, perhaps with on-phone support, webinars, or even live education sessions at local venues (*Note*: See our local sponsorship chapter if you're considering finding local venues or events for setting up a booth!). This effort could justify an online PR campaign.

If you have the time and resources, the best way to get to know customers is to schedule some phone calls. Nothing beats a real-time conversation to determine an audience's needs and pains.

The link strategist may wear several other hats on the link-building team (e.g., content creator, PR manager, social media manager), but the strategist should have the time and resources to spend at least 10 to 15 hours a week researching linker audiences and developing campaign strategy to feed the organization's ongoing need for links.

In the next chapter, we will cover how your team can conduct effective link-building campaign metrics using what you can easily observe in the search engines, as well as other useful tools that can contribute to positive ranking gains.

Chapter 4

Effective Link-Building Campaign Metrics

While "get more links" may be what your boss or your clients or even your SEO strategist recommends, how and why you get these links pointed at your pages will impact the long-term viability of your links as well as the value they pass along to your site. Before designing your campaign, it's important to have a general sense of what you can accomplish with your work as a link builder.

Traditionally, link builders have sought search engine impact and measured their success based on increases in the SERPs. Increasingly though, link builders have begun looking for metrics beyond SERP influence. This chapter looks at goals and areas of influence in both categories (SERP and non-SERP alike) so you can set up a campaign that provides effective results and robust metrics.

LINK BUILDING FOR INCREASING SEARCH ENGINE RANKINGS

Search engine algorithms use links to make decisions about your site as a whole, its particular pages, and how effectively your pages solve the intent of a searcher's query. The classic way of describing a link's value—as search engines perceive it—is that it is a "vote" for the page—and ultimately the domain—it is pointing to. The link out suggests that this other page is relevant and worth investigating. Let's look at some various techniques and impacts of link building for search results.

Increase Perceived Trust/Authority of Your Site

You will see an increase in organic traffic after receiving links from sites that have already earned trust and proved their authority to search engines. These kinds of links help across the board for terms you're targeting, and they benefit sites best if the sites are already well-optimized and without major issues. You'll have little to no ability to guide the keyword impact of these kinds of links (unless you're buying the links or you've developed clever campaigns).

Adjust Perceived Relevance of Your Site

Links can and do send signals to search engines regarding what your site is about, what industries and markets it serves, and the keyword clusters it's most related to. If you're expanding your market focus or if you're just getting started, links that help connect you to "market spaces" will help you immensely. You can think about relevance in terms of your geographic location as well, and links and other types of citations can help indicate to search engines that you can and should appear in the SERPs targeting specific geo-locations.

Direct SERP Keyword Impact Through Anchor Text Manipulation

The classic role of link builders has been to directly impact their site's rankings by buying or placing links with specific keywords in the anchor text. This is still effective and often described as the most effective way to secure rankings. That said, Google's tolerance for manipulating rankings is zero, and they work hard with people and algorithms to punish link builders who overdo anchor text links. So unless you have a site whose rankings you can afford to tank, focus on anchor text that supports the reader and telegraphs the value in visiting the link.

Measure for Search Engine Impact

If affecting search results is your core focus for link building, here are some things you can work on influencing:

- Search rankings for converting key terms
- Percentage of increase in converting search traffic
- Percentage of increase in search traffic from geographic regions
- Increase in number of pages on domain that yield traffic
- Percentage increase in nonbranded search traffic

- Percentage fluctuation in engagement metrics, such as time on site, time on pages, and bounce rate
- Number and location of links from sites/people deemed authoritative
- Number and location of links from sites/people deemed relevant

Any of these can increase the efficacy of your link-building campaign in a way that drives SEO engagement and results.

LINK BUILDING AS MARKET ENGAGEMENT

In addition to impacting search results, links can and do powerfully impact how the market perceives your business. The benefits beyond search are often obscured in SEO-oriented link-building discussions, and often these areas of impact are beyond a typical SEO department's authority within an organization. If you're seeking to drive more links to your organization, it will make sense to learn more about this kind of thinking and be ready and able to discuss it with the appropriate people internally. Here are some ways link building can help boost your brand.

Build Company and Personal Brand

When your link-building efforts include expert engagement as well as content placement, you have an impact on how your market perceives you and your brand. This is especially true if you've done your research and know which publications in your market exert the most influence on your business prospects.

Earning mentions—on a monthly basis—in the top publications in your market keeps your brand relevant. If you've designed your campaign carefully or if you've worked closely with PR and communicated your SEO needs effectively, you can often get great keywords in your anchor text. Check out Figure 4–1, on page 26, for an example of what a successful brand treatment can look like.

SERP impact is just a side benefit here, though; it's more about your perceived importance and value in the market!

Build Your Lead Pipeline

We've found that the links we've earned as a byproduct of building our brand (with interviews and placed how-to content) also generate business leads. In fact, long before we saw search traffic, we saw relevant referral traffic that turned into sales. From an SEO perspective, the links we've earned in this manner are all highly relevant, and many of them are from high-authority sites in the SEO/SEM space. From a bottom-line perspective, these links have been the lifeblood of our growing company.

FIGURE 4–1. Aaron Wall of SEO Book Built an Enduring Personal Brand on the Web

Engage the Expert Community and Guide Conversation

We advocate expert interviews and surveys as a cornerstone of content designed to attract links. If you engage your industry's experts carefully and intelligently, you'll see that you can begin guiding market conversations. Guiding conversations doesn't mean being manipulative; it means pushing conversation forward in a way that benefits the market as well as your organization. The benefit of expert engagement is that the experts are likely to link to content created through that engagement, as well as be more open to your requests to link to or mention your content in the future. You can usually find a topical forum in nearly any subject, where experts are discussing that subject. View Figure 4–2, on page 27, for an example of searching for a forum in woodworking.

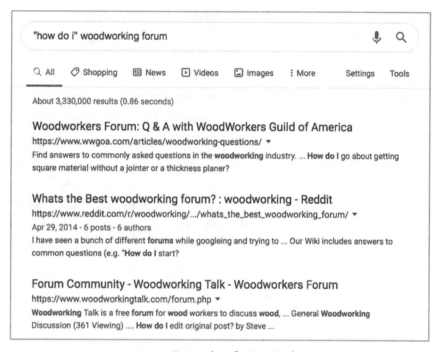

FIGURE 4–2. Example of a Topical Forum

What to Measure in Link Building for Market Impact

Here are some suggestions for data points you can measure when demonstrating link building's impact beyond the SERPs. You can formulate your own metrics to powerfully demonstrate the value of links to other departments in your organization. Try these:

- Percentage increase in targeted referral traffic
- Percentage increase in referral traffic conversions
- Percentage increase in engagement metrics, such as time on site, time on pages, and decrease in bounce rate
- Percentage increase in branded search term traffic
- Percentage increase in unbranded search term traffic
- Percentage increase in social media mentions, shares, and referring visits
- Percentage increase of mentions in target media over competitors
- Number of blog posts and articles about or citing your organization
- Number of customers indicating that media prompted their inquiry
- Number of third-party mentions and community pass-alongs

- Number of positive responses in conversation thread exchanges
- Number of key influencers known to actively suggest your products or services to those who trust them
- Number of positive, goal-focused emails exchanged
- Number of newsletter/RSS subscriptions (a type of web feed that allows users and apps to access updates to websites in a standardized, computer-readable format)

When you track the impact of your efforts in your organic search rankings and beyond, you set yourself up for defensible requests for more budget. Perhaps more important (especially if you're working on your own projects), the discipline of tracking enables you to see a clear path toward positive impacts. In the next chapter, we will cover the concept and creation of linkable assets—the very core of every link-building effort.

Chapter 5

Linkable Assets

Linkable assets are web documents or other digital creations that empower or inform an audience that your target publishers serve. Linkable assets are the in-house experts, information pages, handy widgets, tools, unexpected discounts, valued relationships, or custom data that incentivize others to share a link with their website visitors.

When you understand what's linkable about your organization, as well as what types of assets earn links in your market, you will have a much easier time identifying your link-opportunity types. Knowing these types makes you more effective at prospecting for these types of opportunities.

In this chapter, we go deep on the concept of a "linkable asset," that is, content that's so useful that other publishers feel compelled to share it with their audiences.

LINKABLE ASSET ANALYSIS

Linkable asset analysis is the process of systematically analyzing your site and your competitors' sites, as well as noncompeting publishers' sites in your keyword space, to identify what typically earns links and what *could* earn links but doesn't already. If your site or organization is especially large, this process can and should take some time.

COMMON LINKABLE ASSET CATEGORIES

These linkable asset categories will help get you thinking about what your organization's linkable assets could be. Thinking broadly and creatively at the beginning of a link-building campaign or project engagement can open you to a stronger, more effective campaign design. After all, you could be sitting on a link magnet and not even realize it!

Free Apps and Tools on Your Site

Do you provide any free applications or web-based tools to your site visitors? If so, it's likely that these have already attracted links naturally. If you haven't promoted these tools yet for the purpose of link building, then these assets could help you to develop even more links. Be careful, though, when designing and building a tool or app—they can be expensive (sometimes two to three times what you expect, or what you're quoted), can seem to take forever to develop, and could still flop. That said, nothing demonstrates your expertise like a custom tool you've crafted to make your customers' lives easier. One such tool is BuzzStream, which is shown in Figure 5–1.

FIGURE 5–1. BuzzStream's Software for Link Building

Products/Services to Give Away for Donations/Contests/Review

If you have products or services you can give away, you can earn links through donation thank-you pages, through contests, and via product/service reviews from experts in your market. Often, this asset is one of the easiest paths to developing links. However, it's fairly easy for your competitors to emulate. Further, these approaches to link building can create enormous and unexpected logistical nightmares, such as shipping and packaging, or even getting the winner's contact information from the site conducting the giveaway. Evidence of partner pages can be seen below in Figure 5–2. These partner pages often offer links for the businesses that support them.

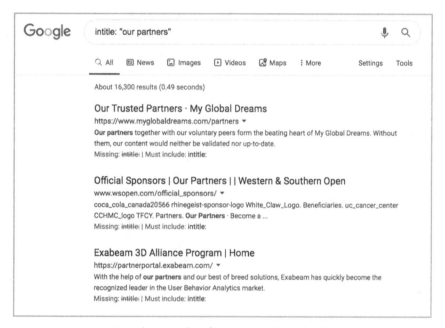

FIGURE 5–2. Google Search of Partner's Page for Organizations

Thought Leaders and Subject-Matter Experts

Are there existing or potential thought leaders and subject-matter experts in your organization? Do they have time to write, podcast, host a webinar, or in some other way share their expertise with the market? What about growing their key contributions into a conference presentation? Thought leaders could generate links in the form of interviews, guest posts, and quote contributions to industry news publications. If you have a PR or social media department, link builders should help them to identify link opportunities that these assets enable.

Widgets, Tools, Images, Data for Publishers (Off-Site)

Have you created widgets, tools, images, or data that publishers of other sites are free to add to their websites? Infographics, embeddable tools, research data, and other types of information created for the express purpose of giving it away is a classic and powerful method for earning links. If you have any of these assets and you haven't aggressively and extensively promoted them, then you're leaving valuable links and relationships on the table.

Partner Relationships

Do you have business partners, vendors, customers, and technology licensees? Each of these represents a potential link in the form of testimonials, published client lists, and "powered-by" buttons. Gather a list of your vendors and partners and look for ways to acquire (and give) links to all of them. Think interviews, link requests for *their* vendors and partners' pages, and updated "powered-by" badges.

Job Listings, Events, and Coupons

If your organization consistently publishes job openings, puts on events, or launches new products, then you've got quite a few link opportunities open to you. Colleges and industry vertical sites are sometimes willing to link to pages that feature new job openings. A good example of a linkable page is the company webpage describing the advantages of working at that company, as seen in Figure 5–3. Many cities have event calendars that will publish details about your event and post links on their site for sign-up and more information. If you consistently offer coupons to your customers, you'll find massive numbers of coupon-listing sites, many of which link back.

Consistent Publishing via Blog, Video, Podcast, PDFs, and Social Media

Does your organization publish content consistently? These linkable assets open you to numerous link-opportunity types from around your industry: everything from blog

FIGURE 5–3. Career Landing Page for Company

directories, niche social news sites, and blog lists to PDF submissions and distribution sites. In some industries, the fact that your CEO blogs is link-worthy and notable in itself.

Budget

Money is almost always a linkable asset, in that if you have the money, you can offer it to another site in exchange for a link. However, the link opportunities that you can purchase are often easy for competitors to duplicate. Further, some search engines aggressively penalize (in the form of lowered search rankings) purchased links that aren't labeled or coded as advertisements, making them a potentially risky investment that could end up costing far more in damages than they bring in search traffic. Some sites, such as directories, require a budget as well.

IDENTIFYING COMPETITOR AND OTHER MARKET-DETERMINED LINKABLE ASSETS

It's also valuable to conduct linkable asset analysis on your competitors' sites and organizations, as well as on the sites of your industry's major news and information publishers. You can do this by running through the linkable asset category types above and determining which ones your competitors have. Here are a couple more ways to identify the linkable assets in your market.

How Do You Figure Out What Gets Links?

If you know your primary competitors, as well as the top publishers in your market, then you can use a variety of free and fee-based tools to identify the pages on their sites that have attracted the most links. These pages will help you get an idea of what your industry thinks of as "linkable." Paste the URLs of your competitors and top publishers into:

- Ahrefs.com
- Majestic.com
- Moz.com

Each of these will help you identify the most-linked pages on sites that compete with you in the SERPs. These most-linked pages can help you find the linkable asset in your space that could be the most beneficial to your campaign—or the asset that's been done to death!

What Gets Tweeted?

When you know your competitors and top publishers in your market, you can begin looking for what content of theirs gets mentioned frequently on Twitter. Unfortunately, social shareability doesn't frequently align with linkability, but it's worth investigating to see which topics are currently hot.

IDENTIFYING AND EVALUATING YOUR EXISTING LINKABLE ASSETS

One of the best ways to identify your existing linkable assets is with a thorough, section-by-section review of your site. This should include not only a personal visit to the major sections and important pages of your site, but a review of your site using your preferred backlink graphing data set: Moz, Majestic, or Ahrefs. You need to identify which pages have attracted links already so that you can earn more links for your site. Further, you must identify what could be linkable but hasn't earned links yet.

Identifying off-site assets can be a bit trickier, often because you don't think of them as potentially linkable, nor do you have any control over them. Your off-site assets include:

- Thought leaders within your organization
- Your PR department
- The web development team
- Existing industry relationships

Running through our list of link asset categories above could spark some ideas, and competitor backlink analysis can also suggest some off-site assets in your organization that you haven't considered or tapped into. Furthermore, your off-site assets typically will require some work on the part of others within your organization, which will require you to build a case for their involvement.

Links generated through engaging people in your organization will often be of higher quality. The value of identifying your linkable assets prior to a link-building campaign is that you can assess what types of sites and opportunities these assets open for you. For example, if your organization puts on teaching or training events around the country, then the events pages themselves are linkable assets. Knowing your linkable assets makes it much easier to identify the link-opportunity types you should prospect for and then pursue via outreach. You'll read more about identifying link-opportunity types in Chapter 6, prospecting in Chapters 8 through 10, and creating an outreach campaign in Chapter 15.

Link-Opportunity Types

L ink-opportunity types are the kinds of web-page types that are likely homes for your links. Link-opportunity types can include sites that accept guest posts—that is, sites that seek and publish content from others. Some link builders look for reporters who've previously covered a specific topic or business. One of the oldest and most frequently mentioned link-opportunity types is a directory, which is typically in the business of linking to websites. Links and resource pages are a key opportunity type as well; these are curated lists of web resources, often on a single topic.

The value of understanding your link-opportunity types ahead of time is that you'll be able to build more accurate and descriptive link-building queries, as well as qualify link prospects more quickly once you have them. Further, certain link-opportunity types will need to be handled differently and by different people in your organization. Your CEO won't necessarily be the person to submit sites to niche directories, nor will your marketing intern be the right person to be interviewed by a prominent blogger. Knowing your link-opportunity types will help you when designing your overall link-building campaign process—and help you determine if a campaign is a one-off or potentially ongoing.

In this chapter, we will outline link-opportunity types and how to best align the different options with your link-building goals.

GOING FROM LINKABLE ASSETS TO LINK-OPPORTUNITY TYPES

In Chapter 5, we discussed linkable assets—the people and web pages associated with your organization that publishers believe will help their audience achieve a task or goal. You identified these assets for the purpose of thinking through their associated opportunity types. Be aware, though, it's possible—and sometimes vital—to go from link-opportunity types back to developing linkable assets. Stay alert throughout your asset inventory and prospecting to new ideas and obvious opportunities.

Brainstorm Opportunity Types for Each Asset on Your List

Brainstorming opportunity types does take a bit of practice and experience, but as the link builder (and the SEO strategist?) you're the best person suited for this job because you're the most familiar with the kinds of linking sites in your keyword space.

Let's walk through opportunity-type brainstorming for your CEO, who has agreed to help with link building. The CEO has been incredibly accommodating and has agreed to write two articles for placement and one for the company blog, as well as participate in any interviews you can dig up. Further, the CEO has agreed to comment once a week on three notable articles at high-profile sites.

In this scenario, your linkable asset is a "thought leader," so your opportunity types include:

- Guest post and other content placement opportunities
- Blogs in your space that write industry or audience-specific roundups
- Industry news sites (assuming their company blog post is suitably noteworthy)
- Sites that have published interviews or other coverage with other industry leaders
- Industry blogs or forums that encourage helpful conversation
- Noncompeting ("adjacent") industry allies that are also publishers
- Podcasts and webinars that empower and inform your audience

Knowing and listing the opportunities you're looking for will help when it comes time to develop your link-prospecting queries.

Here's another quick brainstorm: This time, it's for a company that sells a specialized grooming brush for dogs with curly hair. In this organization, the CEO is distanced from the web side of the business, as they have always been a direct-mail believer. It's just the SEO strategist doing link building, and with relatively little support. Our intrepid SEO strategist has one highly linkable asset at their disposal—free doggie brushes to send out. They also have a video camera and a dog with curly hair so they can make some basic how-to videos.

This SEO strategist's assets include the product, of which they have 50 they can send out. They also have five how-to videos for grooming dogs with curly hair. The opportunities they are looking for include:

- Pet-related charities that have thank you pages for in-kind donors
- Doggy info and community bloggers who review products
- Dog info sites that feature videos
- Any bloggers who might be interested in using one of the doggy brushes as a prize in a contest

Primarily they are looking for nonprofits in the pet space and dog bloggers. With these targets, it will be quite easy to create link-prospecting queries. If they could squeeze in more time every week, it might make sense to participate in a few forums relating to dog grooming as well.

COMMON LINK-OPPORTUNITY TYPES

Now that we've reviewed a couple of sample link-opportunity brainstorms, we'll look at some of the more common link-opportunity types we've encountered in our work.

Content Placement Opportunities

Content placement opportunities include guest posts on industry blogs, op-ed pieces on industry news sites, how-tos placed in your industry's association newsletter, even RSS syndication (basically republishing your blog) on select sites with targeted, relevant traffic. Content placement opportunities require content, which requires writers—ideally great writers who get your industry and know your subject well.

Company Profile Listings

Company profile listings occur typically on aggregation sites that publish job listings, company stock information, PDFs, coupons, events (including sales-oriented webinars), free web tools (including spreadsheets), free downloadable software, and more (we're constantly discovering new aggregation sites, and different industries have different aggregated content types). Some sites charge for publishing your information, and some don't. Some sites follow links to your site, and some add the nofollow tag. Some sites link to you from every page on their site that mentions you, and some only link to you from your actual profile page. If you consistently have job openings, events, new PDFs, etc., then you should investigate this opportunity type. Figure 6–1, on page 38, shows an example company profile link on popular couponing website RetailMeNot.

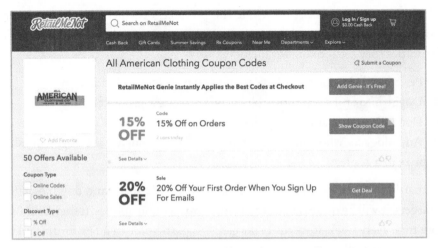

FIGURE 6–1. Company Profile Link on RetailMeNot

Open Conversation Opportunities

Open conversation opportunities include things like:

- Blog comments
- Forum discussions
- Question and answer sites
- Industry social networking sites

These are places where you can register, create a profile, and interact with the community in ways that add value. If you have already created tools and information of value on your site, you can and should direct folks that way via links. Please don't join just to link-drop though—only join the conversation on sites where you can genuinely become a "regular." The asset required here is subject-matter expertise and time. Online forums can be useful places to share your knowledge and links to your asset. Figure 6–2, on page 39, shows an example of an online auto repair forum.

Editorial Mentions

Editorial mentions are links that occur in the body of an article. We're referring here to links that are earned either through merit or persistence, rather than through monetary payment. These can occur in reviews at industry news sites, direct content citations from other how-to writers, discussions of your company's news or blog statements, and even in content you place (see "Content Placement Opportunities" above). These types of links will all be earned through relationships you develop with the industry-expert publishers in your market space. When a site includes a link to you within their editorial

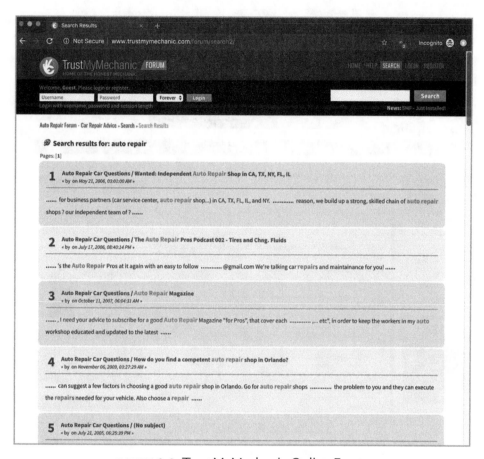

FIGURE 6–2. TrustMyMechanic Online Forum

content, it is considered a trustworthy link. Figure 6–3, on page 40, shows an example of an editorial mention.

Directory Listings

Similar to company profile listings, directory listings are common opportunities across industries. Debra Mastaler, link building and content strategy consultant and coach as well as president of Alliance-Link.com and Keytooles.com says, "Ideally you're sourcing niche directories with high-touch editorial curation. The harder—even more expensive—it is to get listed, the better (usually). The beauty of directories is that typically they're relatively easy to acquire—just add your company's information. That low barrier of entry is also the problem with directories. However, there's no reason to turn up your nose at them. If you can find a few decent industry or geo-relevant directories, you should acquire those links."

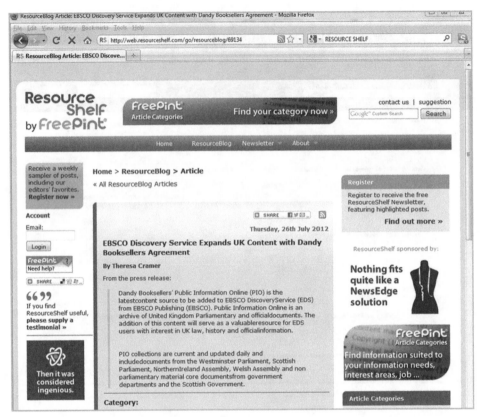

FIGURE 6–3. Editorial Mention

Resource Lists

Resource lists come in many forms. Sometimes they're on library websites, and sometimes they're tucked away on long-forgotten university web pages. Sometimes they're in the form of massive resource aggregation sites (almost directories), and sometimes they get published on a weekly basis in the form of a roundup. If you have created—and continue to create—expert resources for your industry, then you should pursue this opportunity type.

Often overlooked by link builders, many public libraries offer topical link resource lists. These can be very useful links to obtain. See Figure 6–4, on page 41, for an example of a resource list for health.

Sponsored Links

We have not sought experience in purchasing links. It is our understanding that the best purchased links are those that are difficult for search engines and competitors to detect and that come in the body of highly relevant and high-quality content. Avoid sites that

FIGURE 6–4. Sample Resource List

mention or discuss SEO, and definitely don't buy links on sites that advertise the sale of links (unless they are "nofollowing" and you're buying for traffic and exposure, not SERP impact). Sponsoring events or organizations can earn you the appreciation of your market, spread your brand, and drive direct traffic. This type of opportunity (displayed in Figure 6–5, page 42) requires money.

Knowing the range of link-opportunity types gives you a sense of directions your campaign could take. It's just as important, though, to research the market you're in to learn what types of opportunities are most prevalent. In the next chapter, we will explore just that: how to conduct a link-opportunity analysis within your target market, as defined in part by the keywords for which you'd like to rank.

Our sponsors

We are grateful to the generous partners who support our efforts.

By supporting the companies that give to the Animal Humane Society you are actively advancing our mission: to engage the hearts, hands and minds of the community to help animals.

To find out how your business can support the programs of the Animal Humane Society please contact us <u>online</u> or by calling (763) 489-2212.

<u>SidewalkDog.com</u> provides the inside scoop on pet-related & dog-friendly businesses, destinations & events in the Twin Cities and beyond. The only online publisher serving the needs of Twin Cities dog parents, <u>SidewalkDog.com</u> wants to help you get a life...with your dog!

FIGURE 6–5. Example of a Sponsored Opportunity

Chapter 7

Conducting a Link-Opportunity Analysis for Your Keyword Space

Knowing what link opportunities exist for a given market as defined by its keyword space can go a long way toward helping you design a link-building campaign. However, if you don't have the available resources to create new assets, then it may not do you much good to know about these opportunities. On the other hand, if you can clearly demonstrate link opportunities are available, this could open new resources for you in your organization. This chapter provides some thinking and process suggestions for link builders trying to understand, or "inventory," all the link opportunities for their market.

KNOW YOUR MARKET-DEFINING KEYWORDS (MDKWs)

Market-defining keywords (MDKWs) are the keywords you'll be using throughout your link prospecting and market research. They are the "big head" keywords in your industry that will bring lots of traffic but few sales. Here are seven simple guidelines for determining your MDKWs:

1. Probably not converting keywords
2. Words the market or participants use to describe itself/themselves
3. Single or two-word phrases that are very crowded and competitive in the SERPs (not many ads targeting them)

4. Keywords you would not typically target with a pay-per-click (PPC) campaign

5. A root extracted from your PPC/SEO keywords

6. Common names for the practitioners within your industry (what are the experts actually called?)

7. Words commonly used in the names of publications within your market

Because this process requires actual queries in your search engine of choice, it's vital that you've identified your most productive, least "noisy" keywords that will help you really measure and gauge your market space.

DESIGN QUERIES FOR EACH OPPORTUNITY TYPE

Once you know your MDKWs, it's time to create queries and search for them in your favorite search engine. Following are a few ways you can do that.

Look for Blogs, News Sites, and Trade Publications

The existence of blogs, news sites, and trade publications are all indicators of a healthy "expert publication" stratus within your market space. If these kinds of sites exist, especially in large numbers, your campaign design can and should include expert engagement and content creation and promotion, to name a couple. In Figure 7–1, on page 45, we show the results of a search on dog blogs. Notice how huge the dog MDKW space is: 439 million results!

Check for these kinds of publishers with queries such as:

- MDKW blogs
- MDKW "blog list"
- "top MDKW blogs"
- "MDKW news"
- MDKW "Trade Publication"
- MDKW conference or convention (You will have to track back to the trade organization that's hosting the convention.)

How many results in the top ten are relevant? Are you finding lists of bloggers? If not, make sure your MDKWs are broad enough! If so, then make note of "expert engagement" and content creation/promotion as a solid direction for your link-building efforts.

Look for Niche Directories

Niche directories are almost always worth submitting to. Consider them a "covering your bases" link-building effort. Some keyword spaces have niche directories, and some

FIGURE 7–1. That's a Lot of Dog Blogs!

don't. Figure 7–2, on page 46, features search results for dog directories, and Figure 7–3, on page 47, shows a niche directory for all things Elvis Presley.

Find niche directories with queries such as:

- "MDKW Directory"
- "MDKW Websites"

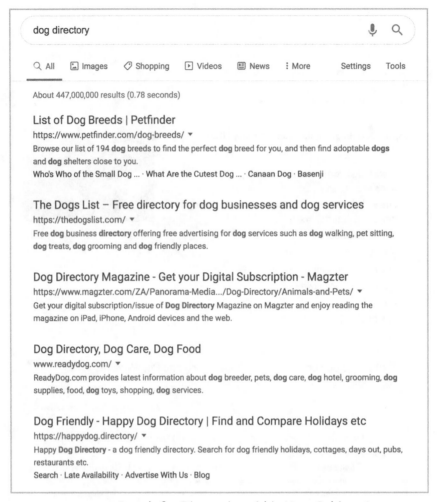

FIGURE 7–2. Search for Directories within Your Subject Area

■ MDKW "suggest * URL"

Look for Interviews with Subject-Matter Experts

The presence of interviews signifies there's an "expert class" within your keyword space. Figure 7–4, on page 47, demonstrates how to search for these by adding "intitle:interview" to the MDKW for which you're seeking experts. In this specific example, we are looking for interviews with expert dog trainers.

If there are a number of interviews, then you should do two things. The first is to get thought leaders in your organization interviewed. Second, you should conduct a group interview of all the experts who have received interviews. Gather the experts' contact information, then brainstorm five to ten great questions and send them out. When they

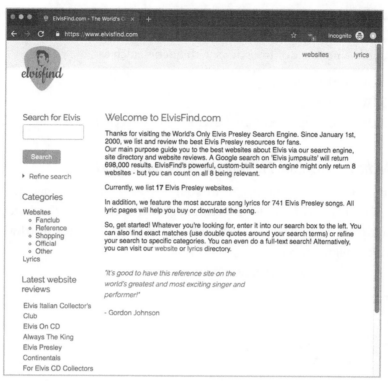

FIGURE 7–3. There Are Directories for Just about Any Niche, Even Elvis Presley

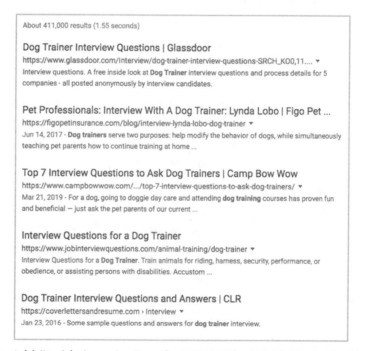

FIGURE 7–4. Add "Intitle:interview" to the MDKW for Which You're Seeking Experts

have responded, aggregate their answers into one article and let them know when it's published.

Check on the presence of interviews with queries such as:

- MDKW intitle:interview
- MDKW intitle:"q&a with"
- MDKW intitle:"tips from" OR "advice from" OR "chat with"

Look for Niche Forums, Social Networking Sites, and Q/A Sites

What is the online community like in your keyword space? Remember, there are hundreds of thousands of people perfectly happy with forums as their platform for web interactions. Find them! This will help you determine whether it's worthwhile to put resources into online conversations.

Find niche forums and social networks with queries such as:

- MDKW community
- intitle:MDKW forum
- MDKW inurl:blogs
- MDKW answers

Look for Professional Associations

Professional associations indicate a high level of business organization within an industry. Figure 7-5, on page 49, shows us the results of a query for dog-training associations. We used the "intitle:association" command with "dog training" to give us search results for dog-training associations on the internet. This results in some great opportunities for link development. First, you should consider joining as a means of connecting formally with your industry. Second, many associations have online newsletters and publications to which you can submit content.

Find professional associations with queries such as:

- MDKW association
- MDKW associated
- MDKW intitle:"of america" (or other locale)

Look for Company Profile Listing Opportunities

Company profile listings—often earned through submitting specific content types to aggregation sites—are a fairly simple way to build links. There are usually paid and

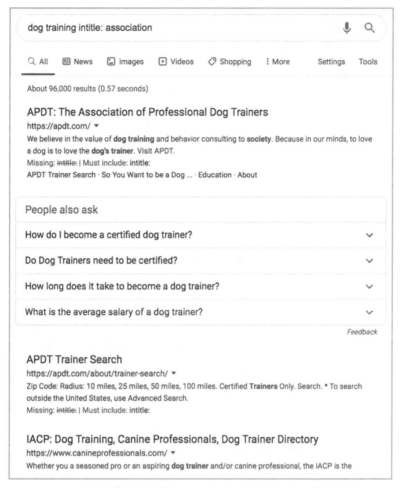

FIGURE 7–5. The "Intitle:association" Command Search

unpaid opportunities. In Figure 7–6, on page 50, Citation Lab's company profile is listed in Moz's recommended company list at: www.moz.com/community/recommended.

Find company profile listing opportunities with queries like:

- MDKW add job*
- MDKW submit software
- MDKW submit pdf
- MDKW add coupon
- MDKW submit contest
- MDKW events
- MDKW free tools

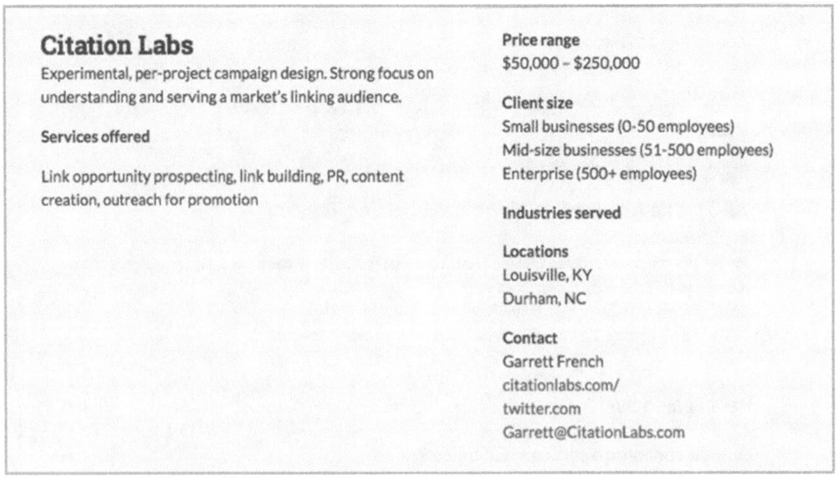

Citation Labs

Experimental, per-project campaign design. Strong focus on understanding and serving a market's linking audience.

Services offered

Link opportunity prospecting, link building, PR, content creation, outreach for promotion

Price range
$50,000 – $250,000

Client size
Small businesses (0-50 employees)
Mid-size businesses (51-500 employees)
Enterprise (500+ employees)

Industries served

Locations
Louisville, KY
Durham, NC

Contact
Garrett French
citationlabs.com/
twitter.com
Garrett@CitationLabs.com

FIGURE 7–6. Moz Recommends Citation Labs

Look for Resource Curators

Resource curation has until recently been the task of librarians. These days it's far more likely that industry expert participants and publishers will build lists of resources either on a one-time basis with continual updates (that is what we mean by "curation") or on a weekly/monthly basis in the form of roundups. We've seen some resource aggregation in the form of exhaustive how-tos that link out to the best industry tools and information as well, so be on the lookout!

Detect resource curators with queries such as:

- MDKW roundup
- "Useful MDKW links" library
- MDKW resources list

Look for Content Placement Opportunities

Guest content placement has been the work of the PR department for years. Times are changing, and it's up to link builders to help lead the company toward content placements that will improve rankings, sales, and brand recognition.

Check your keyword space for content placement opportunities with queries such as:

- MDKW "guest post"
- MDKW inurl:category/guest
- MDKW "guest article"
- MDKW "write for us"

ANALYZING YOUR RESULTS AND SIMPLE RECALIBRATIONS

When you're querying your keyword space to get a sense of the overall link opportunities that exist, one simple, though imprecise, way to compare the relative opportunity size is the number of relevant opportunities in the top ten results. However, for this to work, of course, you'll have to do the same number of queries for each opportunity type. The problem with this method is in the queries themselves—though we use the queries mentioned above, many spaces have different words and variations for their different opportunity types.

That brings us to recalibrations. Try creating your own substitutions for an opportunity type mentioned above. If our queries sound off to you, then they probably are—you know your keyword space best. Also, if you're not getting back many relevant results, your MDKWs could be too narrow—try broadening them. For example, if you used "camping tents," go to "camping" and you should see more relevant opportunities appear.

Once you have gotten some direction from your MDKWs and the actual publisher opportunities that exist, it is time to move onto link prospecting, which you'll read about in the next chapter.

Chapter 8

Link Prospecting

L ink prospecting is the process of discovering potential sites for engagement from which you hope to earn or otherwise acquire links to your site. Link prospecting takes many forms and can be as simple as a quick search engine query or as involved as downloading hundreds of thousands of competitor backlinks. Prospecting, as a task or role, often goes underappreciated in its capacity to discover new directions, so before we get too deep into the "how-to," we're going to discuss a bit of how exactly a prospecting role *should* function.

If you're eager to get into the nuts and bolts of prospecting, however, you can skip this portion of the book. In this chapter, we illustrate the role of what we call the "opportunity prospector," who finds prospective linkers that support the campaign's goals and who can discover and test new potential directions for future campaigns.

TRAITS OF AN OPPORTUNITY PROSPECTOR

Prospectors—if you have the right folks on the job—discover *big* ideas, so this person should not be an intern or virtual assistant, but rather a core team member. They recognize both distinct audience groupings as well as potential content gaps. The prospector may sometimes be the link strategist, or these may be separate roles, but they have a big-picture seat at the campaign operations table. Below are traits of a successful opportunity prospector.

Ability to Recognize Opportunity While Staying Focused

The prospector must have the ability to recognize opportunity while remaining focused on the task at hand. The opportunity prospector needs to live outside of the box. No idea is too zany (in the opportunity phase at least). The prospector lives in constant discovery mode, always finding new directions for content and outreach, but they also need to be focused enough to deliver usable results as directed by the strategist.

Here's an equation we use in training around this concept:

Opportunity = a linkable asset concept + volume of potential linkers

The opportunity prospector, upon securing buy-in for a potential opportunity, works to find every single opportunity associated with that piece of content. Prospectors are in the know about all existing and in-development assets, such as:

- discount codes
- scholarships
- nonprofit programs
- authority content
- partnerships
- upcoming events
- PR developments
- new apps

Internal Subject Matter Expertise

This is another reason the prospector shouldn't be an intern or a lower-level team member. If they're not in the loop about company goings-on, they are not going to be equipped to find every relevant opportunity.

The prospector works with a writer to clearly define content characteristics and specific topics that earn links. This includes providing potential titles, the goals of the new asset, and sample pieces of content that exhibit linkability.

Ability to Find Opportunities in Non-Native Languages

A good prospector understands advanced search operators (inurl:, intitle:, etc...), citation analysis (which domains are most important and who's linking to them), and opportunity footprint KWs (such as blog, links, news, etc...). Using this knowledge, they can, with a translator's help, develop a system for uncovering opportunities in non-native languages. This is more a measure of capability than a must-have, but if you can look for blogs about parenting in English, you should know enough about the process to do it in French, too.

Obsessively Thorough

The prospector can't stop. There's always one more query they forgot or one more URL they find to pull backlinks from. They are out to get *all* the potential opportunities and work relentlessly to get everything that's as good a fit as possible.

A Gut Sense of When to PIVOT

Despite your thoroughness, sometimes you have to say: "This concept isn't working *at all*." And that's OK. Prospectors live and work outside the box, so they can't be afraid to toss some ideas into the recycling bin.

LINK-PROSPECTING METHODS

So far, we've summed up the soft side of the prospector, but people and strategy skills are only part of the job. Knowing how to find thousands of relevant opportunities calls for some pretty specific technical understanding, as well. Finding link prospects is one of the core problems of link building. And typically, the problem isn't in finding enough prospects. You can easily find hundreds or even hundreds of thousands of prospects by cracking open link index database Majestic.com and exporting competitor backlinks (but first, read our section on "Competitor Backlink Prospecting" in Chapter 8). The problem typically lies in finding link prospects that represent opportunity types that are lined up with your linkable assets. Not all the prospecting methods below answer this core link-building pain, but they are the more common methods used by link builders these days.

Link-prospecting queries remain one of the most versatile and powerful tools for link builders. A *link-prospecting query* (also called a "link-building query") is a combination of keywords and advanced search operators that help you discover sites that are likely to link to a page on your site. Link-prospecting queries are highly flexible ways to discover link prospects at large scale and are a fantastic way to quickly determine the quantity and quality of link opportunities in a given keyword space (as noted in Chapter 6).

Link-prospecting queries work because link prospects often have a common "footprint" in the content of the page or even in the URL itself. Discovering these link opportunity footprints and paring them down to only a word or two is the essence of link-prospect query design.

The chief advantage of link-prospecting queries is your ability to align queries to discover only the link opportunities that relate to a linkable asset. This ability is your first line of prequalification and enables you to design narrowly targeted campaigns that focus on a single asset. Thoroughly discovering all the link prospects that relate to a linkable asset is only possible with queries.

The disadvantage of queries is their ease of creation, which can encourage a cursory and unsystematic approach to querying. This unsystematic approach almost always leaves link prospects on the table as you move on to a different asset. A further disadvantage is link-opportunity discovery. If your site lacks a linkable asset, or you're simply unaware of a given opportunity type, you will be unable to create the appropriate queries for discovering these opportunities.

In the past, we've written lists of link-building queries you can use for prospecting. The problem: There are always more queries you could possibly use. Furthermore, you're probably only able to use a small fraction of the queries we recommend due to your linkable assets or the type of link opportunities that you're targeting with your campaign. Ultimately, we don't know your market the way you do. Knowing how to construct queries will help you hunt far more effectively in your target market than a list of queries.

SEVEN TYPES OF KEYWORDS FOR LINK-PROSPECTING QUERIES

Mark Twain said, "The difference between the almost right word and the right word is really a large matter—it's the difference between the lightning bug and the lightning." The same certainly holds true for link-prospecting queries, which is why we've found it really helps to think about the types of words you can use. Finding just the right words will help you prequalify your prospects, which vastly speeds up your qualification phase.

Figure 8–1, on page 57, shows a query for "lightning" combined with the intitle command for "links" that returns prequalified results for sites aggregating links related to lightning. The broad, general topic of lightning inspired many to create links pages for cataloging lightning resources. The intitle: links operator helps find them.

More specialized keywords like "bioluminescence" bring fewer results but more varied link opportunities than general keywords like "lightning" (see Figure 8–2, on page 58, for reference).

For the exercise in this section, we'll pretend we build and sell high-performance kayaks online and from a brick-and-mortar location. Our linkable assets are an extensive guide to the best kayaking spots in the world, our blog with kayaking tips

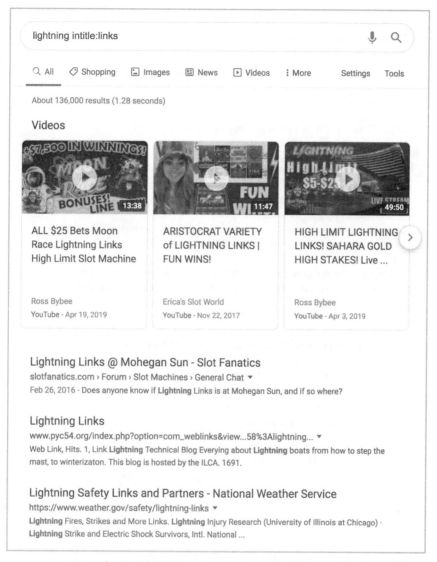

FIGURE 8–1. The Intitle: Links Operator Helps Find Targeted Links

and events, and our in-house kayaking subject-matter experts, who are both builders and kayakers. Let's explore the seven types of keywords you might use for link-prospecting queries.

1. Market-Defining Keywords (MDKWs)

As we discussed in the previous chapter, each market uses particular words to describe itself in MDKWs. What words does your target audience use to describe your industry?

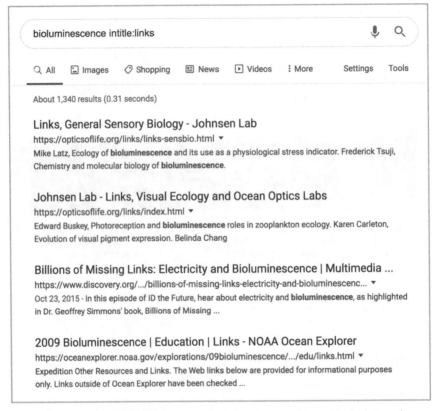

FIGURE 8–2. Specialized Keywords Bring Fewer, More Varied Results

For our kayaking site, these terms could include:

- kayak
- kayaking
- paddling

To find prospects for our guide to the best kayaking spots in the world, we could do queries like:

- kayak blog
- kayaking resources
- places to kayak intitle:list

2. Customer-Defining Keywords (CDKWs)

Customer-defining keywords help you discover prospects that are geared more toward your target audience. Knowing what your customers call themselves and how they refer to fellow group members will help you discover some great prospects.

Customer-defining keywords for our kayak store could include:

- kayaker
- paddler
- playboater
- "paddle bum"

These keywords will help you discover still more prospects who might be interested in linking to your guide to the world's best kayaking spots:

- playboater blog
- kayaker resources
- paddler vacation intitle:list

3. Product/Category Keywords (PCKWs)

Product or category keywords are the high- and mid-level terms that describe what you sell. They're useful because they can help you uncover prospects that could otherwise go undiscovered. For example, on our kayak site we sell a few different types of kayaks. Each type of kayak has its own dedicated enthusiasts:

- sea kayak
- sit-on-top kayak
- playboat
- creekboat
- inflatable kayak
- fishing kayak
- waveski

If you had kayaks to lend or donate for review, you could combine the above keywords with "blog," "news," "review," or even "magazine" to find people to write reviews. Add "forum" to each of the above words, and you'll find people who are avid users of these types of products.

4. Industry Thought Leaders (ITLs)

Industry thought leaders—or, in our kayak case, subject-matter experts—help you uncover public relations and interview opportunities in your space. Here are some names from the kayaking world (people who have given interviews on the subject):

- John Kimantas
- Tyler Bradt
- Harvey Golden

If you're looking for a market's experts, also search in Amazon, or search for "MDKW book" because they often write books. You should also check YouTube for any relevant videos.

Once you know some of your industry's thought leaders, you can look for people who will respond to interviews (so you can interview them and add the content to your site), as well as people who conduct interviews so you can pitch your in-house experts!

Furthermore, you can poke around in forums and see if any thought leaders have participated there. If so, you should consider sending yours there as well. Here are some query commands:

- [ITL] interview
- intitle:"[ITL]"
- [ITL] forum

5. Competing Company Names (CCNs)

Competing company names (CCNs) are wonderful little footprints to track. They can show you a great deal about how your industry's reporters and bloggers treat companies similar to yours. For our kayak company, the list would include other direct competitors.

CCNs are useful in ways similar to the names of industry thought leaders. Our kayak company can see who has covered their competitors in the news, as well as which industry forums happen to discuss their competitors extensively. Furthermore, checking for reviews can show you what you're up against, plus reveal some potential link opportunities. Below are a few helpful CCN search terms:

- [CCN] review
- [CCN] forum
- [CCN] interview
- [CCN] "guest article or post"

6. Geo Keywords (GKWs)

Geo keywords (GKWs) help you discover link prospects that may impact your local search rankings. Our kayak shop obviously wants to rank well locally, and in addition, by discovering and participating with local media, they will drive highly relevant referral traffic that could result in sales.

Geo keywords can include things like:

- state/province
- region

- city
- neighborhood
- zip code

Here are some ways to use geo keywords in link-prospecting queries. Our kayaking shop has monthly workshops for builders, as well as weekly one-hour training classes. It also hosts an annual bluegrass and beer festival for kayakers. We can query for sites related to the broadcast area for events like these. Both events are off-site assets that are ideal for geographic keyword link opportunities offered by the sites returned by the following queries:

- [GKW] events
- [GKW] blog
- [GKW] kayak blog
- [GKW] directory
- [GKW] reviews

7. Related Vertical Keywords (RVKWs)

Related or adjacent verticals are industries in your "ecosystem" that could potentially aid your prospecting and outreach efforts. These could be your suppliers' and customers' industries, perhaps. For example, here are some adjacent industries for our kayaking company:

- canoes
- rafting
- biking
- hiking
- boat building

Our kayaking company will want to make sure that they invite the local canoeing and rafting community to their weekly kayak training events. Bikers and hikers will probably enjoy bluegrass and beer. Further, connecting with boat-building forums, magazines, and blogs will help build links, especially if the company publishes a couple of free kayak plans (and sells others).

Some sample queries could look like:

- [RVKW] blog list
- [RVKW] news
- [RVKW] forum
- [RVKW] "guest post"

- [RVKW] "roundup"
- "[RVKW] resources"
- [RVKW] Twitter list

It would be great if Google could understand (or wanted to understand) that when I search for Customer Relationship Management intitle:"guest post," I need 500 sites likely to publish CRM-related guest posts for a client this month. Instead, I'll get between three and ten decent prospects and start thinking of a new query.

This is the core problem of using Google for prospect sourcing—the relevance of prospects diminishes significantly after the top 10 to 20 results. And going beyond the top 20 results increases time spent qualifying without justifiable returns. With conversion rates being what they are these days, you can start to see why these low numbers of usable prospects is a big problem for large-scale campaigns that have high levels of monthly link commitments.

"Fixing" this problem (besides just returning "more queries," which is, of course, basically the answer) requires thinking through why Google returns so few usable prospects in the top 20 for a single query. We assume Google aims to deliver a few "best" answers rather than provide page after page of great possibilities. They provide a mass-use tool for the average searcher who wants to search and go, rather than a specialized research tool for someone who wants hundreds or even thousands of possible answers.

Think of the fix like this: Systematically and thoroughly alter your queries and force, or "restrict," Google to provide new and still-relevant results in the top 20s that you would otherwise have never seen. Compare the command "crm guest post" to CRM intitle:"guest post." There is some domain overlap, but overall you have a large number of new domains you should consider for placing content. There are three keys to force usable 20-result "segments" out of Google's insanely huge index:

1. Research phrases
2. Advanced operators
3. Tactic-specific footprints

ANATOMY OF A PRODUCTIVE LINK-PROSPECTING QUERY

Let's dig into each one of these and look at ways to build thorough prospecting-query lists. Note: In our query above, CRM intitle:"guest post," "CRM" is the research phrase, "intitle:" is the advanced operator, and "guest post" is your tactic-specific footprint.

1. Research Phrase List Building

The research phrase is what directs Google in the general vicinity of your topic. It pays to spend time brainstorming and developing large lists of research phrases (though tildes can help with this immensely by "thinking" of synonyms for you).

So continuing our CRM example above, you should definitely include "customer relationship management" both with and without quotes. Note: I always create query batches with and without quotes as they often help float new prospects. I also tried ~crm and –crm, which returned some "call centers."

Now, when I looked at the results for our CRM guest-posting query I saw that many of them were about social CRM, and a few were on small-business blogs. These also suggest avenues for prospecting so long as we can tailor content to fit the specific vertical.

So here's our working list of research phrases for CRM-related guest-post opportunities:

- CRM
- customer relationship management
- "customer relationship management"
- call center
- "call center"
- social crm
- "social crm"
- small business crm
- "small business" crm
- business crm

Now it's on to our list of tactic-specific footprints.

2. Tactic-Specific Footprint Lists

Footprints are words or phrases that commonly occur on the kind of page that represents a prospect to you. I call them tactic-specific footprints because ideally you keep them organized by tactic so you can reuse them in the future and continue to add to them as you find new ones.

You can build your footprint lists by closely examining "definite yes" prospects and looking for patterns. For example, in guest posting it's common to include the phrase "about the author." It's so common that it's a solid little footprint in its own right. That said, simply "guest post," with and without quotes, are highly productive as well.

Here are some of the more common guest-posting footprints to combine with the research phrases above:

- guest post
- "guest post"
- "about the author"
- "write for us"
- "blog for us"
- "guest blog for us"
- "guest blogger"
- guest blogger
- guest contributor
- "guest contributor"
- "this is a guest post"

This is by no means an exhaustive list for guest posting, but it provides an excellent starting point.

3. Advanced Search Operators

If you're unfamiliar with advanced search operators, check out this list. Not all of them will be useful to link prospectors, but they're worth understanding because the best ones enable you to restrict the results enough to pinch off another five to ten useful prospects. Here are the ones I use the most:

- *Intitle.* Use this operator to restrict results to documents that contain your phrase in the title tags. It's typically only conscientious or SEO-oriented webmasters who provide useful information in their title tags, so this can be a great way to filter.
- *Inurl.* Similar in usage to intitle, inurl enables you to restrict your results based on what appears in the URL.
- *Site.* I primarily use this operator to restrict by top level domain (TLD). For example, if a query contains site:.edu it will return sites with a TLD of .edu.
- ** (wild card).* The wild card is useful for filling in the blanks on your research phrase and footprint brainstorming. For example, if you type "guest post*" that would include "guest post," "guest posts," "guest posting," "guest posters," etc. The wild card can combine with other operators; for example: ˜wild* returns synonyms of words with the root "wild."
- *– (minus).* The minus operator enables you to remove specific words that you know indicate a non-opportunity. For example, if your CRM results get cluttered with composite risk management results, you could type CRM –composite to remove them. Minus combines with other operators.

- *intext*. Intext specifies that the word or phrase must appear in the text of the page.
- *"" (exact phrase)*. I use this all the time, almost without thinking about it. It's a very useful restriction that tells Google to return an exact match of the phrase in quotes.

It's important to note that not all advanced operators will be productive in combination with all the research phrases and opportunity footprints. This is where experience will help you the most. Furthermore, you'll probably find you use intitle, inurl, and tildes the most.

Next up, we'll look at a huge list of combined queries so you can get a sense of what it will take to get a useful number of prospects for a CRM guest-posting campaign.

4. Queries in Action

To get a solid list of guest-posting opportunities—hopefully enough for at least a month—I combined the following research phrases, operators, and footprints:

Research Phrases
- CRM
- customer relationship management
- "customer relationship management"
- ~ crm
- call center
- "call center"
- social crm
- "social crm"
- small business crm
- "small business" crm
- business crm

Operators and Footprints
- guest post
- "guest post"
- "about the author"
- "write for us"
- "blog for us"
- "guest blog for us"
- "guest blogger"
- guest blogger

- guest contributor
- "guest contributor"
- "this is a guest post"
- intitle:contributor
- inurl:contributor
- intitle:guest
- inurl:guest
- intitle:"guest post"
- inurl:"guest post"
- intitle:"write for us"
- inurl:"write for us"

This netted us more than 200 queries to run. We scraped the top ten results for each query and found 581 domains to check out. And that's only starting to scratch the surface. To really amp up your prospecting efforts, you need to also consider competitor backlink prospecting.

COMPETITOR BACKLINK PROSPECTING

There is a simple beauty to lists of competitor backlinks. You know that each of the URLs listed has qualified itself by doing the one thing you want done for you: link out. This act alone prequalifies competitor backlink lists to some degree. If you merge lists of competitor backlinks and find the co-occurring URLs and host names, you're moving still closer to a qualified prospect list.

Besides identifying individual prospects, analyzing competitor backlinks can reveal new link opportunity types that you may have forgotten, overlooked, or not even known about. Always be on the lookout for new link-opportunity types, and if you have the assets or the resources to create the assets, be prepared to develop queries for finding more of them.

One other great way to use competitor backlinks is by looking at links to individual pages, rather than to the site as a whole. This is most useful when seeking outreach targets for a similar linkable asset that you've created.

A key difficulty with competitor backlink lists—even those with quality metrics as supplied by backlink data vendors—is an inability to quickly line up the prospects with your existing assets because you know nothing about the linking URLs and have very little way to assess why they linked in the first place. Figuring this out for every prospect would take months to do manually, but you can do it easier and faster. There are a number of free and commercially available tools for pulling competitor backlinks. Here are the ones we use and recommend:

- Majestic SEO (see Figure 8–3)
- Ahrefs (see Figure 8–4)
- Moz Link Explorer (see Figure 8–5)

FIGURE 8–3. Majestic SEO's Site Explorer

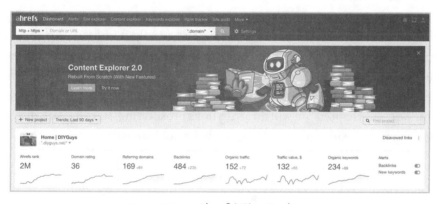

FIGURE 8–4. Ahrefs' Site Explorer

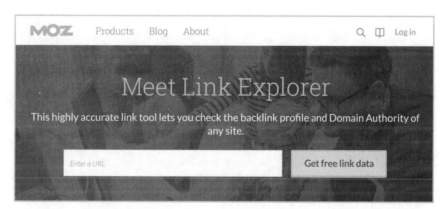

FIGURE 8–5. Moz's Link Explorer

AUTOMATING YOUR LINK PROSPECTING WITH RSS AGGREGATION

Once you've developed link-building query clusters for your evergreen linkable assets (assets that don't expire), it's time to set up and aggregate alerts so you can set yourself up with a steady supply of link prospects. You can do that with RSS aggregation, which basically means that you can control and easily curate the feed of web information you receive through computer programs.

First, you need to select your source for the feed. Here are several potential sources:

- Google Alerts
- RSS Micro
- Google Blog Search Engine
- Trackur

Sign up if you haven't already, and begin reading about how to set up feeds with each of the tools. Then add each of your link-building queries to the tool so it will send you corresponding pages.

You have to send your prospects someplace, and, ideally, it's not to your email inbox. By automating your prospecting using one of these online programs, you can step away for a few days, work through your other prospects, then come back and see what has collected while you qualified and reached out to your link prospects.

In the next few chapters, we will dive into links prospecting, starting with discovering and then scraping already published lists of target publishers.

Chapter 9

List-Scrape Prospecting for Link Builders

Never fear, link prospector, there remain deep wells of link-prospect opportunity, even if you've queried every last prospect from Google and snatched every last link from your competitors' backlink profiles. If you can make the right offer and have a team ready for outreach, then list-scrape prospecting could add a steady stream of powerful links to your portfolio.

We have the great fortune to live in an age in which webmasters aggregate and publish large lists of outbound links. It's as simple as searching Google for lists of XYZ kinds of sites, hand-picking pages with a high volume of outbound links, and "scraping" them with the same type of crawling and scraping software that Google uses to download the internet.

Often these lists are created in directory format for Google AdSense (www.google.com/adsense) earnings. Sometimes these lists—a list of orchestras or of U.S. hospitals by state—are created by passionate curators. And, of course, there are the top 100-plus blog lists, which you can use to search for the top 200 church blogs, for example.

The process of list-scrape link prospecting is simple:

1. Find lovingly crafted lists of websites (list hunting).
2. Brainstorm a valuable, relevant pitch (the only hard part).

3. Scrape the lists and contact information, removing any nonprospects.

4. Outreach, using the pitch you designed in point 2, to sites with available contact information.

Oh, and, yes, you can use our Link Prospector + Contact Finder tools to better automate this approach at https://citationlabs.com/tools/. In this chapter, we'll walk through each of these steps in detail.

LIST HUNTING

In hunting for lists, it's best to let Google's suggest function do the thinking for you. Here are some queries that have worked well for us:

- list of [institution]s
- list of U.S. [institution]s
- list of [a, b, c, etc.] websites
- list of [a, b, c, etc.] blogs
- top 10 [a, b, c, etc.] websites
- top 100 [a, b, c, etc.] blogs

An example of a list search can be seen in Figure 9–1, on page 71. A search of "list of police stations" returns several sites that aggregate police station websites.

I also highly recommend including the Ubersuggest tool (https://neilpatel.com/ubersuggest/) in your searches for lists:

Try searches like:

- list of lists
- list of websites
- list of sites
- list of websites for
- list of sites for

There are more, and your markets will probably have different names for lists, such as "directories" or "resources," too. You're hunting for lists, but they're not always so simply and directly named.

BRAINSTORM A RELEVANT PITCH

If you're genuinely interested in building a campaign around list scraping, we suggest you determine your pitch after you've found a list that could work. It's usually less viable to start with an asset and decide to go look for lists of relevant prospects. It can happen, and you should at least look, but stay open to working with the huge lists that already exist.

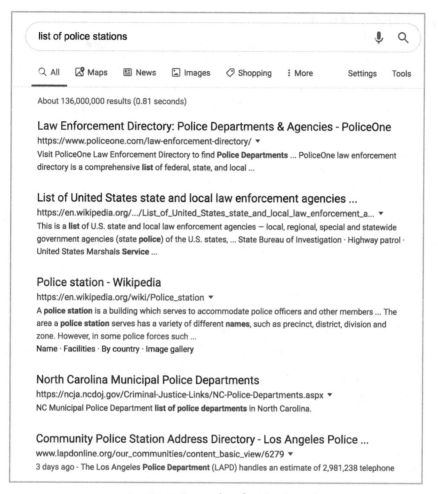

FIGURE 9–1. Example of a List Search

Think of these lists of sites as a target market and start your brainstorming from there. What content would make all the small-town hospital webmasters in the U.S. crack open their CMS and add to their websites? What critical widget is missing from the art museums of the world? Oh, you've got a killer offer for these 400 recipe and cooking sites?

And remember—in this approach you don't stop with one list. You find ALL the available lists of a target type and combine them. List scraping has the potential to be highly thorough.

One last note: Be careful! This approach can cross very, very quickly into spam if you're aggressive in your outreach and don't align the interests of your prospects, their audience, and you.

SCRAPE THE BLOG LIST

Next, scrape your list. I've found that list scraping is faster than scraping Google for popular blog subject areas (health, entertainment, etc.) with hundreds or thousands of blogs.

For example, in a search for fitness blogs, I see the following pages in the top ten results:

- 20-plus Amazing Fitness Blogs to Inspire You
- Top 20 Fitness Blogs
- Top 100 Health and Fitness Blogs

Now start looking for some fitness blog lists using the query list of fitness blogs, and we can throw several more lists on the pile:

- Favorite Fitness Blogs
- Top 100 Diet and Fitness Blogs
- Top 100+ Fitness Blogs
- Five Best Fitness Blogs on the Internet
- List of Weight Loss, Health, and Fitness Blog

From those eight URLs, I found approximately 300 fitness blogs. Even if not all of them are qualified, I can't imagine a single query in Google that would return 300 relevant results.

OUTREACH

Finally, it's time to reach out. My esteemed search marketing colleague Ken Lyons refers to his list-scraping method of prospecting and outreach as the "spray and pray" approach. It is. In an email exchange, Ross Hudgens called it "cold outreach." Yes—it's cold, quite cold. After all, you are emailing these sites without much of an introduction.

Here are some things that can help your response rates in this approach:

- Timeliness of your message
- Aligning your offer with the needs of the publishers
- Clearly demonstrating an understanding and concern for the publisher's audience
- Recognizable, authoritative brand

In the next chapter, we will explore prospecting for blogs, perhaps the single largest and most-accessible link-opportunity type.

Chapter 10

Prospecting for Blogs and Content Ideas Using Auto-Complete Suggestions

We covered blogs as a prospecting target in our initial chapter on prospecting. This chapter digs in even deeper with an approach that enables you to shine a light into all the odd topical nooks and crannies of your audience and, of course, the publishers who serve them.

Here's how it works. Say your campaign requires an estimated 5,000 unique parenting blogs and you only have Google for prospecting. What queries would you type in to get started? I suspect most folks, from seasoned SEOs to prospecting interns, would start running queries like these:

- parenting blog
- mom blog
- parenting advice blog
- parenting tips inurl:blog
- list of parenting blogs

Maybe you get fancier and set Google's time delimiter to the past year—or even month—so you're only seeing pages that are new or have been recently updated. Smart! You're probably kicking up hundreds, if not thousands, of ops if you pull from the top 20 to 50 results.

So your team works through your list of 500 for a couple months, but then you need more prospects because it turns out this particular batch of publishers is getting pretty link savvy and they are asking for money. So, where to next? Here's what we do to really expand the pool of potential publishers.

First, conduct topic research on target sites, use the topic findings to generate and scrape auto-complete suggestions, *then* use these suggestions to build queries that address audience concerns, questions, and objectives. In this chapter, we will unpack that into manageable tasks so you can find your audience where they live.

AUDIENCE RESEARCH: CONTENT TITLE ANALYSIS

First, visit three or more publishers that target an audience you'd like to get in front of. Next, visit each site and copy/paste two to three of their most recent article titles into a text pad. Then go to the next site until you have several titles.

Why? What's in a title? Everything. You'll find all the clues and signals that indicate the facets and aspects of the key experiences of the audience you care about. Titles—in particular, how-to or "non-newsy" titles—provide you with deep prospecting insights for any and every vertical served productively by content.

The title functions as a utility signal to the audience—it indicates what information is inside, who it's for, and how the info could be useful within the scope of the audience's "domain of practice." And these signals seem to have repeatable patterns and categories, at least within their distinct verticals.

Elements of a Title: The Starting Point for Parsing

From the titles of these parenting articles you're reviewing (title sample selection below), you'll notice the following functionality-specific title elements:

- *Practitioner type (e.g., parent, mom, dad, grandparent).* Usually, a fairly static and limited set, but vital for learning how audiences view themselves (see the section on "Seven Types of Keywords for Link Prospecting Queries" in Chapter 8).
- *Practitioner conditions (e.g., busy, depressed, harried, new parent).* Large, practically unlimited potential set.
- *Entity of practice (e.g., "child" is the entity of the practice of parenting).* Again, like the practitioner, fairly static and limited set.
- *Entity of practice conditions (e.g., child has a sensory processing disorder, is 5 years old, hitting siblings).* Large, unlimited potential set.
- *Theatre of practice (e.g., at school, in the car, at the beach, during a thunderstorm).* Usually a large, unlimited potential array of locations or circumstances that govern the utility of the suggested solutions.

■ *Practitioner's objectives.* Often but not always these are objectives for the entity of practice (e.g., potty train, stop eating boogers). In some cases, the objectives can be self-reflexive (e.g., be well so you can be a better parent): large, unlimited potential set.

The above categories reflect the key facets publishers use to signal the utility of a collection of advice (aka an article) to the practitioner (audience).

Article Title: "5 Dos and Don'ts of Shared Custody"

Now let's dig in and see where this takes us by parsing a title we found in the parenting blog space. The goal here is to develop a systematic understanding of the kinds of problems your audience has. We want to find out everything so we can thoroughly search for publishers who help solve their problems. Here's an example:

■ *Practitioner type* (assumptions I made). Parent, mom, dad
■ *Practitioner condition.* Single, joint custody, step
■ *Entity of practice.* Child
■ *Entity of practice conditions.* Step, shared custody, emotional distress
■ *Theatre of practice.* Not apparent from title
■ *Practitioner's objectives.* Raise a resilient, awesome child and avoid unnecessary conflicts

As you go through this title-parsing exercise, you're building a bank of who the title is signaling as its target audience (or, in our terms, the practitioner type), who or what they care for, and other conditions and objectives. These elements become the seeds for the auto-complete scraping we're about to do, and from which we can start to see the needs of the broader audience.

After looking over that parsed title with my seasoned prospector's eye, I think it's worthwhile auto-complete scraping the following "practitioner and entity labels":

■ Single parent
■ Single mom
■ Single dad
■ Stepdad
■ Stepmom
■ Stepchild
■ Stepson
■ Stepdaughter

If you're eager to jump into prospecting, you could select one of the above terms alone and start hunting for nouns that indicate what's being sought by the searcher.

Alternately, you can jump right in and combine them with the following terms, which you would place *after* your selected practitioner label:

- Advice
- Tips
- Problems
- Ideas
- Help with
- How to
- Keeps on
- Won't stop

Put your big batch of terms in a new text file or in the same one. Now, combine your seed terms with these, but place them *before* your seed terms:

- Help for
- Advice for
- How to for

You've finished the hard part of parsing, and you now have a huge list of 108 terms that you could run through an auto-complete suggest scraper. You can also pick one or two of the suggestions just to poke around. Suggest scrapers are all over the place; to find one, search Google for "auto complete scraper."

We built a suggest scraper that you can input hundreds of seeds or "starts" into. You can get by with running a few seeds through a suggest scraper. If you're serious, though, and already a Link Prospector user, let me know, and I'll see if we can find a seat for you. It's an internal tool for now but helps give you quick snapshots of how information demand gets grouped and categorized by your target practitioners.

Here's a selection of nine from the top 50 or so most-frequent results of the 1,500 we got back (with the number of occurrences listed for each):

1. What to do when your mom and stepdad are fighting (12 occurrences in the set—most frequently occurring query of the set)
2. How to get adoption papers for stepdad (9 occurrences)
3. Help for single parent with special needs child (8 occurrences)
4. Best advice for dating a single mom (8 occurrences)
5. How easy is it for a father to get shared custody (8)
6. Ten tips on how to be a stepdad (7)
7. What to do if your stepdad hits your mom (7)
8. How to deal with empty nest syndrome as a single parent (6)
9. How to explain stepmom to child (6)

I love these. We could add an inurl:blog to each of these and head over to Google right now for a large collection of publishers that write for a distinct segment of our target audience. But if you parse these query suggestions in the same way you analyzed titles, you instantly acquire a much broader, diversified vision for this domain of practice.

You can observe—from the first, second, and sixth queries—that the children themselves are often seeking guidance. While this article is written as a prospecting exercise, perhaps you're seeing here how it serves as an approach to content or audience-discovery research as well. If you're writing in this space, have you written extensively for the kids who are actively researching with objectives of their own?

And I love number 8—dealing with empty nest syndrome as a single parent. It's forehead-slapping obvious, but I'd never thought of it. Again—great content direction and a useful query to run with an inurl:blog because it's likely going to find those publishers that are off the well-beaten path and who perhaps haven't gotten quite so many guest placement inquiries.

All that said, there are some limitations. I had to remove false starts like "how to draw something for your mom step-by-step." There were multiple suggests like this, and further down the list, we get into hyper specific or regionally specific queries that I don't think would be useful for prospecting:

- How to calculate child support in Ontario with shared custody.
- How to calculate child support for shared custody BC.
- How to calculate child support in PA when custody is shared.

It's not all keywords and roses, and we still hand-qualify any and all huge sets of suggest scrapes so that when we use them in the prospecting phase, we return pages from sites that are more likely to target our audience or topic area.

We're now done with one of the titles, and we've barely dented the array of practitioner and entity conditions, plus practitioner objectives for the entities, that drive everyone to search in the first place. So, I'd advise you try parsing through some of these titles and building out your auto-suggest seed sets, such as:

- How to respond when your child acts out in public
- How to say sorry: teaching children to apologize
- When my child hurts yours
- My child was a picky eater so here's what I did
- Does your own childhood affect your parenting?
- Sibling jealousy between your older child and baby stressing you out? Read this.
- Child a sore loser? Try these four tips to teach your child to lose gracefully.
- Gardening with toddlers—activities that are fun and easy to do together

The titles above are excerpted from the following sites:

- https://www.empoweringparents.com/blog/
- https://www.ahaparenting.com/blog
- https://www.scarymommy.com/
- https://messymotherhood.com/
- https://bouncebackparenting.com/blog/

Now let's parse another article title. We'll go with the first one from the list above, How to Respond When Your Child Acts Out in Public:

- *Practitioner name.* Parent, mom, dad, grandparent
- *Practitioner condition.* Anxious, angry, stressed, concerned with censure and judgmental assumptions by others of capacity for parenting
- *Entity of practice.* Child, son, daughter
- *Entity condition.* Age, has an unspoken or unknown need, or a need that can't be attended to immediately
- *Theatre of practice.* In a social setting, usually around strangers, *with* parent present
- *Practitioner objectives.* Get that kid to act right

I'm not sure there will be quite as many obvious starts as the previous title we parsed. So, let's single out some practitioner and entity labels and conditions that are likely to return some great auto-complete suggestions:

- my child|son|daughter|toddler
- my grandchild|son|daughter

Note that we neglected "my stepson|daughter" for this exercise for the purposes of simplifying our example—they should absolutely be added for thoroughness. Now, we need some behavior-oriented starts that will help us fish well in the auto-suggest:

- won't stop
- misbehaves
- acts up
- disrespects me
- is disrespectful
- won't listen

In this instance, it might be productive to sandwich our entities in this way:

- help to
- how to

. . . plus . . .

- make my <entity>

. . . and close with . . .

- behave
- be respectful
- listen

Once we combine everything (into 105 starts) and run them through our auto-complete tool, we're likely to see results that take us far outside the scope of the initial title we started from. Again, that's because we isolated and extracted the title's key elements and used them to help find more of the common circumstances, conditions, and labels facing those in charge of caring for unruly children. Here are some of the most-frequent results we got from adding those 105 starts to our suggest scraper:

1. How do I make my son listen to me (7)
2. How do I make my daughter listen to me (7)
3. My boyfriend disrespects me in front of his son (6)
4. How do I make my child listen to me (6)
5. Why does my child only misbehave at home (5)
6. What should I do when my child misbehaves in front of others (5)
7. My mother disrespects me in front of my child (5)
8. My 4-year-old child won't listen to me (5)
9. My child misbehaves in public (5)

And though there are few surprises in the top results, we have branched out into some rich content directions. For example, I would have never thought to write for the mother whose boyfriend is being disrespectful in front of his son. And consider the one about the mother/grandmother being disrespectful. Where does that take us in terms of queries for discovering publishers? It takes us far and away from simply searching for parenting blogs. Parenting, and every other domain of practice that we participate in or write into, contains far deeper avenues than most of us have ever appreciated.

Now it's time to use our results for prospecting . . .

Build Queries Using Your Suggested Topics and Audience Info-Needs

Take all the auto-completed queries you've harvested and combine them with [inurl:blog]. Just be sure to remove those brackets: []. If you have more time for qualifying, you could also add simply the word [blog]. Between those two, you'll be relatively sure that the top 20 results or so will be swarming with useful publishers that will help your target practitioners with content, and they're less likely to be publishers you or other content marketers/SEOs have seen before.

Still using the Link Prospector Tool for mass querying, here are some sample queries to run based on the above extracted suggestions:

- What to do when your mom and stepdad are fighting inurl:blog
- How to get adoption papers for stepdad inurl:blog
- Help for single parent with special needs child inurl:blog
- Best advice for dating a single mom inurl:blog
- How easy is it for a father to get shared custody inurl:blog
- Ten tips on how to be a stepdad inurl:blog
- What to do if your stepdad hits your mom inurl:blog
- How to deal with empty nest syndrome as a single parent inurl:blog
- How to explain stepmom to child inurl:blog
- How do I make my son listen to me inurl:blog
- How do I make my daughter listen to me inurl:blog
- My boyfriend disrespects me in front of his son inurl:blog
- How do I make my child listen to me inurl:blog
- Why does my child only misbehave at home inurl:blog
- What should I do when my child misbehaves in front of others inurl:blog
- My mother disrespects me in front of my child inurl:blog
- My 4-year-old child won't listen to me inurl:blog
- My child misbehaves in public inurl:blog

One last test I've neglected: Is it better to search for "step parenting inurl:blog" than to use something like [how to explain stepmom to child inurl:blog]? In other words, how similar or diverse are the domains that return for those two different queries, and is it worth doing both of them? At a glance, I notice several similar domains on both queries, but I think they're different enough to justify running both of them. And if you have a strong qualifying process in place, you'll be fine.

If you've been wondering where to go next for blog prospecting and content idea generation, then you're now well situated to dig back in to the spaces you thought were so familiar to you with new, finely granulated queries that align with information demand and all your previously unknown facets of this demand.

In the next chapter, we will discuss automated and manual ways to qualify link prospects for a targeted project.

Chapter 11

Qualifying Link Prospects

I f "Excel Hell" exists, then there must certainly be a level in it specifically for lists of link prospects. Those people who've had to find prospects worthy of outreach from lists of thousands of URLs know exactly what we're talking about. In Chapter 8 we discussed several ways to prequalify your prospects, including targeted queries designed to discover prospects in line with your assets and finding co-occurrences among competitor backlinks.

This chapter investigates both "automated" and "manual" ways to qualify link prospects once you've gathered them for a project. We recommend you use automated methods to focus on easily measurable factors to cull the list to a manageable size. Then manually review the list to further qualify and highlight the best link opportunities for the proper segment of your campaign. You can also gather contact information at the this stage, if applicable to your campaign.

QUALIFYING LINK PROSPECTS BASED ON AVAILABLE METRICS

The first place to begin attacking hundreds or thousands of prospects is with any readily available metrics. If you've used the SEObook Firefox plugin to scrape search engine result data, you can source metrics that way. Additionally, we suggest using the following Google Chrome extensions:

- Data Scraper—Easy Web Scraping
- Web Scraper

Many of the commercially available link-prospecting services also have their own metrics that will enable you to qualify in a more "automated" way. Here are more methods you can use to quickly remove prospects from large lists without actually visiting and looking at the web pages (yet).

Keyword Occurrences in URLs

If you've copied and pasted your list of link prospects into a spreadsheet program, one way to determine relevance is to simply search for your market defining keywords—and potentially keywords associated with the link-opportunity type—in the URLs themselves. For example, if you've been looking for link lists on .edu sites, then the word "link" or "list" appearing in the URL is a pretty good identifier. If you want the blogs, then "blog" would be a fantastic place to start searching your spreadsheet. Any URLs that contain the keywords should be set aside for a manual review later.

Authority of Host Name or URL

Page rank (PR) remains the simplest, quickest, most scrapable metric for freely assessing the authority of a URL and its host name. We don't practice or preach chasing high-page rank links, but we firmly assert that you can make broad generalizations about a link prospect data set based on PR. If you've sourced your link prospects either from link-building queries or competitor backlink data, then sorting your list in descending order of host name PR can help you immediately spot the strongest, most authoritative sites for potential outreach. Other authority measurements are available from other link-prospecting tools and can be used to sort in much the same way.

Inbound Link Count to Host Name, Inbound Link Count to URL

Like page rank, the number of links a site has can be easily manipulated and should never be a sole decision point for whether to establish a relationship with a site. And, like page rank, if your link prospects have been prequalified with queries or backlink co-occurrence, then inbound link count becomes a more useful number. In addition to helping you make decisions about which sites to approach for engagement, inbound link counts to nonhost name URLs can help you identify content to which your market responds well.

Distribution Metrics: Twitter Mentions, Facebook Likes, Reddit Mentions, Stumbles, Etc.

The SEO Toolbar for Firefox also enables you to quickly pull data points, such as the number of times a domain has appeared in Twitter, Facebook, Reddit, and StumbleUpon. These metrics are strong signals that the site owners are active social media participants and may have developed a following. These sites should certainly be set aside for further consideration, especially for content placement, interviews, and news-related engagement.

MANUALLY MAKING PROSPECT QUALIFICATIONS

At a certain point, it becomes necessary to visit prospect sites by hand. We believe you should do as much work as possible to minimize the number of sites you visit by hand, as this is one of the most time-consuming and tedious parts of link building. It's also the point where you're likely to have the most inspiration for your campaign, so be sure to schedule ample time and be ready to capture the ideas you have. Following are some things to keep in mind as you qualify prospects in this way.

Asset Relevance

Sometimes the presence of a link-opportunity keyword in the URL can indicate possible relevance to a linkable asset. And sometimes you have to visit the page and look the site over to make sure the owner/curator is likely to be receptive to publishing a mention of your asset.

Reach and Influence Assessment

There are a number of ways to assess a site's influence and reach. To our knowledge, few of these are readily capturable in an automated, per-URL fashion. The number of blog and/or newsletter subscribers can tell you a great deal about how long the site has been around, as well as how far your linkable asset is likely to travel should it get mentioned. The Twitter followers of the site's publisher is another decent metric, but if you're pursuing guest-post opportunities, then the number of times the domain has appeared in Twitter is an even better metric of the site's reach. Further, you should check to see if the site has badges for voting for its pages on niche social news sites. If so, search that social news site to see how often your prospect has appeared and to get an idea of how often their content has gone "hot." Go for reach and influence whenever possible!

Oops! It's a Competitor!

Sometimes competitors appear in your link prospect data sets. This can be tough to discern ahead of time, especially if you're new to a market and/or a client. Sometimes it requires a site visit to make that distinction.

At-a-Glance Site Quality

Is the design and layout pleasing, or at least not distracting? Are you bombarded with ads and AdSense links that force you to scroll to find the content on the page? Are there obvious misspellings and atrocious grammar? Again, these could all be strong signs that this prospect should be discarded (no matter what the metrics tell you).

TOOLS FOR FASTER MANUAL QUALIFICATION

There's only one tool that we're aware of that considerably speeds up the process of manual qualification. It's a free and very simple tool that we developed—the URL Reviewer Tool. Here is the step-by-step process for using the tool to speed up the final manual qualification of your link prospects:

1. Turn off images in your browser. You'll move faster if you have multiple tabs (or windows) open, and your computer will work faster if it doesn't have to handle all those images. You can usually do this by opening your browser's settings/options.

2. Use a "URL Reviewer" tool, which opens a list of URLs in new tabs. Search for "open sites in multiple tabs."

3. Only add 10 URLs at a time at first to test the strain on your computer. If it handles 10 well, try 20, then 30. You're testing for bottlenecks here, which can occur in your RAM, your router, your internet connection, etc. You want to find the optimal speed so you can get at as many prospects as possible at a time.

4. Use Chrome, which manages RAM allocations more efficiently than Firefox, Opera, or Safari. Some link builders are wary of using Google-based products in link building, especially if they are researching link buys. If you share this concern, then don't use Chrome.

5. Save yourself a mouse click and use Ctrl-W or Command-W to close tabs.

6. Only make a mark for confirmed, definite prospects in your spreadsheet. Once you've finished going through your list, you can sort by that column and mark all the others as "Not Prospects." Your nonprospects are at least as valuable as your prospects—they will help you qualify prospects even more quickly in the future.

Using these methods, focused link builders can hand-qualify up to 250 URLs an hour. Garrett, who suffers at times from ADD and inspiration-induced reveries, can often plow through 100 or so. Your times will vary.

55 LINK-OPPORTUNITY QUALIFIERS

This list of 55 qualifiers should help to get your brain turning regarding metrics and methods for qualifying your link prospects, whether you are automating your qualifying process or doing it by hand and looking at each site individually.

24 Automated Qualifiers

1. Keywords appear in target URL
2. Keywords appear in target URL title tag
3. Keywords appear in H1 tags
4. Keyword occurrences in body text
5. Keyword occurrences in meta keywords and description
6. Number of outbound links on target URL
7. Number of inbound links to target URL
8. Number of inbound links to domain
9. Followed/nofollowed outbound links
10. Competitor URLs
11. Excessive AdSense placements
12. PageRank of URL
13. PageRank of domain
14. Domain age
15. Page type (social network, blog, answers page, forum, links page, etc.)
16. Number of comments in comment threads
17. Inbound links from news sites, .edus or .govs
18. Inbound links from blogs and other sites within your prospect set
19. Forum signature inbound links
20. Inbound links from niche/industry news sites
21. Inbound links from industry groups and organizations
22. Social media inbound links (Twitter, StumbleUpon, Reddit, Delicious, etc.)
23. Social media/industry group badge outbound links
24. Page type (blog, review page, links page, etc.)

31 Manual Qualifiers

1. Is there genuine relevance between the page and the page you're building links to?
2. Is it a previously unidentified competitor?
3. Is the text human-generated?
4. Are there excessive, obtrusive ads?
5. What motivated the current links on the target URL?
6. Recent posts, recent site updates, updated copyright date?
7. At first pass, does the text look correct in grammar and spelling?
8. What is the design and image quality?
9. How thorough and well-tended does the resources/links page seem?
10. Is there more than one link page?

11. When was the last update?

12. Is the site owner/moderator easily accessible by email or phone?

13. Is there a comments box?

14. What is the quality of comments and conversation there now?

15. Does it contain discussion related to your product or service?

16. Is there an established community evident in comments or an adjunct forum?

17. Are there Q/A forms on the site?

18. Does it have strong content?

19. Does the site have editors?

20. Are there links out to other known influencers?

21. Does the site contain written reviews?

22. Does it include an email newsletter or other signs of reach and distribution?

23. Is there an "In the News" section with quotes by major newspapers and industry publications?

24. Is the person's name the URL?

25. Is it an industry analyst/consultant site?

26. Is it a niche industry news coverage site?

27. Does it have a robust commenting community with a great deal of response from author?

28. Is there writing about recent industry news and developments?

29. Obviously attends conferences?

30. Does it use multiple media formats?

31. Have you seen this URL on multiple blogrolls?

Now that you've got qualifying under control, it's time to talk about trust. Link trust, that is, which is what we'll cover in the next chapter.

Chapter 12

What Is Link Trust?

O n the web, where engines index URLs by the billions (the good, the bad, and the ugly), signals of trust, merit, and intent of source will be crucial to any search result, including a personalized search result.

Signals of trust, merit, and intent of source can be determined in a couple of ways with an algorithm that looks at onsite or off-site signals, or without an algorithm at all, using offline factors (rarely discussed, by the way).

So links, citations, inclusions, and connections, along with confidence, intent, credibility, and veracity aren't going anywhere, because what other signals are there? Seriously, if you had a billion dollars and wanted to start a search engine, what signals will your big fancy algorithm measure in order to produce useful results?

What's likely true is the sources of all signals are getting more and more algorithmic scrutiny, and end users play a larger role in this process in many ways. The links you depend on for both traffic and rank better be bulletproof and not a house of cards waiting to crumble. If your link-building tactics and targets have not been wisely chosen, the day will come (or already has) when you will not be happy. The value of certain types of links cannot be underestimated.

Why? Because they are so hard to get and are based on a decision made by a person who is a passionate subject expert. They don't have to be a Ph.D., librarian, or a famous blogger. They just have to be able to provide algorithmic confidence signals. And you need to know what those signals are. I know what many of them are because I've sat in front of a computer screen for way too many years studying and working at it.

The ability to identify who and what a true influencer is, and why, is crucial for both broad and narrow topics. It's just as important as knowing how to interact with each one of them in the right way to get what you seek.

At a search industry conference in 2002, during a Q&A session, a panelist (me?) was challenged for being too cautious and unrealistic with his tactics. The panelist had just told the entire room that link-building tactics, like mass directory submission, or article syndication/submission, or indiscreet reciprocal linking, or press releases, or paid links, and even some forms of linkbait, were all doomed to failure sooner or later, that any website basing its long-term success on such tactics would fail.

It would be unfair to point fingers at any company in particular, because to some extent we have all helped perpetuate the link-building myths that Google innocently fueled when it first gave us PageRank. At the same time, I find it hard to believe anyone who earns their living by building links is really surprised by what has happened over the years and continues to happen; for example, the devaluing of directory links. Are you really shocked that Google no longer thinks a link from link-o-matic, link-to-my-loo, and LinksForNoGoodReason.com are of any value?

How about deep links inserted inside articles, then syndicated to hundreds of other sites? It's junk. The only thing you should be shocked about is how long it's taken the search engines to devalue this spammy link-building approach. It's the same with reciprocal link networks, or blog link networks. In fact, any linking tactic not driven by merit but rather by deception cannot be trusted.

Many link-building services mistakenly consider a steady stream of new clients to be an indicator that they are effective link builders.

Google's focus on trusted sources is your worst nightmare. At the heart of the trusted link model is the word *trust*. But the mistake being made is missing the true origin of that trust. It is never the page itself that is trustworthy. Neither is it the domain nor is it the IP block or the number of co-hosted websites present or some other silly metric. Trust originates with the steward of the content like the page editor, author, or curator. Trust originates from people and manifests itself on the web as links. The engine that figured that out first was Google, then others followed.

My favorite saying is as accurate today as it was in the 1990s: The engines already know how to count links. What they don't know, and what they will get better at, is knowing which of the links they have counted actually matter.

In this chapter, we will discuss link-trustable websites and what makes them trustworthy. Additionally, we will cover a contribution by Ross Hudgens, where we learn about building links from commonly recognizable news and media outlets—also known as tier one link building.

SPOTTING SIGNS OF TRUST

What signs do you look for when seeking a good link target site? There is a generic answer and a specific answer.

- *Generic answer.* A good link target will be different for every site you are seeking links for.
- *Specific answer.* Let's say the site you are seeking links for is devoted to every-thing about the history of jazz music, like the one shown below in Figure 12–1: www.apassion4jazz.net.
- An example of a high-quality and trusted target site would be a university library database, like the one featured in Figure 12–2, on page 90, from the University of North Carolina that contains a page of links for blues music research.

FIGURE 12–1. If This Was the Site You Were Seeking Links For . . .

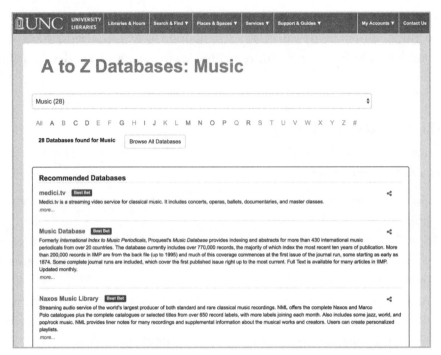

FIGURE 12–2. Then This Is a Great Target Site to Find a Link

Why? Many reasons. First, always look for the intent of the target site. In the example above, the intent of a university music web guide is evident. That site isn't there to sell links, barter links, swap links, trade links, triangulate links, or any other silly link scheme. The intent has nothing to do with any search engine. That site exists as a resource to help people. A link from that site and others like it sends incredibly powerful signals of trust to the search engines.

The beauty of this is it doesn't take many such signals/links to get to a point where the engines will then, by extension and association, trust apassion4jazz.net as well. And as the search result on the following page shows, they obviously do. The search results for "history of jazz music" (see Figure 12–3, on page 91) shows apassion4jazz.net at the top, thanks to its high-trust content links.

HOW TO GET TIER ONE LINKS
by Ross Hudgens, founder and CEO of Siege Media

There are no links more powerful than tier one links. CNN, *New York Times*, and CNET are just a few of the sites that fall into this bucket. That is, they are news organizations that fit the "parent test": publications you could mention to your parents that they'd immediately recognize.

FIGURE 12–3. Search Results for "History of Jazz Music" Shows Apassion4jazz.net at the Top, Thanks to Its High-Trust Content Links

In quantitative terms, these are normally sites that fit in the upper 10th percentile of the link metric of your choice. They also have the potential to be "seed sites." In other words, they're a great place to get a link (which is awesome), but the subsequent reality that they can drive real traffic and, thereby, additional links from other publications that read them is often even more powerful.

Traditionally, links and coverage of this type are done through old-school public relations (PR). Create a story, build a relationship with the reporter, then pitch it to two to five people. PR firms would often spend years building these relationships to leverage for their clients, which made getting coverage from SEO firms somewhat of a black box.

Today, the best way to do this is through creating and promoting surveys to 20 to 40 people instead. In this section, we'll get into that process and give you the toolkit to generate tier one link placements.

The Requirements for Success

While it is true that relationships help you get more tier one placements, they aren't required. That said, there is a general set of standards that this type of publication looks for.

First, the company the story is coming from must be credible. If you run an affiliate site with no LinkedIn, a shoddy looking website, and no noticeable backstory, that immediately creates pause with a reporter. If they're running your story, they want to feel confident it won't come back to bite them because of an insufficient sample size, sloppy data, or a poor source.

You can still generate links if you're one of those businesses, but for the most part, it's recommended to avoid doing so if tier one is a strategy. Building a business that's credible to the press is a similar path to building a business that's credible to users, so it's worth pursuing even if press isn't something that immediately makes sense for you.

Next, the content being generated must be newsworthy. In general, you need to be saying something absolutely new to be covered by the news. CNN is not going to cover a beginner's guide or a resource page—that's old-hat in their world.

Therefore, you need to generate something breaking. There are several routes for doing this in the traditional PR sense, such as raising a round of funding or launching a new product. However, for the purposes of this discussion, we'll focus on creating press coverage from scratch rather than something likely outside your control as a link builder.

When generating something breaking, the focus must be almost entirely on generating survey content, because it's the easiest way to create news from nothing. Consumer surveys allow you to ask different types of questions of the public. These questions lead to interesting insights about how people think, which can then be sliced and diced into different demographic segments. Hopefully, you can illuminate interesting tidbits about the world and drive reporters to want to cover it.

Some examples of successful surveys include:

- Only one-third of drivers clean their car each year.
- Men with moustaches are more likely to cheat on their partner.
- Millennials are the worst tippers in the United States.

Thankfully, you don't need to ask people these questions to get responses. Online tools allow you to do this easily and affordably. We'll get into how to do that later.

That said, to make your surveys coverable, there is a final requirement of the work that's worth highlighting. The data being generated must be significant and trustworthy. One thing every major reporter will ask for is the methodology of how the data was generated. They do this to understand two important points that could affect the data:

1. *Statistical significance.* With surveys under 500 people, there is a large margin of error due to the small sample size. Running into a grumpy set of 25 people can significantly throw the results. This is why reporters look for large sample sizes to make surveys more credible. On average, we suggest over 1,000 respondents. In

certain industries, 500 is acceptable if it's a niche enough audience that reporters don't usually get access to. Examples of this may be tech CEOs or sales managers in San Francisco.

2. *How the survey was conducted.* Who, what, when, and how you asked it can all throw the results of a survey. For example, if you asked, "Do you love coffee more than life itself?" of a group of people at 4 A.M. that you forced to wake up, you'd likely get more "yes" responses than if you asked the same question at 2 P.M. Other examples are asking leading questions or forcing people into one or two responses, which can push people into answers they maybe wouldn't have otherwise given.

Because of this, it's smart to include this methodology wherever you host the survey so you don't have to wait to be asked.

How to Create Winning Surveys

Now that you know the core tenets of what tier one press looks for, you can start thinking about creating a winning survey that generates links and press online.

We like to stick to the "S.U.C.C.E.S.s" framework from the Heath Brothers, authors of *Made to Stick: Why Some Ideas Survive and Others Die* (Random House, 2007). That is, ideas that are "made to stick" check as many of these boxes as possible:

- Simple
- Unexpected
- Credible
- Concrete
- Emotional
- Stories

When thinking of a potential idea for a survey, you should ask yourself if the potential answer you're going to get will check most of these boxes.

When thinking of a question to ask respondents, stick to three frameworks:

- *Do you know the answer to this question?* If you asked people in San Francisco, "What's your favorite NFL team?" you could get responses, but you'd already know the answer for the vast majority (the 49ers). It's best to ask questions you don't confidently know the answer to, because that's more likely to lead to unexpected results.
- *Can you imagine a marketable title?* In an earlier example, "One-third of drivers haven't washed their car in the past year" was cited as a successful survey. This is a result you could assume from a question like, "Have you washed your car in the past year?" If you can't imagine a question that would make you want to click a

post or an email, then you probably have the wrong question. Regardless, it still somewhat needs to fall in line with bullet one: a general feeling or intuition without the absolute certainty to make it obvious.

■ *Does it illicit an emotional reaction?* Although it's recommended to hit every letter on the S.U.C.C.E.S. framework above, it's particularly recommended to strike a chord emotionally in some way. In the above example on how rarely people wash their cars, the emotional reaction would likely be "ewww!" which still counts and makes people want to share the story. If you bore people, you won't get coverage.

If you stick to these three frameworks, the survey title will check most of the boxes described previously. It will tell a story about the person who answers, elicit an emotional response (I didn't know that/wow!), and be simple enough to distill quickly into a subject line.

The main point missing is if the story is credible. That is, if a credit card company wrote that story about how infrequently people wash their cars, would that make sense? Comparatively, what if Match.com wrote a dating survey? You'd take that as absolute fact, even if it didn't easily match all the suggestions described.

It's critical to make sure the questions you're asking make sense for your business. While this is prudent from a link generation perspective, it's even more important for good marketing. It should make sense for your business to run a survey and arguably generate secondary value from the effort, even if the primary key performance indicator (KPI) is links.

Once you understand that, there are a few things to consider with the potential direction of your surveys:

■ *Who are the audiences that link to things like this?* That is, if you run a survey on the perception of SEO, who are the actual publishers that would cover it? Are there enough?

■ *When is this kind of subject covered?* If you sell student loans, there is an increase in discussion of them when people go back to school, which makes sense in the content calendar for news publications. If you pitch these surveys into an off-season for a particular topic, you're more likely to have issues. That said, there is also a potential positive: You may have less pitch competition, so there are multiple factors to weigh.

■ *What's the likelihood you'll get marketable responses?* It's common that you may think a question is good, but the responses you get back are dull and you don't have much to work with. For this reason, it's sometimes suggested to "test" questions and see how a sample of 50 to 100 folks respond to them before investing in 1,000 respondents.

With this information in hand and a good direction for your question or set of questions, you can get to the nitty-gritty: asking the questions.

Which Online Survey Services to Use

The internet changes quickly, so I won't bore you with overly granular suggestions of where to ask these questions or how the tools are structured, which could easily change by the time you read this. But there are two relatively evergreen sources which are likely to still be around for the long term that we recommend leveraging:

1. *Google Surveys:* Google asks questions on online news articles in exchange for allowing the reader to view the full article. This warrants relatively cost-effective surveys, but with the potential loss of respondents being in a rush or less likely to give you a credible, thoughtful answer.
2. *Survey Monkey:* As the world's leading survey tool, Survey Monkey allows for advanced demographic segmenting that you can't get with Google Consumer Surveys. That said, this comes with a higher cost on average. Typically, reporters seem to trust Survey Monkey results more than Google results, but not to a significant degree.

Overall, the more you refine your audience, the more expensive your question is going to be. Therefore, to get the highest impact for the lowest cost, the ideal Venn diagram is to think of a question or set of questions anyone can answer that is still marketable.

The service you use will depend on how often you plan on asking survey questions and the kind of data you regularly need. We use both Survey Monkey and Google Surveys (depending on the client need), and both are great and relatively affordable.

To create a marketable survey, expect to pay somewhere between $500 and $1,500 to get interesting, reliable data. That's the cost of entry to make something compelling.

Survey Content Formats

There are three different ways to leverage survey data; each have their pros and cons.

1. *The single-question survey with data visualizations.* The most common option, the single-question survey, allows you to ask a punchy question, then summarize it in an article. For ideal marketability, you want to build "shareable assets" into any content you create. For surveys, that means data visualizations. You'll want to build small images, as reporters are unlikely to share infographics in the tier one area. Here are some examples:
   - https://www.creditcards.com/credit-card-news/worst-tippers-survey.php

- https://studentloanhero.com/featured/survey-student-loan-borrowers-and-divorce/

2. *The single-question survey with data visualizations and an infographic.* Depending on the topic, it's also possible to use a survey question as the backbone of an infographic in addition to smaller data visualizations. This is especially lucrative when you know the topic appeals to a set of mid-tier bloggers who would also be interested in the subject but are unlikely to write a full article on it. By using both asset types, you won't turn off the press, while also including a second audience. Here are some examples:

   - https://www.carrentals.com/blog/driving-with-germs-study/
   - https://www.personalcreations.com/blog/new-mother-statistics

3. *The multi-question survey with data visualizations and/or infographic.* Another popular, lower-risk option is the multi-question survey. This option takes a wider approach and asks multiple questions of the same audience. It allows for various narratives to be pulled out, while also increasing the likelihood that one of the responses returns something interesting for a reporter to craft a narrative around. The downside to this kind of approach is that it's significantly more expensive, both in time and money. The positive is that it can come off as more authoritative and be crafted into a report-type format, such as "The State of Online Dating in 2020." For the right business, the data can be reused and create interesting year-over-year changes that can be developed into their own story. Here are some examples:

   - https://www.nitrocollege.com/research/remake-the-school-system
   - https://www.nitrocollege.com/research/typical-american-financial-life

Survey Post Structure

There's more than one way to skin a cat here, but the overall best practices that create successful surveys are as follows:

- *The post is scannable and filled with rich images.* Your data visualizations and content should create a post that's a joy to read. If you're a reporter, you should be able to pull out the main story without reading too much, but you should also be able to find more depth if needed.
- *It includes survey methodology.* Most frequently cited at the end, your methodology should list the number of respondents and when/where/how you generated the data. Some reporters may ask for this, depending on the question.
- *You lead with the best story.* In other words, don't bury the lede. Find the most interesting data in your story and state it up front, whether it's in the post title or in

the first data point you summarize and/or visualize. Don't make people work to find the story.

- *You include [Survey] or [New Data] in the title.* HubSpot did a study on the click-through rate and found that titles with brackets perform better than those without. For surveys, it adds helpful context to use one of these two descriptions to describe the content they're about to cover. It may also make sense to include the best statistic in the title as well.

If you ask a great question or set of questions, structure the post properly, and make it enjoyable to read, you've done most of the work to create a successful post to drive tier one links.

Next comes the fun part: promotion.

How to Promote Surveys

Once you've built your survey and you're confident in it, it's time to think about getting the word out. There are a few approaches to doing this.

The Exclusive

Before hitting publish, we suggest reaching out to a reporter or a small set of reporters, and offer an exclusive of some sort. This creates a feeling of importance for that reporter that may make them more likely to cover it.

A suggested process would be to email your preferred reporter and offer them the exclusive with a 48-hour timeline of response needed. Include the nuts and bolts of your post and, ideally, the post in PDF form so they can get a sense for the full study.

Some reporters may decline or not respond for various reasons, so you should have a timeline of around seven days before publishing to account for this step. Once you've emailed the first reporter and not heard back, you can email a second with the same exclusive opportunity.

The email pitch for this will look very similar to your normal pitch, which we'll cover below. That said, make sure you include "exclusive" in the subject line and attach the post in some form.

If you're not getting bites from your ideal two or three reporters, it's time to move on and just hit publish, then let the dogs out in terms of promotion.

The Press Release

Another tactic of promoting survey content is a press release. While these aren't going to make or break your piece, distributing through a wire service can be helpful for getting one to two more pickups from a tier one. If they end up costing under $300 per placement, that's an investment that's commonly worthwhile for your business.

Write your press release as you would an email, just not directed to a specific person. Summarize the best parts of the story, give people clear contact information if they'd like to discuss, and link to the article.

Reddit Submission

Reddit is another powerful vehicle for promoting surveys that appeal to the right audience. Try searching for the subject of your survey in Reddit's search engine and look for highly trafficked subreddits that may be interested.

When doing this search, you'll want to make sure the subreddit posts links from third parties and frequently cover news. If you don't see a lot of that on the first page, there's a good chance your post will be flagged, and you will never get traction if you post there.

Advanced tip: Try submitting to the people or press that cover you. Often, if you submit as a publisher instead of yourself, it will be better received because it isn't directly coming from a commercial entity.

Email Outreach

By far, email outreach will be the cog that keeps the gears turning for most of your survey promotion. If this process strategically makes sense for you in the long term, it's worth building relationships with the people you're reaching out to.

Many reporters are on Twitter. Follow them, engage with their articles, and get to know their tastes.

This knowledge and relationship building will make you much more likely to be successful in the long term with survey promotion. However, you will not always have a relationship to build from, so you'll need to approach some people cold.

Here are a few suggestions for getting in front of the right people:

- *Do a news search for your topic or similar topics on Google.* This is a great first source for finding reporters who cover topics similar to you. That said, you don't want people who cover topics that are too close. If someone has covered your survey recently, it's likely they won't cover it again.
- *Search by reporter after searching by publication.* If you pitch tech news, there's a good chance you'll end up on The Verge. But if you're covering Apple specifically with your survey, you don't want to pitch Verge's catch-all email. To have the best chance of success, you want to find the reporter(s) who cover Apple most frequently. You may still get lucky if you pitch a tips@targetpublisherdomain.com email for a big publication, but you shouldn't rely on that strategy to be successful.

■ *Confirm the type of coverage or news they handle.* Ideally, their "beat" will be as close to one that's fits with your idea as possible. If you want to build a long-term relationship, you need to be confident that they cover your work. Do not just take a chance, or you risk burning that reporter's confidence. For example, The Verge may cover Apple product news, but have they ever covered a survey? You can find out by doing a search on Google, such as "site:theverge.com apple survey." If you aren't seeing results, that's a good indicator they don't.

Once you've found potentially interested parties, you're ready to start pitching. As a general suggestion, email people Monday through Wednesday. However, in the right industry, news can get picked up on weekends as well.

An ideal email template for a survey pitch looks something like this:

Subject: Survey for [*Website/Name: Punchy Stat*]

Body:

Hey [*Name*],

[*Custom Sentence About Reporter's Beat/Alignment with Survey*]. Given that, I think you may be interested in a [*Description*] survey that I helped put together for [*Business Name*]. There were some interesting takeaways:

Stat 1

Stat 2

Stat 3

You can see the survey in full here: https://website.com/survey

If you're interested in the story, we'd love if you considered it for a piece on [*Website Name*]. Happy to send through the data as well if you're interested!

Thanks, [*Name*]. Looking forward to your feedback!

In practice, here is how that same survey may look for a fictional Apple survey:

Subject: Survey for Doug: One-third of Apple users lack confidence in brand

Body:

Hey Doug,

Appreciated your coverage of Apple's earnings report last week. Seems like sales are slightly trending down in China.

Given your coverage, I think you may also be interested in an Apple consumer confidence survey I helped put together for Apple Junkies. There were some interesting takeaways:

- One-third of Apple users lack confidence in the brand.
- In Washington specifically, 1 in 4 Apple users lack confidence.
- Texas has the highest degree of consumer confidence, with 4 in 5 users showing strong confidence.

You can see the survey in full here: https://applejunkies.com/consumer-confidnece

If you're interested in the story, we'd love if you considered it to be a piece on The Verge. Happy to send through the data as well if you're interested!

Thanks, Doug. Looking forward to your feedback!

With email outreach for news, there are generally not many high-end targets to reach out to, which is why it's important to get each email right. Depending on the market, you may only have 20 to 30 highly qualified targets to contact.

If you combine your survey with an infographic, you can sometimes open that audience to 100 total. Regardless, it's worth considering the old maxim: The wider the audience you target, the worse you target them.

Make sure you reach out quickly with your survey. Reporters want news, after all, which means time is of the essence. You should aim to end your outreach cycle in no more than seven to eight business days after publishing.

Who Can Generate Tier One Links?

Tier one links aren't easy to come by for every business. They coordinate strategically with a certain kind of business that aligns to frequent news cycles. For example, in finance there is a big appetite for news and a lot of potential topics to cover.

But if you're in the business of selling flowers, there may not be as many angles to take with a survey. You can still create them, but there may not be as limitless of a supply as there would be with something like credit cards.

This is something to keep in mind when thinking about tier one links. They're always nice to have, but they're occasionally difficult to align to your content strategy in a way that makes sense at scale. If you rarely do them, you're more likely to not do a good job, and the issues compound from there.

Success from an SEO standpoint can come from many different angles, and you don't have to have a ton of tier one links to succeed online. Consider it as a tool in your belt and proceed appropriately.

In the next chapter, we will explore relationship building that helps you create a content promotion network.

Chapter 13

Building Relationships

There is a tendency among SEOs to have a "drop-and-dash" mentality when it comes to links. This is why there are so many comment and forum spamming bots, long lists of sites where you can snag social media profile links, and a huge market for paid links. This chapter focuses on philosophies and tactics that, although time-consuming, will ultimately result in a steady flow of high-value inbound links that your competitors won't be able to duplicate.

Good reciprocation and relationship-building targets include reporters, bloggers, industry experts who publish consistently, even respected and prolific forum posters. From the link prospects you qualify, look for active sites and individuals mentioned frequently in social media, as well as those who have established authority. If there's a "secret" to our biggest successes in link building (outside of dramatically reducing prospecting and qualification time), this chapter contains it.

THE PRECIPROCATION CONCEPT

The "preciprocation" concept is simple: Promote the best content of others (especially including your link prospects) before they ask for it via links from your site and placed content, votes, newsletter mentions, tweets, or whatever platform or medium you have at your disposal. Link out lavishly to deserving content, even from competitors, if appropriate. Use followed links. Expect nothing in return, though certainly do occasional outreach to let folks know that you appreciated and cited their work.

Preciprocation provides several advantages:

- By continually watching for and promoting great industry content, you will know what you should be aspiring to in your content creation.
- Your audience will trust you as an expert curator of industry content. Though the content isn't yours, your "brand" will still pass along a bit as the referrer.
- You keep tabs on what your competitors are doing in the content marketing and social media arena.
- The experts creating the content you promote will, in some cases, reciprocate by promoting your content to their network.
- Some experts may be relied on to link to you with anchor text best suited to your SEO goals.
- The experts and other publishers you promote will be more open to interviews, surveys, and other highly linkable content collaborations.

The disadvantages of preciprocation are:

- Not every market contains a layer of active, expert publishers (such as bloggers), who are the link prospects most likely to respond to this method.
- It's a lot of work, requiring dedicated daily work of about an hour or so.
- It takes a long time to get "rolling" to the point where you're genuinely impacting your chances of increasing links.
- If you're pushy or expectant in your requests for promotion of your content, you will come off as rude, even if you've been preciprocating for weeks or months.

BUILDING PRECIPROCATED RELATIONSHIPS INTO LINKS

Once you have begun warming up your link targets through preciprocation, you can start to formulate ideas for turning these contacts into links. We recommend that you do this primarily through content that, again, promotes your link targets while adding new information and value to your industry's thought space.

Here are some core concepts that illustrate how to develop your preciprocated relationships into content and links:

- *Good ol' content promotion.* If you already have expert-grade content on your site and it hasn't gotten much industry attention, a simple mention to a few of your preciprocated contacts could result in links. Because the relationships are already warmed up, they're more likely to spend a minute considering your request!

- *Top 100 (blog posts, Twitter users, PDFs, podcasts, etc.) of 20XX.* If you create content on your site that highlights the experts in your space that you've preciprocated, they are likely to help you promote it. Sometimes this will be through tweets, and sometimes through links.

- *Expert publisher group interview.* Ask great questions of a large group of industry experts (including those competitors with whom you've developed rapport and respect), and you're sure to create content that gets others thinking and sharing. Plus, the experts themselves will benefit by promoting the content.

- *The "writing assignment."* Create an interesting and engaging writing project and ask your preciprocated experts to publish their assignment on their site—be sure to link to their assignment from the assignment announcement page, which is on your site. For example, Rae Hoffman publishes an annual "expert interview" on link building, which in turns helps her site attract links and publicity. See Figure 13-1 for this example.

FIGURE 13–1. Rae Hoffman's Annual "Expert Interview" on Link Building

■ *Promoting your customers.* This old PR technique works well for link building. Source, share, and promote their stories and expertise, and you'll earn links from them and their networks.

■ *Solicit expert content.* Some experts will want to use your blog as a place to reach a new audience with content (and earn a new link or two). Consider opening your platform to content placement from others, and they are likely to help promote it for you.

In the link-building campaign templates (see Chapter 17) you'll find these concepts developed in actionable detail.

DEVELOP YOUR CONTENT PROMOTION NETWORK (TO TAP INTO OTHERS' NETWORKS)

The more reach you develop for your organization—the more RSS/newsletter subscribers, the more followers and friends, the more votes you can wrangle on niche social news sites, the more forums you contribute to, the stronger the forum you create on your site—the further your content will go and the more links it will earn. From a tactical perspective, this will require you to be an active publisher in multiple mediums, and it requires dedicated daily effort from at least one employee with a strong "curatorial" eye.

You will find, as your distribution network grows, that you will earn links and mentions from the people paying attention to you. Furthermore, you will find it much easier to establish relationships with other major players in your space who have created similar networks. As you discover and promote rising stars in your market space, you will earn the appreciation of future giants. Developing your link distribution network is a long-term project and something that you do gradually as you discover and qualify new link prospects, "preciprocate" them, publish new content, and conduct outreach for it.

Here are some of the pillars of a content distribution network:

■ *Twitter/Facebook.* This is probably the simplest channel to set up and get running for the purposes of promoting your industry experts' best content.

■ *Company blog.* While fairly simple to set up, the real challenge comes in developing a sustainable and effective content strategy. Starting with some of the concepts from Chapter 5 will help you build links.

■ *Email newsletter.* While not a direct link-building tool, an email newsletter filled with great content gives you more reach and impact. Plus, it becomes a way to preciprocate—and to say thank you—to your link prospects. See Figure 13–2, on page 107, for an example of using a newsletter as a marketing tool.

FIGURE 13–2. Larry Chase's Newsletter, *Web Digest for Marketers*

- *Forum/community platform.* Participate (answer and ask questions) in the important ones in your industry, but also consider launching your own as a means to develop links and embed yourself more powerfully in your market.
- *Niche social news sites.* Discover the niche social news sites most relevant to your target audience, and if there isn't one, consider creating one and adding it to your site. Like a forum, this project is not to be undertaken lightly or without resources to promote and build it.

While your content distribution network will earn you links organically, it's important to remember that each independent channel you develop is its own linkable asset. There will be new link opportunity types you can acquire links from as you launch new channels.

OVERPRECIPROCATING: THE DANGERS OF ALWAYS BEING THE "PLATFORM"

As this chapter demonstrates, we are firm believers in promoting the content contributions of an industry's experts. This is because we've seen the impact it's had on our business, our links, and our relationships in our own space. However, if you're not careful, you can over-preciprocate and get a little too wrapped up in promoting others, rather than seeking ways to add value to the conversation that comes directly from your experience.

We generate a great deal of our business leads through publishing unique content in leading industry publications. We once did a series of group interviews on a leading industry blog and discovered that our lead flow stopped entirely. Why? We stopped being the experts and let the spotlight shine on our peers in the industry. The upside, of course, is that the experts (including competitors) we interviewed have remained friendly, if not become our out-and-out supporters.

This entire chapter has been about shining the spotlight on others. Just remember that the platform you're building for yourself must benefit you, too, and the best way to do this is by publishing fantastic content that helps your industry solve its pains in new and more efficient ways.

In the next chapter, we will explore this issue further by really digging into your market's key pain points and creating highly linkable content.

Chapter 14

Analyzing Market Pains to Create Highly Linkable Content

I n the previous chapter, we discussed preciprocation and warming up your market. This chapter expands on the warning at the end of Chapter 13: Be helpful, promote your link prospects, but don't always be the platform for others to tap dance on. You have to also demonstrate your expertise—you have to add your own unique value and voice to the conversation. This chapter will help you identify what kinds of content you should be creating to not only attract links from your prospects, but to also get some conversions with your content.

Chapter 5, the linkable assets chapter, includes a good overview of what to look for on your site and in your market but doesn't go into content creation; this chapter does, with an emphasis on written content, as that's what we're most familiar with. We highly recommend you experiment with the medium that works best for you and your organization's strength. If you have developers, your content can and should look like free web tools that relate to your market. If you have graphic designers (and access to unique data and talented data interpreters), then perhaps it's infographics. But no matter what bells and whistles you add, remember: Content is king.

HOW-TOS, GUIDES, AND OTHER INFORMATIONAL WONDERS FOR DIYers AND CURIOUS PROSPECTS

Fresh and up-to-date how-to content has and will have eternal appeal in a market. That's what makes it the standby for the linkable content creator. How-to content guides readers through a process for achieving a specific goal that's relevant or related to the target market. It's through this type of content that link builders (or your content strategists and PR folk) establish your company's experts as thought leaders and people of influence. This content travels in all sorts of media wrappers, from PDFs and podcasts, to videos and tweets. In the search results for "woodworking 'how to'" (see Figure 14–1), we see a small selection: plans, forums, videos, and tool guides—all valuable content.

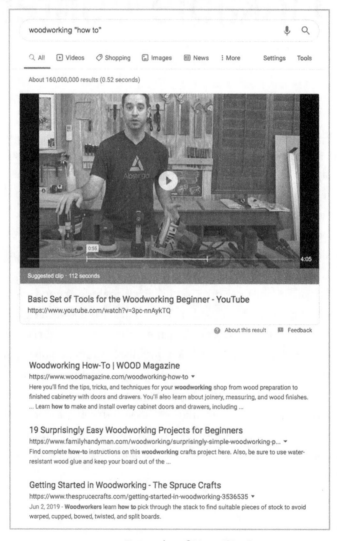

FIGURE 14–1. Example of How-To Content

Effective how-to content solves a market's pains. If you're already familiar with your market, you probably know the core pains. However, you will still be surprised at pains you weren't aware of if you conduct a "pain-point survey." If you're new to a market space, then this survey will be invaluable. Note that this survey only looks at pains that content creators have addressed.

A How-To Survey for Market Pain-Point Analysis

First, you will need to refer to your market-defining keywords (or MDKWs). Your MDKWs help you guide your queries toward the information that will be most useful to you. Start by combining MDKWs with the types of words listed below. Your market is likely to have different words to describe helpful content, and it could make sense for you to search Twitter, Reddit, Facebook, or other social sites where content related to your market is shared.

Here are some sample queries:

- [MDKW] how to
- [MDKW] advice
- [MDKW] tips
- [MDKW] process
- [MDKW] tutorial
- [MDKW] about
- [MDKW] recommended
- [MDKW] recommendations
- [MDKW] tricks
- [MDKW] basics
- [MDKW] guide
- [MDKW] definitive guide
- [MDKW] hints
- [MDKW] what you need to know
- [MDKW] ideas

Also play with these (but only concentrate on titles!):

- [MDKW] article
- [MDKW] book
- [MDKW] video
- [MDKW] podcast
- [MDKW] PDF

Begin with some manual queries and check the top ten for one or two MDKWs. If you find queries with lots of unique, decent looking content (just by looking at the SERPs—don't visit pages yet), set these queries aside for a larger batched query.

Conducting How-To Oriented Pain-Point Analysis

Now you have, laid out for you in plain numbers, the most commonly occurring phrases in the SERPs for the how-to content in your market. This is your starting point for creating a pain-point framework. This pain-point analysis should be fairly stable—core pains in a market rarely change. That's part of what unifies the market. Here's how to lay things out and start getting a sense for the most important types of information in your space:

- Make a list of the distinct phrases that stand out.
- Think about each phrase you extract as if it were going to be an entire section of your site or a category on your blog.
- Be as thorough as possible, and lay your preconceptions aside as much as possible.
- Once you've assessed the main phrases that define the pains in your market, you can run each pain phrase in place of the [MDKW] queries above to flesh out each category.

You can use your pain-point analysis in a number of ways:

- Identify what information is missing or poorly presented in your market.
- Create a content calendar for your writers.
- Identify interview questions or general interview directions for experts.
- Create a content site or site section architecture.
- Aggregate the best and most-linked pieces of how-to content for each pain point.
- Develop free, web-based tools or downloads targeting specific pains, and create content describing how and when to use them.

IDENTIFYING LINKABLE CONTENT IN YOUR MARKET

The process outlined in the how-to discussion above provides a broad and informational look at what causes your market pain, and therefore, what your market cares about. It's reasonable to assume that if you solve these pains with content, your site will attract links over time. There's more than one way to analyze content in a market, though. This section looks at how to identify and analyze the *most linkable* content in your market. This will help give you a sense of what factors matter to the linkers in your space (assuming your space has a community of organic linkers).

Further, this analysis will help you weed out which market pains matter the most and which ones are created by content farms to respond to emerging keyword demand (these could be useful, too, but aren't likely to have links).

At its core, this process revolves around analyzing inbound links to individual pages and *not* the site as a whole. Why? This leads you directly to important and valued pieces of content (they were cited by others), and it gives you a list of ready prospects when you create better content. Like the how-to analysis above, there are not yet any tools that execute this process on a systematized basis, so you will have to do it by hand.

This is a fairly lengthy process, but well worth the time invested.

Identify the Top Publishers in Your Market

In Chapter 7, we discussed queries for identifying blogs and news sites. Add in a few of the how-to queries above, and you can use these to assess the strongest content and publishing players in your market. Start with queries like these:

- [MDFK] blogs
- [MDFK] news
- [MDFK] trade publication
- [MDKW] how to
- [MDKW] tips

And then . . .

- Make sure SEO for Firefox is fully engaged—you will be extracting URLs from the SERPs of your favorite search engine.
- Make sure your search engine of choice is returning 20 results at a time.
- Run your first query, then extract the results (be sure to save it in a meaningful, easy-to-remember way).
- Repeat until you've run through all your queries.
- Paste *only* the URLs into the host name and URL occurrence counter.
- Manually check the top occurring host names and URLs—these are most likely to be your industry's top publishers.

Analyze the Top Publishers' Most-Linked Pages

Now that you have a rough idea of your top publishers, you can begin to analyze their most-linked pages. You can and should use this process to analyze your top competitors to see which of their pages have attracted the most links—not only will you discover their linkbait and linkable content, but you'll uncover pages with paid links pointing to them as well. Figure 14–2, on page 114, shows what this process looks like. Try these steps:

1. Take your list of top publishers and run them, one by one, through Ahrefs.com, Link Insight, Open Site Explorer, or Majestic SEO.
2. Examine the top 50 or so results for each site.
3. Explore URLs that appear to be informational or contain something other than sales content.

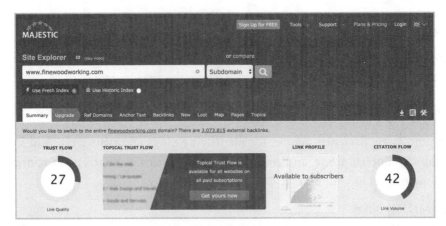

FIGURE 14–2. Majestic Site Explorer

4. Record URLs of note, along with their link count and title of the content in a spreadsheet.

5. Now you can see the URLs in your market's top publishers that have attracted, earned, or begged for the most links in your market. Here are some of the things you can start to identify now:

- What is the pain addressed (and how does it line up with your pain map)?
- What is the target audience (knowledge level of target audience, reading level, etc.)?
- What is the content type (article, PDF, video, podcast, infographic, etc.)?
- How is the content structured?

There's an added bonus to this sort of analysis, too. If you pull the backlinks to these top URLs, using Ahrefs or Open Site Explorer, you have some fairly well-qualified targets for outreach as you begin to create content of your own.

HOW RECIPROCAL LINKS CAN BE VIABLE

A reciprocal link is when two sites agree to give links to each other: I'll link to your site if you link to mine. But it's not quite that simple. People have tried to game the search engines with reciprocal links schemes, so the search engines have to look deeper to determine the intent of the reciprocity.

The rules of reciprocity cannot be perfectly defined. In other words, if you state that going beyond 30 percent reciprocity with your links is bad, I will tell you that's insane, besides being incorrect. Having a high reciprocity percentage (RP) is considered a red flag that the engines can use to devalue your links. The math is simple. If 100 percent of any site's inbound links are reciprocal, then those links can't really be trusted as an indicator of quality because it could simply be a case of "you link to me, and I'll link to you." (This can and does happen, but it isn't a quality-specific occurrence.)

For some subjects, it is perfectly normal, almost expected, that the link reciprocity percentage should be extremely high, approaching 100. The more niche your subject matter, the more likely it is you will have a high RP with sites that have the same or similar subject matter.

Case in point? Consider the Southeastern Bat Diversity Network (sbdn.org), an organization with a goal to "conserve bats and their habitats in southeastern North America through collaborative research, education, and management." Very noble, indeed. I've always felt bats needed help.

If you look at other top sites within this subject area, you start to notice something. The other sites devoted to bats have a tendency to link back and forth to all the other sites devoted to bats. While this should not be surprising, many people miss a key point about what this means. Reciprocity link spam cannot be determined by a fixed number. A reciprocal links percentage cannot be set in stone. What's reciprocally spammy for one topic is perfectly natural in another.

Study the backlinks to a few related sites, such as Batcon.org, BatResearchNews.org, and North American Society on Bat Research (NASBR.org), and you see that each of these sites tends to link to the other and vice versa. The reciprocal linking percentage across the top five sites is more than 80 percent, and for the top three, it's 100 percent. And this RP is perfectly natural, believable, and in no way an attempt to fool any algorithm or improve rank. These sites link to each other because they share the same passion for a specific topic and want to make sure people visiting and reading their content find the other sites about the same topic.

Now, if I examined five or ten sites devoted to another (broader) subject and found the same 80 percent or higher reciprocity rate, that would be suspicious. For example, if the subject matter is NFL jerseys, where hundreds of sites fight for SEO supremacy, it would be an absolute red flag for the engines if we found any ten NFL jersey sites linking back and forth to each other with the same high RP as our bat example.

In fact, I'd argue that 80 percent reciprocity among a collection of NFL jersey sites was a signal they might be operated by the same people. That's the very definition of a link network and link spam, yet the RP was no different than my bat examples. The only difference was the subject matter.

Which brings us to those absolutes. You simply cannot make any sort of absolute statement as to what constitutes reciprocal link spam. Nor can you say that reciprocal links are always good, bad, suspicious, or helpful. They are never any of these, and they are always all of these. What you have to do is look at each case and and recognize the logical, natural-linking potential and reciprocity tendencies.

It's not rocket science, either. Some of what you just read seems so obvious to longtime link builders that it's easy to forget. The cult of reciprocal links advocates and enemies would do well to call a truce and stop looking for absolutes, and instead start looking for illustrative examples to help each site know if, how, and when to implement reciprocal links properly, or at all.

LINKABLE CONTENT CAN GENERATE CONVERSIONS, TOO!

In a perfect world—which you as a link builder should be striving for, obviously—linkable, shareable content also generates conversions of some fashion or other. Whether newsletter subscribers, ebook downloads, ad clicks, or even sales, your linkable content should be moving folks along a funnel. The great part is, though, if your linkable content can convert, you know you're generating *relevant* content. There are some link-builders who specialize in irrelevant linkbait. It attracts links and impacts SERPs, but chances are good that this impact won't last forever.

If every link you earn brings in targeted traffic to content that leads folks along a funnel toward increased value interactions with your brand, then you're way ahead of the game. SERP impact is your gravy. The good news is that all your how-to pain-point and linkable-content research has prepared you with a massive list of topics and potential titles. Your job now is discovering how to work your company's brand and buy cycle into the topics.

Here are some types of conversions you can drive with content:

- PDF downloads
- Newsletter sign-ups
- Community sign-ups
- Free tool usage
- Webinar sign-ups
- Social follows
- RSS subscriptions
- Increased time on site
- Sales

ENGAGING YOUR INTERNAL THOUGHT LEADERS AND SUBJECT-MATTER EXPERTS

Unless you, the link builder, are your organization's subject-matter expert, you're going to have to work with the folks in your organization who *are*. Content that enables an audience to gain access to these subject-matter experts is more likely to result in links.

Primarily, you will be engaging them with interviews, though if you have a strong team, willing experts, and the blessings of the management, you could have them write—or assist them in writing—the pain-based linkable content you've identified. Furthermore, your organization's subject-matter experts may have already developed their own online platforms. There could be folks in your organization who have relevant followings already that you could ask to become more involved in your linkable content creation. If your CEO is already on Twitter, by all means ask them to tweet about your latest guides to accomplishing more with less!

TIP-BASED CONTENT: HOW TO RESEARCH, SCALE, AND PROMOTE

Tips are the smallest documentable unit of "how to" do something. Their presence— or absence—within a target market's SERPs provide phenomenal opportunities for link strategists and other content marketers. Here's a proposed definition of "tips" for marketers, along with ideas and direction for link strategists and other content marketers on how to use tip-based content to meet marketing goals.

Importance of Tips to Marketers

You know what a tip is, but they've become so mundane, you may not have examined them at close range. Tips are tiny concept vessels for preserving and passing along distinct units of practical advice from subject-matter experts. From the information seeker's perspective, tips provide a perceived shortcut to subject matter mastery and provide a solution to their painful inability. See Figure 14–3, on page 118, for an example of some woodworking tips.

By providing a tip that enables someone to complete a task, the marketer builds trust and creates further promotion opportunity—from links and shares, to downloads and sign-ups. When researching a space, "tips" can include other units of knowledge, such as "steps," "checklists," "worksheets," "guidelines," and more.

Four Tips on Understanding the Significance of Tips within a Vertical

Tips tell marketers a great deal about a given vertical—its publishers and audiences and their pains. As you hone your tip-research skills, here are four things to look for:

1. *The presence of tips in your vertical demonstrates that there is task-based information demand.* Even if your content isn't tip-based, the presence of tips indicates that your market needs information on how to execute relevant tasks. Gathering and

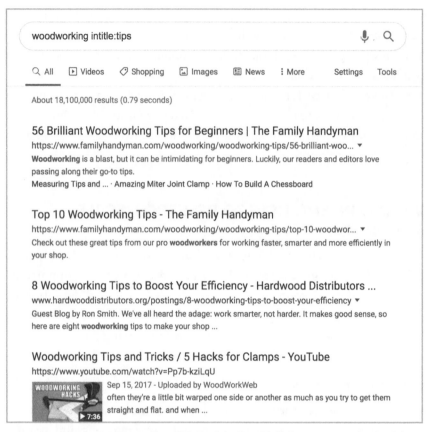

FIGURE 14–3. An Example of Google's "Intitle" Operator Paired with the Keyword "Woodworking"

organizing tips will help you understand the range of information demand, as well as the various tasks that are problematic for your audience.

2. *The absence of tips indicates subject matter mastery may require understanding principles rather than following tips.* From a content perspective, this will require from you and your writers more effort to create successful content. Assuming you're an agency specializing in tip-based content creation, you may be doing the principle-to-tip distillation based on conjecture or—better still—interviews with subject-matter experts.

3. *The absence of tips indicates a content opportunity.* Even if subject-matter expertise in a vertical requires the understanding of principles, or even an advanced college degree, years in the field, passing a bar exam, etc., the absence of tips means that a smart content marketer can begin the work of distilling general principles into distinct, task-oriented directives. You will have difficulty sourcing your tips but being first-to-market with tips can create significant value for a company.

4. *Markets with tips are likely to still have "tip gaps."* Being able to identify these gaps—especially as they overlap with your content marketing objectives—requires a systematic inventory and categorization of existing tips.

Three Tips for Research and Categorization

Digging into a vertical's tips provides a rich well of direction and source material for your own tip-based content. Here are three tips to help you maximize your research capabilities:

1. *Inventory tips by combining your subject matter phrases with tip-discovery stems.* Your subject matter phrases are typically non-pay-per-click, big-head keywords that describe your target market, its various practitioners, and/or core concerns that can serve as a root for your tip queries in Google. Tip-discovery query stems are words like:
   - "tips"
   - "ideas"
   - "techniques"
   - "ways to"
   - "how-tos"
   - "advice"
2. *Identify any standard, codified groupings of information in your vertical!* For example, verticals typically have unique names for types of "tips." "Recipes" are common collections of tips in the cooking vertical, "drills" are ideas for exercises that sport coaches can implement at practice, and "lesson plans" are a sort of education recipe for teachers to follow in class.
3. *Create a "tip-lopedia," or tip inventory, for your vertical's body of tip-based knowledge.* If you're working in a vertical for the long term, or at least for a 6- or 12-month content-oriented engagement, it makes sense to build your own tip-lopedia for cataloging and categorizing all the tips and their sources in your vertical. Then, when it comes time to create content, you can parcel out your tips based on the requirements of the given piece. When you've thoroughly collected tips from a vertical, you can more easily discover appropriate categories and groupings for them. These categorizations can become a value-add to a body of knowledge.

Five Tips for Scalable and Unique Tip-Based Content

Simply rewriting tips doesn't help differentiate your content—or add anything new to your vertical. Here are some ways to use existing tips as a starting point rather than an end goal:

1. *Tip clichés in your vertical can be "unpacked" and/or "debunked."* As you build your vertical's tip-lopedia spreadsheet, track the number of times a tip is mentioned or suggested. The most frequently mentioned tips can potentially be split into even smaller tips, or at least written about with more depth, deliberation, and care. It may also be possible or useful to debunk, disprove, or in some way debate the most frequently promoted tips in a vertical.

2. *Many subject-matter experts haven't reduced tips and advice to their smallest form.* Your vertical's most prominent and important subject-matter experts—your niche celebrities—have probably come up with some amazing, if not fully articulated, tips. It's also probable that they haven't broken these tips down to their smallest possible form.

3. *Tips and tip categories can serve as a basis for group interviews.* Knowing the most regularly published tips can be a great place to start an interview with your niche expert celebrities. Ask them to debunk the common tips or to provide their unique spin on them. You can also ask, "What tips besides the most common ones would you recommend?"

4. *Tips can serve as a basis for infographics or other "utility enhancers."* Providing new wrappers for old or standard tips can give your content new life in a vertical. Can offering your tips in a printed form improve their utility? Can you turn your tip-lopedia into a simple fact-finding or diagnosis application?

5. *If forum-based tip sharing happens frequently in your vertical, this is a huge opportunity for tip-sourcing.* While forums and other social media sites can provide the most useful, actionable tips, they are often poorly organized, incompletely explained, and have no "architecture" to them.

Four Tips for Promoting Tip-Based Content

Tip-based content can earn links, shares, and other citations with no promotion. Tip-based content can also perform poorly, even with extensive promotion. Here are some tips on promotion:

1. *Cite and notify your tip sources.* You are rewriting, rearticulating, and reorganizing their tips to the point that they are no longer recognizable to their originators. However, citing your sources provides an anchor of trust and reliability to your content, and it provides you with a promotion opportunity as well when you write to the esteemed subject matter expert to let them know that you referenced them in your humble work.

2. *Target roundup writers.* If your vertical has roundup writers, these are some of the first folks you should target for mention, share, or link requests.

3. *Distribute it yourself.* Tweet it, share it, put it on your homepage, link to it from guest posts, include the URL in relevant comments, and add it to your monthly email newsletter.

4. *Make sure your content targets a conversion.* Tip-based content conversions can include things like sign-ups, downloads, installs, follows, friends, shares, links, and even sales if you have ebooks or other content for sale.

In the next chapter, we will cover link acquisition and how to best illustrate the value of your linkable content to the publishers who choose to link.

Chapter 15

Link Acquisition

L
ink acquisition is the process of conducting outreach designed to induce people or sites to publish links to your content (and, in our methodology, without paying them). Link acquisition is sometimes referred to as "link begging," but this is a misnomer. In effective link acquisition, you always—*always*—illustrate the value of your linkable asset within the context of the needs of the publisher's target audience. Our most effective link acquisition emails typically don't even use the word "link." In this chapter, we will cover how to set up and choose the appropriate terminology for your pitch.

DESIGNING THE PITCH: BEFORE SENDING YOUR LINK ACQUISITION EMAILS

The first and most important stage of link acquisition is in your pitch design. Effective pitch design also relies on a thorough, linkable asset inventory (so you know what you're pitching) and effective link prospecting and qualification (so you know who you're pitching to and why).

You have a list of prospects, but do you know which of your linkable assets lines up with their interests, audience, and editorial agendas? For scalable and effective link-building campaigns, we recommend that you organize the campaign with your inventory of assets at the core. The more relevant your asset is to the prospect, the higher your conversion rates will be.

WARMER RELATIONS: SENDING "PRECIPROCATION" SIGNALS IN EVERY EMAIL

There's a reason this book goes from link prospect qualification to building relationships, and not directly to link acquisition. Preciprocation (which you first read about in Chapter 13) is one of the strongest indicators you can give someone that you're invested in moving your industry forward with enthusiasm and optimism. Furthermore, it shows that you're listening to them, which is one of the most powerful ways to open the hearts and minds of your industry's publishers. We recommend that you build preciprocation, in some way, into every email you send.

For example, if you haven't contacted someone yet, you could send preciprocation signals like this:

> I really enjoyed your piece on X. In fact, I mentioned it in our email newsletter, to my Twitter followers, and added it to this massive roundup of our industry's top resources (URL). Check it out, and if you think it's worthy, please mention it to your readers! Also, I'd like to interview you for an upcoming article. Are you open to answering some questions for my readers?

If this is your second or third contact, you can tone down the preciprocation, but always remember to indicate your future willingness to help out. If you know your expert is writing a book, for example, your letter might be more along the lines of:

> Hey [*Contact Name*]!
> Just writing to let you know that we dropped another little bomb on the X industry. ;) It's really picking up steam on Twitter and causing a lot of discussion. Check it out and let me know what you think! [*insert your URL*] Also, let me know when you're done with that ebook so I can tell my readers about it!

DEMONSTRATING CONCERN FOR THEIR AUDIENCE'S NEEDS

When promoting your own content to publishers, one of the strongest ways to signal that you're worth listening to is by demonstrating concern for their readers. If the publisher is a good and worthy steward of your industry's community—and they will be because you've prospected and qualified well—then the readers will be their primary concern.

Of course, these folks are going to be few and far between. However, they are the most valuable and influential links and relationships you'll find in your space because they will have developed *trust* from their readers. And you can be sure they will have developed trust from the search engines as well.

Another way to demonstrate concern for the reader is by expressing how your readers and site visitors have responded to your content (whether by links, mentions in Twitter, actual written responses you've received, etc.). This shows you've been listening. Finally, by using language like, "If you think your readers could learn from it," or, "Because your readers responded so well to X," you demonstrate that you, too, care about readers.

It's always best to err on the side of concern for readers. If the publisher is publishing a blog or industry news site, you could try saying "visitors" instead of "readers."

SUGGESTING "MENTIONS" OR "SHARING" INSTEAD OF REQUESTING LINKS

The word "link" has gotten some bad connotations of late. You have to remember that publishers not only get bombarded with link-exchange spam, but there's Google pushing the "nofollow" tag and threatening to end a website's supply of organic traffic if that site does any "unnatural linking."

And think about it—the word "link" itself is abstract, too technical, and doesn't convey the value that your content will bring to other publishers' readers. No one wants to link. They want to share valuable content. They want to be the conduit for someone's life-changing (or business-process-changing) epiphany. They want to earn still more trust and adulation from their readers. Asking for a "link" just mucks up their thinking about this goal and makes them suspicious of your true motives.

Therefore, we recommend—in most situations involving content promotion—that you stay away from the word "link." Use words like "share," "mention," "let your readers/ followers know," etc. This language also leaves them open to share your URLs in the ways they see fit.

HOW MUCH CUSTOMIZATION IS ENOUGH FOR YOUR OUTREACH?

In the early stages of preciprocation, there's no level of customization that is too much, especially for the most influential publishers and prospects in your space. Your first few contacts with your link prospects should, ideally, be as customized as possible.

Ideals are one thing, and the reality of contacting 250 publishers, or even 2,500, is a circumstance that calls for some time spent adjusting your ideals. At a certain point, you're going to have to resort to using some templates. A decent rule of thumb is that the more preciprocation you build into your outreach email, the less customization you have to do.

To illustrate, we found that when we asked people to participate in interviews, they were more likely to mention our content to their readers, especially when the content highlights them in some way. Further, the more you've already mentioned and promoted a prospect or even someone who already links to you, the more you've already earned their trust, which ups your chances that you can dash off a quick templated request for an action that benefits you. As in all relationships, this should be done sparingly.

Customize your engagements as much as possible, and in cases where you have to resort to templates, make sure you're building in some strong reasons for them to listen to your pitch and respond by mentioning you.

SENDING YOUR EMAILS

Clicking "Send" on a link-request email is an exciting and terrifying moment. It's worth listening to your gut instincts the moment before you send an email because it may lead you toward a stronger pitch. Either double-check their name, their site's name, or something along those lines, or think of a way to bolster your pitch (e.g., you remember a related post they did and hunt it down to demonstrate that you have done your homework). We highly recommend you cultivate and listen to this little voice.

Send Three, Wait 30 Minutes, then Reread Your Email

In the case of automated outreach, we recommend sending only a few, waiting a standard amount of time, then going back to the emails to double-check them. You may even get some early feedback that helps you tighten your engagement. Of course, you've already spent hours on the template.

It's tight, reads well, and you feel like it's going to elicit some solid mentions and links. But you misspelled a name that spellcheck couldn't catch, and in your hustle to get the email done, you missed it. Or maybe some of your interview questions aren't as clear as you thought, and you end up with five people asking for clarification and 500 people putting the interview off until never. These are examples of conversion killers.

Pay special attention to the subject line, especially after sending off your first burst of 5 to 10 percent of your emails. Does it entice people to open by expressing the benefit to them or their readers? Does it contain a misspelling?

While we've never gotten openly flamed, we have deserved it a time or two. Here are the mistakes we no longer make in content-based outreach for acquisition:

- Wrong name
- Wrong site name
- Subject lines that don't entice
- Misspellings in subject lines
- Poorly worded or confusing interview questions
- Too many interview questions
- Contacting sites that sell links with content-oriented outreach
- Cold outreach without preciprocation
- Not aligning link prospects with linkable assets
- Requesting homepage links from expert publishers
- Using the word "link"

HANDLING OUTREACH RESPONSES: IGNORES, ACCEPTS, DECLINES, AND COUNTERS

Once you've sent all your emails, it's time for the links, responses, and tweets to come rolling in . . . right? We certainly hope so, but we never count on it, and we hope you don't, either. This section will help you to prepare for what could happen after those emails go out. We hold that, broadly speaking, there are four possible ways for someone to respond to your email. They can:

1. Ignore it.
2. Accept it and take action to mention your site.
3. Send an email declining your request.
4. Counter your request.

Let's explore some tips for each possibility.

Ignores: If at First You Don't Succeed . . .

You can try one more time—maybe your email got swept away under the deluge of daily emails this person gets. Try them again. Here are some tips:

- Always send a custom second email. Always. If you don't have the time to make your second request custom, then you shouldn't be sending it. Don't just resend your original request!
- Do include the original email text, though! Just make sure it's underneath the custom note you send.

- Mention any "big names" who have responded to your request so far. This helps demonstrate value.
- Maybe they're just busy, not ignoring you. Give them a few days to get back before sending something again.
- Consider looking for a different contact at the organization.
- If you still don't get anything back, take their name out of your contact rotation. From now on, the only time you should contact this person is if they write to you first.

Accepts: Woo-hoo! Now What?

Congrats! You got the link, you got the tweet, you got the Facebook update, you got the cover story of *Time* magazine! Now what? There are a number of things you should be prepared to do:

- Say thank you. Emails are nice. Tweets are nice. Future links from you are nicest. Keep that fire going!
- Ask if they need content (assuming you have writers).
- Ask if you can interview their expert.
- Depending on click-throughs and traffic value, ask what other kinds of content they would be interested in sharing.
- Ask if they're interested in interviewing you (assuming you have a thought leader in your organization).
- Offer to make any personal introductions that you perceive could be useful to them.
- Follow/friend them if you haven't already.

Declines: Wait, What? Why Not?

It happens. Sometimes people write you back to thank you for thinking of them but say they're not interested in sharing what you sent to them. The bare fact that they responded—even though it was in the negative—is a positive and powerful thing. Here are some things you should do when you receive declines:

- Say thank you. And mean it.
- Put on your "objective scientist" pants and ask them, in as few words as possible, while expressing your boundless delight in their decision to respond, why they have declined your request.
- Learn what they would be willing to share in the future.
- Confirm their willingness to hear from you again ("When/if I create *x*, may I ping you again?").

Counters: Some People May Negotiate

In spaces in which publishers are highly aware of the value of a link, you're likely to encounter some counters to your emails, especially if you're going the request route and haven't adequately preciprocated your space. They may add a few hoops for you to earn your link. It's probably worth it, unless those hoops are money. Then you need to double-check your agenda and decide whether you want to be an organization that pays for links. But if those hoops are, say, a special discount for the site's readers, then let them know that you'll talk to the appropriate folks to decide whether you can move forward and offer a discount in exchange for a link.

ACQUISITION TRACKING: KEEPING TABS ON YOUR EFFORTS

Depending on your specific goals for outreach, there are many things you can and should track. We created an outreach spreadsheet that contains the following tabs. This is a good starting point for your brainstorm regarding what you will track:

- Targeted Host Name/Link Page
- Contact's Name
- Email Address
- Date of 1st Contact
- Date of Follow-up
- Link Placed? Y/N
- URL of Placed Link
- Date Link Placed
- Linked URL
- Anchor Text Used
- Site Type
- Email Subject Line
- Opening Line
- Offer Made
- Growing the Relationship
- Twitter Address
- Notes

SUBMISSION ACQUISITION: COVERING YOUR BASES

While this chapter focuses on links that are earned via great content and relationship building, you've probably already brainstormed some link-opportunity types that will require more one-touch submission type of actions in order to earn them.

These are likely to be opportunities like event aggregators, niche directories, PDF submission sites, etc. There's rarely a reason *not* to go for these opportunities. Just remember that they have a low barrier to entry, meaning that just about any site can get them without having to earn all that trust we talk about building and leveraging in this chapter.

Submission acquisition is a grind, but you should do it anyway. Here is a preparedness checklist that will make it go faster for you:

- List of your qualified link prospects
- An email address for the person who is responsible for the link to your site
- Spreadsheet for recording logins/passwords per site
- Ideal anchor text and variations for each URL
- Description snippet prepared and variations thereof
- Ideal categories
- Physical address of company
- Credit card billing information (when applicable)

The more info you can gather ahead of time, the faster this kind of work can be. Grit your teeth, grind it out, and get it done. And always err on the side of relevance to your target keywords, especially relevance to your target audience.

FIGURE 15–1. Submission Acquisition Checklist

EVERYTHING YOU NEED TO KNOW ABOUT SUBJECT LINES FOR LINK-BUILDING EMAILS

by Gisele Navarro, Director of Operations of NeoMam Studios

Much has been written about the perfect subject line to increase open rates of email marketing campaigns. There's less advice, however, about subject lines for link-building emails. Cue link builders banging their heads against the wall after applying email marketing tips to their outreach emails. They spent hours prospecting, building the perfect list of sites and contacts, but once they sent out their emails, nothing happened. Nobody replied to their outreach. Heck, nobody opened the email in the first place.

All these awesome email marketing tips don't deliver on links because email marketing and link building are two very different worlds. In one of them, you're likely to be contacting people who have subscribed to you because they want to receive your emails. In the other, you're pitching content to webmasters/bloggers/journalists who don't know who you are, all in the hopes of getting a link.

The scenario is different, so your mindset needs to be different. In this section, you will learn tried and tested formulas that will get you the opens you need to start a conversation about links.

Applying Principles of Social Psychology to Link-Building Outreach

Have you ever done something you didn't really want to do simply because someone else asked you to, like buying something after being persuaded by a pushy salesman or agreeing to going out after receiving a group WhatsApp (even though you wanted to stay home)? Those are two examples of what is known as *compliance*.

In the field of behavioral psychology, there are many different strategies link builders use to obtain compliance from others.

One strategy that can be applied to link-building outreach is the foot-in-the-door technique. The theory behind this technique says that agreeing to a small request will increase the likelihood of agreeing to a second, larger request, as long as the big request is consistent with or similar in nature to the small request.

The effectiveness of the foot-in-the-door technique was demonstrated in an experiment at Stanford University, in which a group of women received a request to answer some questions about their use of soap products (the small request). After answering the questions, a larger request was made that they would permit a group of men to enter their home and take an inventory of the products they owned. A second group received the larger request without the preceding small request to answer the soap survey. Jonathan Freedman and Scott Fraser found that those in the group subjected to the foot-in-the-door technique were far more likely to agree to the more demanding inventory request than those in the group that had been only asked the final question.

Every subject line formula you'll learn in this section is based on the theory behind the foot-in-the-door technique. Our small request here is to open the email; the larger request will be to get that link.

Regardless of the formula, the key to making our small request is always the same: Your subject line must clearly state what the email is about. Any recipient who clicks on it is confirming that they are interested in learning more about your message. At that point, you'll have your foot in the door—and the big request of linking to your site won't seem like such a crazy request.

The Top Tip to Get Your Foot in the Door (Regardless of the Link-Building Approach)

Before I jump into the subject lines you should try, I'd like to share the basics that apply to every formula you'll learn in this section. But bear in mind that I'm assuming your list of prospects is spot-on and you're reaching out to the right person based on the type of link you're trying to build.

Regardless of the type of link-building strategy you're working on, there's one rule your subject lines should always follow to get your foot on the door.

Be Honest and Specific About the Intent of Your Email

If you start your interaction with a subject line that clearly conveys the purpose of your email, then it won't come as a surprise when you ask for a link. In other words, your subject line needs to be straightforward, clear, and specific because it will set expectations for your email.

Don't resort to faking a reply or a follow-up in your subject lines. If your plan is to make them think that you are having an ongoing conversation just to get your email opened, I've got news for you: They will realize that you tricked them as soon as they read the first sentence of your email.

If you write subject lines that are completely unrelated to the intention of your email, there's a big chance that the recipient will open your email out of curiosity. However, there's also a big chance that your link request will get ignored because your email didn't match the expectations you've set with your subject line.

Nobody likes to be lied to—don't forget that.

23 Subject Line Formulas for Different Types of Link-Building Emails

Next time you sit down to write an outreach email, give these subject lines (which I've categorized in the following sections) a try, and you will increase the number of conversations with potential link targets.

Guest Posting

More often than not, sites that accept guest writers will specify how they prefer new guest posts to be pitched. If the site you want to contribute to has a dedicated page (or section) about guest-posting opportunities, make sure to follow their guidelines; there's no need to reinvent the wheel. However, in those cases where there's no clear guidelines for wannabe contributors to pitch their guest posts, use the following subject lines:

- *I'd like to write for [site name] (here's X article ideas).* This is perfect for those cases where you've written a series of articles and you're searching for the right home for them.

- *Interested in article contributions about [topic]? I'd love to collaborate.* This a great subject line for when you prefer to discuss content ideas on a specific topic with the editor before submitting written articles.
- *Contributing to [site name]: sharing my clip portfolio.* If you've developed a strong portfolio of articles, you can let your previous work do the talking.
  - *Pro tip.* Journalists use platforms, such as Clippings.me and Muck Rack, to showcase their articles, so editors are used to seeing clip portfolios presented that way.

Broken-Link Building

Before reaching out to a website about broken links, make sure there's someone on the other end who is responsible for the site. The internet is massive, and there are many sites that are unattended, so keep an eye open so you avoid wasting your time as a broken link can also be an indicator of an abandoned website.

Check out the subject line formulas below for reaching out to active sites with broken links that could be replaced with links to your site. To learn more about Broken Link Building Campaigns, please refer to Chapter 19.

- *Broken link on [site name]: Are you the right person to report this to?* If you couldn't locate the webmaster responsible for maintaining the website, use this subject line when approaching the best contact for this request (e.g., an online editor or digital marketing manager). Ideally, you want this person to point you in the direction of the colleague responsible for fixing errors on the site.
- *[Name of page] needs updating: X broken links and one suggestion.* If you landed on a page by analyzing all the sites that linked out to a specific URL that is offline, take an extra minute to identify any other broken links on that page before sending your email. When reaching out to the webmaster, you will then be able to list all the broken links that you've found along with the resource you're suggesting for inclusion (the link to your website). After realizing there are multiple broken links, webmasters are more likely to want to update the page right away.
  - *Pro tip.* You can use an add-on, such as the Broken Link Checker extension on Chrome to quickly highlight broken links on a page you're visiting.
- *Found an error on [site name] that you might want to fix.* An alternative to the previous formula, this subject line would be perfect when contacting a site owner that might not understand what a broken link is. In those cases, you want to avoid jargon to quickly deliver the message that there's an error on a page that needs the website owner's attention.
- *Do you handle website errors? (broken links on [site name]).* This is a hybrid between the previous subject line and the first formula at the top of this list. I've used it

when reaching out to writers who are listed on the About page of content hubs inside university websites.

Link Reclamation (Brand Mention)

Always read the context in which your brand has been mentioned in order to avoid contacting someone who will not only refuse to link to your website, but also could get upset with the request. An example could be someone who has written a negative review of your company on their personal blog. In such cases, the best practice is to flag the review for your customer care department and avoid reaching out to request that a link be added when mentioning your brand.

The formulas below will come in handy next time you need to reach out to a site that mentioned your company without linking to your website:

- *Thanks for mentioning [brand] on your [topic] page (quick request).* Always start link reclamation emails by showing your gratitude. After all, the person you're reaching out to didn't have to mention your company, yet they have done just that, so a thank you is in order. This particular subject line could be used when contacting a webmaster or site owner who has dropped a brand mention within the core pages of their website (e.g., their About page).
- *Thank you for mentioning us! ([title of their article]).* This is a formula for those cases when you're contacting a journalist who has mentioned your brand within an article (e.g., a round-up of recommended products). In those cases, you want the recipient to spot the title of the article they have written to quickly engage them into opening your email. I strongly recommend using this subject line formula when you're reaching out to one of many writers who regularly contribute to a website.
- *Quick question about your latest post (on behalf of [brand]).* This is the formula I use when reaching out to a blogger who has mentioned my company in a blog post. You can use tools, such as Ahrefs, BuzzSumo, or Google Alerts to set up daily alerts for your brand name so you can reach out to bloggers as soon as the mention occurs.

Link Reclamation (Content Marketing)

Much has been written about link reclamation as a link-building strategy. There's less advice about the technique in combination with other off-page SEO efforts (a term that includes every SEO-related task or activity that happens off of the site), such as content marketing for links. For teams who build links with content, I always recommend that they add a layer of link reclamation to their campaigns to maximize the number of links.

Here are three tried and tested formulas to help you turn those unlinked brand mentions into links back to your content:

- *Attribution request: [title of their article].* This is my go-to formula for contacting journalists who have featured the content I produce for my clients and have mentioned the brand but have failed to credit the content with a link back to the original source (aka, my client's website). It's simple and to the point, including the title of the article in question to quickly get the writer's attention.
- *Credit to original source: [title of their article].* This is the subject-line formula my team uses when a journalist has picked up a piece of content after seeing it published by a media outlet and has credited them as the original source instead of linking back to our client.
  - *Pro tip.* Your email should be short and clear. Start off by thanking the writer for sharing your content and include a link to the article they have written. Instead of simply asking for a link, ask for the credit to be fixed so it points to the original source of the content, and include the URL they should link out to.
- *License infringement and Attribution request: [title of their article].* If your content campaign includes images, make sure to license them under Creative Commons License 4.0 International, which states that publishers can share and/or adapt the material as long as they credit the creator with a link back to the material. Use this subject-line formula when doing link reclamation for images that are licensed under Creative Commons and have been used by other sites without linking back to your website as the source.

Resource Link Building

The subject lines for this type of link building will highly depend on the type of resource you've built.

That said, here are three subject line formulas that are suitable when reaching out to webmasters or editors who curate resources around a specific topic:

- *Suggestion for [name of resource page]: [name of your resource].* Straightforward and to the point, the recipient of this email will quickly know what page on their site you're referring to and what type of resource you're pitching. If your email gets opened, then it's very likely that you'll get a link—as long as your resource is of good quality, of course!
- *Are you accepting new resources for [name of resource page]?* This is a good choice when reaching out to a site editor or webmaster about a page that doesn't seem to be updated on a regular basis.

■ *New resource for [name of resource page]: [name of your resource].* This is an alternative to the first formula on this list that incorporates one of the most powerful words in advertising. Everyone wants to have something new, because it's an improved and nicer version of the old. In addition, research has found that our brains react to novelty by releasing dopamine, which makes us want to go exploring in search of a reward: a great start for a link outreach email!

Round-Up Inclusion

Many bloggers and journalists publish weekly and monthly round-up articles where they handpick resources and content connected to a specific topic. The subject lines below will come in handy next time you're pitching content you think should be included as part of one of these round-up posts:

■ *Tip for [name of round-up]: [title of your article].* If the round-up has a name, you should use it to show that you have done your research. In many cases, the article will include a short blurb at the beginning or at the very end of the post where the writer specifies an email address to pitch new stories for inclusion. Use this subject line when contacting the specified email address.

■ *Do you take suggestions for [name of round-up]?* Unlike the previous case, this is a subject line for contacting a blogger or journalist who publishes a round-up but doesn't make it explicit whether they are open for suggestions. In case the answer is a yes, it's better to approach the person with a question and mention the piece of content you'd like to suggest inside the email.

Content Marketing for Links

One of the go-to link-building techniques today involves creating content that can be pitched to other sites in the hopes that they will reuse it and link back to your website. I call this "content marketing for links" because it's not quite the same as resource link building. However, there are many people who refer to this technique as "digital PR," because, more often than not, the main goal is to build hard-to-get media links.

The content is usually a visual piece that can be easily shared: a simple static image (infographics, maps, charts, illustrations, photographs, etc.), an animated asset (videos or GIFs), or an interactive feature that uses an iframe or embed code (interactive data visualizations, quizzes, calculators, etc.).

Next time you're pitching this type of content with the goal of building links, try opening your emails with the following subject line formulas:

■ *Tip: [title of your content] ([format]).* I always advise including the word "tip" to help journalists immediately identify your email as a pitch. This can be crucial if the topic of your content could be mistaken for a different type of message, such as a sales pitch or junk mail:

- How to lose weight this summer
- Tip: How to lose weight this summer (infographic)

- *Tip for [site name]: [title of your content].* When contacting someone who writes for multiple publications, include the name of the site you're targeting into your subject-line formula. Keep this formula in mind when your target site is a company blog and you're unsure of who manages it, so you're pitching the most suitable contact based on their position within the organization (e.g., content manager or digital marketing executive).

- *Story idea: [title of your content].* When pitching content to an editor who assigns stories to journalists, you can use this as an alternative to the first subject-line formula on this list.

- *Tip: This [format] will show you [brief description about the topic of your content].* My team has been incorporating emojis into subject lines when the topic allows and the content is aimed at Millennials and Generation Zers. Note that the subject line has been written in a click-bait tone; see the difference:

  - Tip: The college degree of the top earning CEO in every US state (interactive)
  - Tip: This interactive will show you what the top CEOs in America studied in college

- *Exclusive for [site name]: [title of your content] ([format]).* Make sure to mention the word "exclusive" when you're ready to offer exclusivity over your content to a specific publication. This will give your email priority as media outlets love to break the news about a story before anyone else.

Set the Right Expectations with Your Email Subject Lines

The majority of the advice you've read before today about subject lines comes from the world of email marketing, but link building is a different ball game, so it requires a new mindset. The foot-in-the-door technique is a tried and tested theory from the psychology of compliance that will help you develop the mindset you need for writing subject lines that will get you links.

Next time you're writing an email for a new link-building campaign, try to be as specific as possible in your subject line so your small request (opening the email) is consistent to your big request (linking to your content).

12 ELEMENTS OF IRRESISTIBLE SUBMISSION REQUESTS

A link request sent via email should include several elements. Collectively, these elements serve two key purposes. First, they let the person you are contacting know that without a doubt you took the time to look through their site, and second, they make it as easy as possible for that person to make a decision about whether to give your site a link.

Email inboxes are busy places, and you need a way to make your email stand out from the hundreds of others. Here are 12 elements your link requests should contain, followed by the logic behind them. Although these may seem obvious once you read the logic behind them, the majority of link requests we receive do not contain them, so adopting these practices will set you apart from the competition for your target's attention.

1. *A subject line that follows any stated directions given on the site you want to link to yours.* On many sites with collections of links to other sites, the editor in charge of link evaluation/selection often states that when asking for a link, you should follow specific directions. One of these directions is typically a special subject line, such as, "Request for editorial consideration." If you have not taken the time to look at their site carefully, or even if you have, and you do not follow their stated link request directions, don't be surprised if you never hear from them and don't get the link. If the site gives exact instructions for submissions, then you have a bigger challenge. Do not put the words "link request" in the subject line, simply because there are probably about 100 million emails with that exact subject line or something similar hitting inboxes and getting deleted every day.

2. *The site owner's name.* It seems simple, but take the time to look through the site where you want the link, and find the site owner's name. Address this person by name immediately in your email. If you begin an email with "Dear Webmaster" or "Site Owner," you can expect your email to to be deleted immediately. Can't find a name on the site? Look for a phone number, then call them. Yes, use the phone. Think about it: If you have a website with a personal URL in your name, and someone sends you a "Dear Webmaster" link, it will be immediately obvious to you that the sender has not been to your site, even if their email indicates otherwise. If this person really had been to your site, your name would have been the first thing they would have seen. People might overlook the mistake, but you'll increase your chances of getting your foot in the door if you take the time to address the site owner.

3. *Your name.* Again, it's just common courtesy. The person requesting a link is a human being and so are you. A first line like, "Hello, Mr. Ward, my name is Bill Thompson," tells Mr. Ward that Bill looked at his site and respects basic human conversational etiquette. It also shows Mr. Ward that you didn't send that same email to 4,000 other people, unless by some bizarre coincidence their names were all Mr. Ward.

4. *The URL of their site.* Using wording, such as "I see that on your site you have the following content at the below URL," allows you to use a template approach but

also shows the site owner you know their name, site, and a specific URL. You are obviously not lying to them or spamming them. And while we're at it, don't show fake sincerity or imply friendship when you've never met. Be professional, courteous, and to the point. People get turned off by email from strangers who act like their buddies.

5. *Your site's name and the URL you are hoping they will link to.* For example, "I am contacting you about my site, called [SiteName], which is located at [URL]."

6. *The exact URL on their site where you think the link is a fit.* Using a line, such as "with regard to your page located at https://www.[page URL]," is especially helpful for those people who maintain large sites with hundreds or thousands of pages. Help them to help you.

7. *A short paragraph that describes your site.* Do not oversell your site or give them 76 reasons why they should link to it. If they link to it, it won't be your email that convinced them. It will be because they looked at your site and determined whether it's link-worthy to them based on their criteria.

8. *The exact URL from your site that you want them to link to.* Be as specific as possible: "Since I have a splash page that has some Flash elements, you may prefer to use this URL for linking: https://www.SiteName.com/noflash.html."

9. *A valid email address and response to any requests made to that address.* Here's an example: "If you would like to contact me about this, please feel free to reach me at my personal email address below." (Then list your email address.)

10. *Your phone number.* Always give them an option: "Or, if you prefer, you can also call me at this phone number . . ."

11. *Confirmation that you have added a link to their site.* If you are seeking a link from a site where a return link is required (I don't, but many do), also include a confirmation.

12. *The URL on your site where they can see the link to their site.* This way, you can show them that you fulfilled your end of the agreement.

What your email doesn't say is just as important as what it says. Any webmaster, editor, curator, or site manager who receives the email outlined in Figure 15–2, on page 140, can tell immediately several crucial things about this link request:

- It was sent by someone who took the time to look at the site. How else could they call it by name?
- It was sent by someone who took the time to find out who runs the site.
- It was sent by someone who reviewed the site for appropriateness. How else would they have known the site had a "links" area related to their own content?
- It was sent by someone who followed the site editor's link-request instructions.

- It was sent by someone who couldn't have sent that same email to 25,000 people.
- It was sent by someone who respected the website owner's time by making it easy for them to know just what URL they wanted linked.
- It was sent by someone who looked at more than just the prospect domain's homepage.
- It was sent by someone who was not afraid to put a phone number in the email; spammers don't do that.

To:

From: You@yourdomain.com

Subject: Site submission

Dear [*Site Owner Name*],

I am contacting you regarding your [*full title of the site, not URL*] site at [*URL*].

I'm working with [*URL*] to announce and link a new section on their site called [*title of the site you want the link for*].

Per the link request instructions on your site, I would like to request a link to our homepage in your Links to [*website descriptor*] Websites section located at [*URL*].

Please feel free to let me know if the above provides you with the information you need to review and consider our site for linking. I can be reached via email at you@yourdomain.com, or, if you'd like to talk about this by phone, my direct number is (123) 456-7890.

Best Wishes,

Your Name

FIGURE 15–2. Sample of What a Full Link-Request Email Might Look Like

There are many more subtle points to the exercise illustrated in Figure 15–2 and many additional things you might need or have to include, but these are not right for every scenario, so let's keep things as simple as possible for now. This letter was designed for a link builder working on behalf of a site owner; if you were the site owner yourself, you would delete the sentence beginning "I'm working with" and edit the rest of the letter accordingly.

The bottom line is that by recognizing the individuals on the receiving end of your link requests, you immediately move out of the spam realm in their minds. When most folks receive link letters, they look for telltale signs that they were not singled out individually. If they spot an obvious bulk link seeker, they usually delete it immediately.

This means you cannot automate this process and you have to create and send each link request one at a time—as you should. Sometimes each site takes an entire three clicks and two minutes. Big deal. This is a lifelong link you're seeking.

In the next chapter, we will analyze BuzzStream Data to discover outcomes across customer bases and show what the baseline response rates look like for outreach campaigns. This is the information we wish had been available 20 years ago when link building started!

Chapter 16

Analyzing BuzzStream Data

by Stephen Panico, Chief Growth Officer of BuzzStream

Outreach is at the heart of any strategy geared toward getting links, building buzz, or increasing brand awareness. Still, despite the fact that almost every company that cares about promoting their site or content sends outreach, there are tons of questions. Some of the ones we hear most often are:

- What level of response rates should we expect? How much variation should we expect from campaign to campaign?
- Do we need to personalize our outreach to get results? If so, how do we do this and still conduct outreach at a scale that moves the needle for the business?
- What can we do to improve our response rates?

To provide some answers to these questions, in this chapter, we've analyzed campaigns across our customer base to show what the baseline response rates look like and to determine whether (and how) certain organizations are able to consistently outperform the industry. Spoiler alert: They are. And we're going to show you the tactics that let them do it.

KEY TAKEAWAYS

In reviewing our customer campaigns internally, we found the following results:

- *The top 5 percent of groups conducting outreach can consistently get 40 percent or higher reply rates across their campaigns.* This is dramatically higher than the median reply rate for companies we researched (12 percent). The primary differentiators for top-performing accounts are the amount of time spent prospecting for highly relevant contacts and customizing messages to make them personalized and contextually relevant.
- *Groups that send outreach using only templates with merge fields receive an average reply rate of 16 percent.* Reply rates are decreased by 1.3 percent if a group personalizes the outreach in an irrelevant or cursory way. If those emails are contextualized with relevant personalization, the reply rate is boosted by an average of 10.7 percent. And if a past promotion is referenced, reply rates get a further boost of 2.3 percent.

METHODOLOGY

We aggregated outreach data from over 12,000 campaigns across 2,000 active BuzzStream accounts and analyzed it to understand reply rates by campaign. We then averaged the reply rates for all campaigns in a given account that have been completed over the past year. After that, we analyzed over 30,000 anonymized and coded individual emails to understand the impact of different approaches to outreach and personalization.

Finally, we followed up with top performing accounts (those in the upper 5th percentile of campaign reply rates) to understand commonalities in their specific processes.

OVERALL REPLY RATE TRENDS

The most striking aspect of the data we analyzed is the sheer range of the distribution that can be seen in Figure 16–1, on page 145. Although the median reply rate hovers around 12 percent, there is a large chunk of our customer base that dramatically outperforms, with the upper 5th percentile averaging a staggering 40 percent reply rate across their campaigns. Similarly, there are accounts that clearly do not perform well, with a comparatively paltry 3 percent reply rate across the campaigns we analyzed.

To quickly summarize the data:

- Roughly 50 percent of BuzzStream accounts regularly receive a reply rate of over 12 percent for their email campaigns.
- The upper 25 percent of accounts regularly receive a 20 percent or higher reply rate.
- The bottom 25 percent of accounts receive under a 7 percent reply rate.
- The best performers (top 5 percent) receive reply rates of over 40 percent.

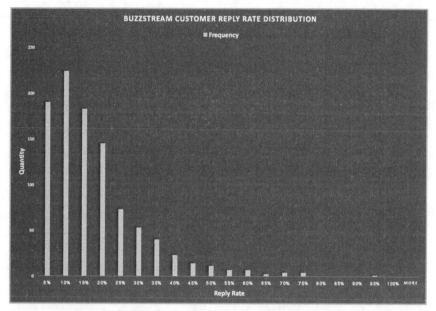

FIGURE 16–1. BuzzStream Customer Reply Rate Distribution

■ The worst performers (bottom 5 percent) receive under a 3 percent reply rate.

This data covers the breadth of BuzzStream customers, which includes agencies and independent companies across a wide range of industries. To discover the common success factors of top performing accounts, as well as elements that lead to underperforming campaigns, we examined the messages that were being sent to contacts across 12,000 campaigns.

THE IMPACT OF PERSONALIZATION ON REPLY RATES

Of the campaigns we examined, the overwhelming majority (slightly over 95 percent) sent their initial outreach using a template with merge fields. When reviewing emails that were sent using only a template with merge fields and no additional personalization, we saw a baseline reply rate of 16 percent (see Figure 16–2, on page 146).

Once we knew the average base reply rate for people who did not personalize, we could assess the impact of different personalization strategies. Although personalization can be diverse in its application, most of the messages we reviewed fit pretty snugly into three approaches, as illustrated in Figure 16–3, on page 146:

1. Fake personalization
2. Contextual relevance
3. Reference to past promotion

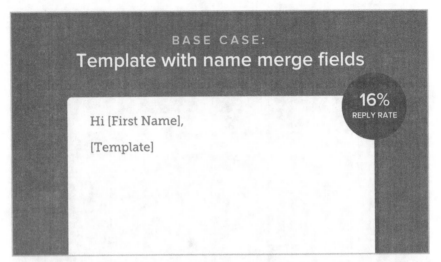

FIGURE 16–2. Percent Reply Rate Template with Name Merge Fields

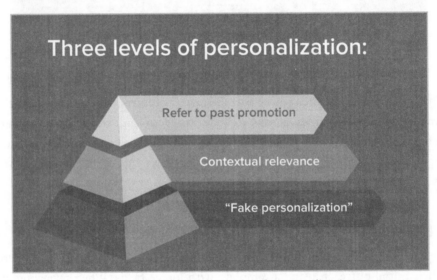

FIGURE 16–3. The Three Levels of Personalization

Fake Personalization

Fake personalization is a generic reference to an article or some other piece of information that's meant to signal that the outreach professional has some knowledge of the contact they are reaching out to, when in actuality, they don't have any context about that individual at all.

A common example of this type of outreach is any email that begins with some variation of: "Hey FNAME, I just saw your article at XYZ.com. Great post! I've written something your audience would like . . . "

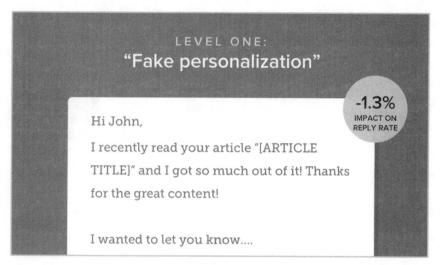

FIGURE 16–4. –1.3 Percent Impact Reply Rate with Fake Personalization

Unfortunately for those groups that use this process, they'd be better served by not personalizing at all. Based on the data, fake personalization generates a –1.3 percent impact on reply rates compared to the base case of people only using templates with merge fields (as seen in Figure 16–4).

Contextual Relevance

Contextually relevant personalization shows clearly that the person sending the outreach has a good understanding of the author by specifically referencing not just their article or info, but tying it directly into the request. This type of personalization depends on a tight prospecting process as well as a good understanding of the outreach audience.

This type of personalization, in stark contrast to fake personalization, offers significant improvements to the base case with an average reply rate improvement of +10.7 percent; refer to Figure 16–5, on page 148, to see the difference.

Reference to Past Promotion

References to past promotion are precisely what they sound like. This type of personalization requires a well-updated contact database that teams can reference in order to know which of the contacts in their campaigns have shared or linked in the past. If you've had a good working relationship in the past, that contact is much more likely to promote again.

However, when analyzing this type of personalization, things get a little murky because it is almost always completed in concert with contextually relevant outreach.

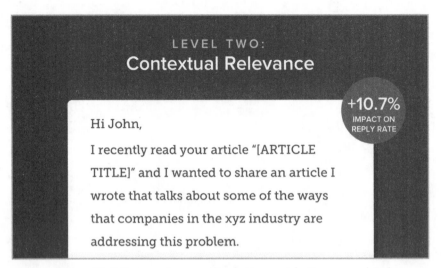

FIGURE 16–5. +10.7 Percent Impact Reply Rate with Contextual Relevance

So, to isolate the average improvement of references to a past promotion, we analyzed those instances and compared them to those instances of contextual relevance without said references. When doing so, we found an average improvement of +2.3 percent on reply rates (see Figure 16-6).

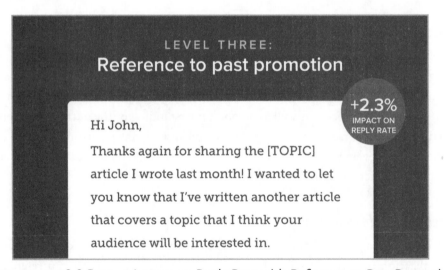

FIGURE 16–6. +2.3 Percent Impact on Reply Rate with Reference to Past Promotion

CAMPAIGN RESULTS BY OUTREACH SENDER TYPE

When aggregating the types of outreach people are doing, three types of profiles occur most often:

- *Volume Senders.* This group consists primarily of link builders who are relying on links from specific page types to their content/site. They are mostly doing things like resource page outreach and link reclamation (unlinked mention) campaigns.
- *SEO Content Marketers.* This type of outreach team blurs the line between traditional SEO and PR, using a range of tactics, including blogger outreach, infographic placement, and broken link building.
- *Pure Digital PRs.* These accounts focus their outreach almost exclusively on high-authority media sites by targeting journalists and high-level influencers with exclusive and/or newsworthy content that aligns with their niche.

Although these approaches are nearly all aimed toward getting links to sites or content, the approaches differ significantly. To understand those, we reviewed the average list size, reply rate, average number of replies, and average domain authority of the sites that replied.

These strategies highlight significantly different campaign logistics, but an interesting (and slightly unexpected) element in the data was that Volume Senders and Digital PRs seem to get the same reply rate (see Figure 16-7). It seemed like there was more to this story than was being told in the reply rate alone, so we turned to Ahrefs with a representative subset of these campaigns to understand the impact of these approaches on downstream placement rates.

This analysis showed that although replies might be similar for two outreach types, actual placement rates differ significantly (see Figure 16-8, on page 150).

Reply Rate			
	Volume Senders	SEO Content Marketers	Digital PRs
Average list size	468	97	47
Reply rate	13%	23%	13%
Average # replies	59	22	6
Avg. Domain Authority	21	38	78

FIGURE 16-7. Reply Rate

Placement Rate

	Volume Senders	SEO Content Marketers	Digital PRs
Average list size	468	97	47
Avg. placements (outreach)	8	5	1.7
Avg. placements (organic)	0.6	2	14
Avg. placements (total)	8	7	16

FIGURE 16–8. Placement Rate

First, let's clarify what we mean by "outreach" vs. "organic" links. Outreach placements are simply links that were earned as a direct result of outreach itself. Organic placements were earned by people subsequently linking as a result of the impact of content or pages created by the contacts who were initially reached out to.

These results can be summed up as follows for each of the groups you read about earlier:

- *Volume Senders.* Nearly all the value of the outreach in terms of link placements is derived from the initial outreach itself. Due to the general lower authority of the sites and the lack of editorial value for things like resource pages in general, there are fewer organic placements with this approach.
- *SEO Content Marketers.* A mixed bag, but it shows that the majority of value is still derived from the initial outreach campaign. Subsequent organic links do happen, but it is not the backbone of the strategy because the range of authority and search value of those sites is scattered.
- *Digital PR.* Here, in the initial outreach campaign, placement rates are very low, averaging one or two placements. However, because those sites generally have a very high authority and the linking articles are often newsworthy based on current trends, subsequent organic links make up for the low initial placements.

To summarize the impact of these different campaign approaches, see Figure 16–9, on page 151, for the blended average placements and domain authority for the different approaches.

I should note that these results do not point to a superior outreach sending type. Although it appears that the better long-term strategy is a pure Digital PR play, the

Authority of Placements

	Volume Senders	SEO Content Marketers	Digital PRs
Total Placements	8	9	16
Avg. Domain Authority	23	32	53

FIGURE 16–9. Authority of Placements

reality is that each of these approaches have their place in an SEO strategy and must be tied to the specific needs of the organization.

Let's briefly review some of the pros and cons for each group:

- *Volume Senders*. This process offers the fastest results and the clearest path to links. Further, it is the most consistent process because there is usually a clear reason for the link request. That said, in general, the authority of those sites is lower and subsequent links don't generally happen.

- *SEO Content Marketers*. This blended approach gets solid authority links and builds relationships with niche influencers. Done correctly, this approach will align closely with search intent and can also be used to establish an up-and-coming site as an authority in a vertical. However, it will be more difficult to earn links with this approach than in a volume sending campaign, and usually those links are not received from the most authoritative sites.

- *Digital PR*. This approach is all about targeted outreach to high-authority sites and is great for established brands or agencies that can offer proprietary data or exclusives to publications. These links get major buzz and can lead to tons of follow-on links. However, this type of outreach can be difficult for brands or agencies that don't have solid reputations, and the targeted those publications will only be interested in exclusives. One other downside to this approach is that the primary benefit comes from increasing a site's authority. However, it is not likely to result in a significant increase in page authority and may not get as much direct traffic value as the other approaches.

TRENDS OF TOP PERFORMERS

Given that there are teams that consistently get strong reply rates, we wanted to reach out to a few representative groups across the range of our customer base in the top 5 percent to understand the commonalities in their process. The goal was to understand those elements that are not dependent on specific niche, industry, or team size. Ultimately, the groups we talked to shared most of the following traits:

Process-Oriented

These outreach teams have a well-defined process, and they stick with it. This does not necessarily mean that they structure their outreach rigidly, however. It means that they ensure that they find specific information about a contact, leverage this information in their emails, and follow up on replies and unread messages in an orderly manner. Many of these teams have scripted their processes so they can easily share them and onboard new team members as they grow.

> *"High touch outreach [at scale] is a unique blend between business processes and creative tasks. On one hand, having a set of efficient processes helps us stay organized and helps simplify the education process for new team members. On the other hand, there's a million ways you can customize an email and a million directions the conversation can go in, so it's more about teaching a way to think than it is about having strict templates to use. That's why we have a library of outreach examples and utilize analytics tools to assess ongoing performance in order to maintain a high standard on outreach success rates."*
>
> —Jon Cooper, Hyperlynx Media

Significant Time Spent in Contact Prospecting

This is probably the most common and significant differentiator of top performers. These groups spend most of their time prospecting, qualifying, and researching prospects to ensure they are going to be interested in their outreach.

> *"At Siege we like to make 100 percent sure that the people we're reaching out to are a good fit for the piece we are pitching. We first review their site to make sure they are high quality and not loaded up with paid sponsorships or anything that feels remotely spammy. We then determine how exactly the content we are pitching will be of interest to them. That means that for each prospect, we need to confirm the topical relevance and specific details of our piece that we think will interest them. For instance, maybe they've covered the same topic last year and ours has new data for this year. The more time we spend vetting prospects and crafting our pitches up front, the easier and faster the outreach becomes."*
>
> —Ross Hudgens, Siege Media

Customized Email Messaging to Each Contact

Simple to grasp, but perceived as difficult to execute, this was another common differentiator of top performers. In reality, the difficulty of customized messaging (meaning templates that are customized, not unique emails to each contact) is tied closely to time spent prospecting. The more time spent in the prospecting and segmentation phase, the easier it is to quickly personalize each message with relevant content.

> *"Some managers become so consumed in economies of scale, by proxy, they end up devaluing the person who is on the receiving end of a pitch. However, when it comes to placements with high-authority publishers, taking the time to personalize each pitch is key to success. By scouring personal blogs, social media networks, and author archives, you establish knowledge that allows you to nurture an authentic relationship with each writer. This long-term relationship-building strategy fosters name recognition and affinity for individuals on your team as well as your business. Over time, you'll go from sending individual pitches to seeing top-tier writers reaching out to you for content and quotes."*
>
> —Kelsey Libert, Fractl

Leverage Existing Relationships

Groups that have an established outreach program and a well-maintained contact database regularly leverage their relationships for future progress in two ways. First, as previously discussed, they will reference their relationships in their outreach to boost replies. Second, they will use their database as a source to build their lists for subsequent similar campaigns, building on the success of their campaigns and making results more beneficial and predictable over time.

> *"In our experience, targeting the right journalists is paramount—what makes a great story for a finance journalist looks very different to a great story for a travel journalist. In addition to writing a great pitch, you need to send it to the right people. We use our database to help us build media lists based on similar successful campaigns, which enables us to be more targeted. Plus, as we frequently have multiple people working on the same campaign (and multiple campaigns being promoted at the same time), it important for us to keep our database well maintained so we know whether or not a particular journalist has already been contacted about a campaign we're working on."*
>
> —Hannah Smith, Verve Search

In the next chapter, we will walk through outreach templates for link-building campaigns that we have found successful.

Chapter 17

Putting the Pieces Together: Link-Building Campaign Templates

t's always helpful to have some examples of link-building campaigns when designing your own. These are some general templates we've found useful in our work. If you're ready to get started right away, you may have skipped directly to this chapter. That's fine—just note that the underlying concepts we've already covered are more important in campaign design than the templates, but the templates are great for seeing where the concepts can take you. In this chapter, we'll walk you through some of the best practices of campaign design.

THE ULTIMATE RESOURCE AGGREGATION PIECE

In the ultimate resource aggregation piece, you're creating a massive list, or roundup, of an informational resource that your market finds useful. Ideally, you're also recontextualizing it in some way that adds more value than if a reader found one of the individual pieces alone. This can be in the form of a process walk-through or some other framework that your market will find useful. Remember, you're ideally selecting your resources for this piece from among the link targets in your keyword space.

Resource Aggregation Examples

Here are some additional examples of resource aggregations that you can check out on the web. Note that each one has its own framework or context for the resources that introduces them and makes them more accessible. See Figure 17–1 for an example of link aggregation content.

FIGURE 17–1. An Example of Link Aggregation Content

Resource Types

There are a number of resource types you can and should consider aggregating (see Figure 17–2, on page 157, for an example). These include, but are not limited to the following:

- how-tos and guides
- videos
- top (your industry) Twitter users
- blogs
- PDFs
- free tools/paid tools

FIGURE 17–2. Example of a Tool Aggregation Piece That Will Attract Links

- podcasts
- classes
- all the "top #" lists for a topic (top 10, top 100, etc.)

People, Work Hours, and Cash Required

This one is all about applying your talent and work hours. What's nice about the resource aggregation piece is that it's fairly fast if you're already an expert in a space, and it's a fantastic "crash course" to the top thinkers and publishers if you're new. Ideally these are not pieces you dash off, but rather spend time looking for new and more useful ways to organize the information. What will make your collection of links more useful than others? Can you come up with a score for each link or a rating? Do you have personal information you can add to each resource mention? Can you present the links within the framework of a process, or within some other framework recognizable in your industry?

This can take someone who's an old hand in a space about a day to research, categorize, find new patterns, and publish. Someone who's new to a space could/should spend two or more days, ideally.

Link Prospect Sources

Ideally the resources you link to in the first place are your link prospects. It is probable that the expert publishers in your space will take interest in a new configuration of previously existing resources.

Here's where your title and pitch come into play! Further prospects include sites and pages linking to the same resources *you* linked to.

Finally, you can try some of these queries to turn up some new prospects for you:

- [MDKW] blogs: You'll want to let your industry's bloggers know about you, even if they're not in the resource.
- "[MDKW] news"
- [MDKW] community: Some forum owners might be interested in sharing your resource, or give you permission to share it within their communities.
- [MDKW] roundup
- "useful [MDKW] links"

Tips and Helpful Hints

Resource-list inclusion makes a wonderful introduction to experts in your market and is a great way to start off a campaign if you're completely new to a keyword space. To up your chances of getting links from this kind of piece, include resources from writers who consistently create roundups of the space. If they're writing about the space consistently anyway, they're more likely to link to you.

We've created badges for bloggers in our resource lists before but found that these badges ended up making the linked-to pages on our clients' sites look spammy. We suspect this is because they were site-wide.

Numbers—as in the number of resources—can be an effective way to communicate the size and enormity of your resource list. There are some SEOs who believe that numbers and lists are losing their effectiveness. We suspect that this could be true in some spaces, and especially if the resources are not organized in a new, interesting, and more useful way.

Figure 17–3, on page 159, is an example of an outreach email template for your next "Ultimate Resource Roundup." Add to it and subtract from it as you see fit!

THE GROUP INTERVIEW/SURVEY OF EXPERTS AND OTHER MARKET PARTICIPANTS

We've found that interviewing the expert publishers in a space—that is, the frequent writers, contributors, and active participants within a given industry, hobby, or other

---

Subject line: You're in [Title of Resource Roundup]! Yay! ;)

Just a quick note to let you know that we included you in [*Title of Resource Roundup*]

https://www.hostname.com/YourResourceRoundup

We linked to: https://www.theirsite.com/theirresource

Will you help us spread the word about your inclusion in the roundup?

What really sets our roundup apart is that it [*customize your message*].

Also, if you're a member of [NicheSocialNewsSite.com], will you consider voting for this post?

https://NicheSocialNewsSite.com/YourResourceRoundup

Thank you!

Your Name

FIGURE 17–3. Sample Outreach Email Template for Ultimate Resource Roundup

"thought space"—is an excellent way to build links, create great content, and connect more powerfully with your market. We've engaged expert/hobbyist forums in this way as well, to fantastic result.

Examples of Group Interviews and Expert Surveys

Any time you can create pleasing presentations for your data, your link traction will improve. Below are some examples of group interviews and expert surveys. Note that there superficially appears to be a relationship between the quality of the graphics and the overall presentation and links.

- Search Engine Ranking Factors
- Interview: 12 Top Online Entrepreneurs Share How Hard They Work
- 21 Link Builders Share Advanced Link-Building Queries
- 30 Link Builders Discuss Backlink Analysis for Campaign Design—Part 1
- ToolCrib.com's Ultimate Guide to the Top Ten Most Dangerous Woodworking Power Tools

QUESTION DESIGN: WARNING . . . YOU GET WHAT YOU ASK FOR

On a number of occasions, we've asked way too many questions of our experts. In one instance, we sought to publish a single article, asked 10 questions of 30 experts, and got back 30,000 words (enough for over 30 articles).

We've never asked too few questions. In fact, here's a great example of a group interview article with only one question: "(44 Experts Discuss) Social Media Strategy Before Tactics." However, if you ask your questions in a way that forces your experts to explicitly quantify their answers (with numbers, for example), you can create this kind of a result: Link Value Factors. Wow! What a beauty! In this piece, the survey creator wasn't overly concerned with too much input; because the answers got quantified and graphed, it helped reliability of data to have more input! Also, when possible, focus on hot, potentially even controversial, topics. This will help you get some interest from others in your space.

People, Work Hours, and Cash Required

When it comes to group surveys, the bigger, the better, usually. Ideally, you're gathering enough input, thought, and wisdom that you can create multiple pieces. It's tough to put numbers on this, but something like "(44 Experts Discuss) Social Media Strategy Before Tactics" could probably take around a day to aggregate and publish. Something like "Interview: 12 Top Online Entrepreneurs Share How Hard They Work" probably didn't take forever, either.

Link Prospect Sources

In this case, your best prospects are the participants themselves. In markets where we've gone in cold, we've found about a 20 percent rate of links and mentions from participants. In every case, we've found that the number of links is at least double the number of participants.

Tips and Helpful Hints

Ask people if they will participate in your group interview/expert survey *as* you're asking them to mention or link to something else. Also, as in the resource roundup described above, make sure to include roundup publishers in your group of experts. They are most likely to link! See Figure 17–4, on page 161, for a sample outreach template.

Subject line 1: May I Interview You? and Potential Article for a Roundup

Subject line 2: Group Interview—You In?

Hello!

I have two requests: 1) to add your voice to a group [*subject matter*] interview I'll be publishing and promoting next month, and 2) to consider a recent piece I wrote for a mention in one of your upcoming roundups!

To be included in the interview, I will need your answers by [*date*]! If appropriate, feel free to provide links to any blog posts you've done that answer questions more fully!

1. What's your "[*subject matter*] story?" In other words, how and why did you get started in [*subject matter*]?

2. What [*subject matter*] skills were the hardest for you to learn and why?

3. Have you ever taken [*subject matter*] too far or failed spectacularly in some way? How so?

4. What resources (blogs, books, websites) would you recommend to someone who's new to the [subject matter] arena?

5. What question did I leave off/what message would you really like to get out there?

6. Who else should I interview?

>> And here's the article I hope you'll consider for a roundup:

[*article title*] [*article URL*]

Or will you give us a tweet? [*article title*] https://bit.ly/articleurl

Or just a vote on NicheSocialNewsSite.com? :D
https://NicheSocialNewsSite.com/titleofthepiece/

[*Pitch the value of your piece*]

Thanks for your consideration, and I look forward to getting your answers!

[*Your Name*]

FIGURE 17–4. Sample Outreach Template for the Expert Interview/Survey Piece

YOUR OWN HIGH-QUALITY, LEAD-GENERATING, BRAND-BUILDING CONTENT

Ideally, by the time you get around to pushing your own content on others for link consideration, you have amply warmed up your link prospects by promoting them, helping them spread their message, and demonstrating that you both care about the audience and the industry as a whole. By engaging your link prospects in this manner, you have sown the seeds of trust. They are now more likely to consider mentioning work you have done—work that does not directly promote them in some way, especially if it's great content.

Examples of High-Quality, Lead-Generating, Brand-Building Content

Ideally your content pushes your industry's thought forward, delivers relevant traffic, confers a bit of reputation on your brand by association (from where you earn mention and links, or, if you publish it off-site, from the publisher's brand), and even generates business leads. That's quite a tall order, right? Isn't this supposed to be a book about link building? Well, we believe that this sort of content is the highest form of link building because it satisfies so many different objectives simultaneously. It's what we strive for in our own marketing, and it's what we urge our clients, prospects, and the market as a whole to work toward. No, it's not easy, and it takes a lot of attempts before you start really getting it right. Here are some examples of content that does it all right (forgive our hubris in mentioning some of our content here—note that it should also help you in the content-creation phase):

- Link Building with Content: How to Attract Links and Leads
- 101 Ways to Build Link Popularity
- How to Research, Create, and Distribute Highly Linkable Content
- The Link Prospector

People, Work Hours, and Cash Required

Creating this kind of content—whether it's a tool, article, video, or whatever—requires significant investments of time. There's no easy way around this one! At some point you have to put your position or your organization's position out there in a format that's going to help you achieve multiple business goals simultaneously.

Notes and Tips

To make your content more linkable and reputable, you may have to go to the experts in your organization and lean on them to share their time and expertise (the same way you initially went to the expert publishers in your space). For our own marketing, we've found that free tools and process-oriented spreadsheets are highly linkable, and demonstrate our capacity for deriving value from link-prospect data. Remember that you have to *give* to your industry to *receive* the links and leads!

It's vital to not always be the platform and the connector. Though this does serve to build links, you also have to be an originator. This is what builds the leads. Prospects want to see your original thought, not just that you can recognize and cultivate great thought in others! In Figure 17–5 you can see an example of how you can position yourself as an originator.

Dear [*Contact Name*],

I'm writing today to introduce: https://citationlabs.com/36-broken-link-building-resources/.

This URL collection walks motivated readers through the methods and processes of large-scale, research-intensive broken-link building.

We include a number of your writings and resources there. In addition, we promote [your tools] as good data-gathering alternatives for link builders without crawler/scraper technology.

My request to you is that you check out our new guide and mention it if you find it noteworthy.

Thank you for your consideration!

Best,

[*Your Name*]

FIGURE 17–5. Sample Outreach for High-Quality, Lead-Generating, Brand-Building Content

EXPERT ENGAGEMENT: THE "WRITING ASSIGNMENT"

In creating a writing assignment or prompt for your expert publishers, you first come up with an intriguing concept or question—perhaps one left over from your interview questions. Then you answer this question yourself on your site and implore your visitors to do the same. The goal is to make it something that others would genuinely have the urge to write about in their next blogging session. Then you promote the heck out of your question. Furthermore, as part of the promotion, make sure that contributors know you'll be linking to their answers.

Some Examples of Expert Engagement Writing Assignments

Here are a few samples of expert engagement writing assignments we've found "in the wild":

- A Letter to Myself
- Create Your Own "Bloggers to Watch" List and Tell Us About It Here
- ToolCrib.com's Guide to Your 31 Most Influential Woodworkers (a hybrid writing assignment/expert survey)

People, Work Hours, and Cash Required

This method is fairly simple to execute, though it will require maintenance as you correspond with experts and add their contributions to your site. Also, it's not likely to work as well if you're entering a space "cold." This method will be much more effective when done after building relationships in your space with the expert publishers and other contributors.

Notes and Tips

There are a number of ways you can spin this approach to link building. If you've done a massive survey, you could give away your data and ask others for their interpretations. You could also combine this effort with your group interview and simply ask people to answer your questions on their site. Then your job as the editor/curator will be to collect and aggregate the most interesting and important data as you see it.

We've only done this technique once, after a group expert interview piece we created for a client got mentioned in Time.com. We took the "distributed group interview" approach and asked a large number of experts to weigh in. We also told them that we'd be sending their answers to our contact at Time.com, which we did. We did *not* ask them to link to the original, though many of them did.

FREE PRODUCTS AND SERVICES: CONTESTS, DONATIONS, AND GIVEAWAYS

This is about the closest we get to buying links in this book. And, yeah, it's pretty close. It happens on calls with clients and prospects, especially those seeking our link prospect data and not our agency services; they have no time or desire to contribute great content to their space in exchange for links. Furthermore, there's often an SEO-driven mentality to acquire links with some sort of immediate and direct value exchange. To protect the innocent, we don't point out sites accepting donations in exchange for links. Instead, we like to focus on the fun contests we've seen that leverage giveaways! Figure 17–6, on page 165, shows one way you can create this kind of sample outreach, offering something as simple as a shout-out on a major media site.

Subject line: Share Your Hard-Earned [*Subject Matter*] Lessons with Time.com!

Hello!

I'm a new [*subject matter*] blogger, so when I emailed interview questions to famous [*subject matter*] bloggers like [*expert*], [*expert*], and [*expert*], I got pretty nervous. After all, I only started blogging a few months ago. Why would these pros answer my questions?

Well, I'm glad I faced my fears and emailed them because they *did* answer my interview questions, and after I published their answers ([*link to client site where story appeared*]), Time.com picked up the story!

I know there are more than just their lessons out there. And I know that you must have some of them!

Here's how to add your wisdom to the group interview and get a shot at a mention in Time.com!

1. Answer the questions below and post them to your blog.

2. Tweet @[*client*] and email [*your address*] to let us know they're up.

3. Add a link to your answers in the comment section of our group interview in order to share it with visitors from Time.com!

4. I will email Time.com on April 15, send a complete list of who else responded, and ask them to check out our group interview again!

We had [##] responses to our original interview. To get Time's attention again, I'd really like to add at least 100 more! Here are your interview questions:

1. What's your "[*subject matter*] story?" In other words, how and why did you become a [*subject matter*] expert?

2. What, if anything, tempts you to do [*subject matter*] poorly, and how do you resist?

3. What [*subject matter*] habits were the hardest for you to adopt and why?

4. Have you ever taken [*subject matter*] too far? How so?

5. What resources (blogs, books, websites) would you recommend to someone who's new to [*subject matter*]?

Thank you for your consideration, and I look forward to writing to Time.com with your contribution!

FIGURE 17–6. Sample Outreach for the Writing Assignment

In the next chapter, we will cover the guest posting tactic and how to run highly effective guest post placement campaigns.

Building Links and Expertise with Guest Post Placement Campaigns

A guest post is an article, written by you, that is placed on someone else's site. PR professionals call this a "bylined article." SEOs like guest posts because they enable links to very targeted pages, namely, sales pages that contribute directly and immediately to revenue. A guest post campaign occurs when you increase the scale of the processes required for a single placement of a guest post.

This tactic was specifically called out and presumably penalized heavily by Google's Matt Cutts in early 2014. It's still alive, well, and contributing to rankings increases by teams who follow best practices, such as the ones you'll find in this chapter.

We start out a bit philosophical but get practical soon enough. Hang in there—it's all vital to running a highly effective guest placement campaign!

If you're manufacturing outbound links—particularly via guest placements on third-party sites—your work must bear potential scrutiny from Google-quality raters (people who hand-investigate links to determine if there was intent to manipulate rankings), not to mention your peer competitors. How you build links—to your own or client properties as well as other supporting resources—matters tremendously. And how you link out is about more than just Google and your competitors.

You're making task and process recommendations to real folks—with the full expectation of them following your direction. Outbound linking provides the basis for earning your readers' trust in your carefully considered advice, explaining how they can reach their goals, seize their dreams, and achieve any number of other conceivable goals—and it all starts with properly citing your information.

CITATION JUSTIFICATION

This section explores circumstances where citations are required—academically or journalistically—and where citations just "feel right." It closes with a checklist we recommend for the content that you intend for off-site placements.

Citation Required Circumstances

These are the instances in which you absolutely must include citations, both to honor the work of others and to boost your own ethos as a purveyor of information:

- Data or "findings" (a recent study shows . . .)
- Direct quotation of a source (according to expert individual or organization/ brand . . .)
- Indicating the source of a summary of key concepts, philosophy, or approach
- Further, fuller, supplemental resource on topic (for more information visit)
- Embedded material credit (image/graphic/video from)
- Defining jargon and industry terminology for the layperson (definition)
- Indicating the source/discoverer of a fact
- Indicating the development or course of a concept as it gained acceptance/adherence (concept originated with Bob, but picked up and extended here by Barbara)

So now let's get into the spirit of citations. The citation required list above just feels a bit flat and uninspiring. The "spirit" side of citations is a bit more joyous and reverential—breathless and excited for the web of connections and relatedness that every topic contains.

The Spirit of Citation

In some cases, you want to give credit where it's due not because you have to, but because you want to. Some of those instances include:

- Gladly giving credit where credit is due: respecting the "elders" and authorities of the practice, and acknowledging the shoulders of giants
- Giving credit because author was inspired in some way by the document/document's author

- Each link out establishing and anchoring an overall assertion that leads the reader to a desired, healthy, safe action or mindset
- Enable or speed task completion of a task that's associated with the article but not directly required
- Call out the linked document's authors by name because they're awesome— expressing gratitude, connecting readers to larger practitioner community
- We don't have enough space to fully dig into the topic—here's more
- We got the spark of an idea for xyz from this document
- A funny, fun, or inspiring aside
- Wry or sarcastic aside, supported by a related document

So we hope that list gets you more in the mood to link out. And better able to conceive of methods that will actually benefit your readers rather than just your search rankings. Citations can provide a fun interplay between the author and reader.

We'll leave you with a return to the practical side. Here are some of the questions we ask about every document we create for placement—our "Citation Justification Checklist":

- If we remove this link, will the article's utility or pleasure to the reader decrease?
- Have we indicated to the reader how the link adds utility or pleasure to their lives?
- Does the anchor text help the reader understand the cited document?
- Can the text near the outbound link thank or call out the linked document's author or brand in some way?
- Is the reader alerted that there's a link, and why—and when—they should follow it?
- Is the link academically justifiable/required in some way?
- Does the linked document genuinely support a position or the completion of a task related to the article?
- Do we link out consistently within the article, supporting all the key assertions, not just the one related to our site/client?

BUILDING LINKS TO SALES PAGES

Sales pages, whether they sell products or services, lack citability. In other words, there's rarely a justifiable (much less scalable) reason to cite a sales funnel page from a guest placement (not to mention a curated resource list) or any other tactic you may be using.

This section closely follows citation justification for a reason: As you strategize your way forward, you must think carefully on how an off-site writer would conceivably justify linking to your sales content. You're still selling from your sales page now—just adding a new "customer" persona: the off-site writer whose job it is to inform and delight audiences while citing your documents.

Building Citation-Worthy Elements into Your Sales Pages

Link building to sales pages becomes increasingly viable (that is, justifiable to the potential linker) when you add what we call "citable elements" to the page.

The balance between sales and citability is a delicate one, though. If you do pursue this course, it's likely you'll use anchor links (no, not anchor text) to help tuck these elements beneath or beside the funnel and still be able to send the visiting reader (and editor, publisher, and even a Google-quality rater) directly to the cited element that supports an assertion in the placed article.

There's also the concern of skewing the page's topic as perceived by search engines, which could potentially diminish rankings for targeted terms. Again, there's a balance here that will require discussion and debate across several stake-holding teams.

CREATING "CITABILITY"

So, how do you create citability on your sales pages to justify including links from off-site writers? Here's a quick list to get your brain going:

- *Data or "findings."* Any data you publish to a sales page is first and foremost ideally yours and yours alone, derived from your findings as a business. Also the data ideally fits into the flow of purchase decision by your customers—namely it supports and justifies your product or service within the task accomplishment cycle of your target customers. Your busiest or slowest times of the week or day? Times when you have the most or least inventory? Most popular color or size? These types of data points can be woven neatly into off-site content.

- *Direct quotation of a source.* A source here could be a customer use case story or a brief interview with your internal experts that provide some new insight into effective task completion—in the context of the product or service. Marketers typically want products and services to be the hero on the sales pages, but for linking purposes, you're better off letting the customer or expert shine a little brighter and give off-site writers something gripping to quote that illustrates concepts or inspires a redoubling of efforts.

- *Defining jargon and industry terminology for the layperson (aka definitions).* A sales page may not be the spot you'd typically think to drop some definitions. That said, if there's any dense or even slightly obscure terminology related to your page's products or services, then you'd conceivably benefit your customers by defining them. You should also have a proper glossary, but that's a whole different article. Defining words remains a highly justifiable reason to link out.

- *Pricing guides or generalized pricing information.* In much of the online how-to publishing space, opportunities to cite pricing information abound. Most tasks require materials or services to complete, so how much should these things cost? Pricing remains top of mind with consumers, no matter where they are in the buy cycle. Any information that helps contextualize or convey the parameters that impact cost can serve as a highly citable page element.

- *Images, videos, widgets, downloads.* Could your sales pages benefit from some graphics? Are you already using graphics to sell? Got case studies and sales PDFs? Great! Think beyond (but still within) your sales funnel into elements that could illustrate task completion or service execution best practices outside the context of sales.

- *Detailed, multi-faceted metrics-based reviews.* Reviews remain highly citation-worthy so long as they can fit into the task-completion how-to narrative that most publishers churn out. Even better—facet out and metrically-rank the benefits of your products to different audience segments. How much better is this shoe for someone with bunions than another shoe? How much compression do these socks actually provide? If you happen to work with any off-site writers, check in with them on audience facets for whom you could provide more thorough insight. Seniors, parents, pet owners, fitness buffs, and other mundane sufferer categories have large bodies of corresponding publishers.

- *Tips/advice directly related to products/services on the page.* Can you enable or speed task completion for a goal that's related to your products or services? Just good, old-fashioned how-to content here, but with your products or services as central to the context of the information. So on your dog chew toy page, you have some key detail on helping your dog to stop chewing your furniture. On your plumber page, you have a simple step-by-step guide to unclogging a drain with baking soda.

- *The origin story.* Talk with the designers, manufacturers, artists, and whoever else helped design or perfect this product or service. The origin itself can be highly citable, and it's almost certain that the story will have citable internal elements as well. Inspiring the audience to reach higher and try again remains a highly justifiable citation purpose for off-site writers.

- *Supplemental outbound resource links.* Just kidding—who'd put outbound links on a sales page? Well, what if they somehow served the purchase cycle? Still probably no, I know, but they would be highly citable, especially if the on-page sales narrative included something like: "We collected these resources based on client recommendations and questions related to our products."

RECOGNIZING THE PRACTITIONER ACTION CYCLE

If, in reading through the suggested citable elements above, no clear direction stood out, it may help if we take a step back from the buy cycle to address what's really going on in this exercise. In the above examples, we've stepped up a category from the buy cycle into what we call the Practitioner Action Cycle.

Practitioners in our model are your customers and audience. But they don't think of themselves that way. They are currently in active practice doing their job, hustling, working hard, getting ahead inch-by-inch in their day-to-day. Your site is a way station along their day's arduous task list, and you will be ruthlessly selected against based on your page's capacity to enable task completion.

So, this is a sort of fancy way of saying that you don't define your customers—their to-do list does, along with all the context this implies. It helps to think this way, though; it pushes us out of the flat interpretation of the seller and into a more compassionate appreciation of the day-to-day of the practitioner who may become a customer. Further, it's this line of thinking that enables us to find our supporting elements that will be citable throughout the publishing ecosystem where your audience goes daily for information and inspiration.

So if your page converts, you're clearly speaking to your target practitioners. No question. But if your page lacks citable elements, then you could benefit by following these questions through to concrete-as-possible answers. Even if you don't know what to do with your answers, your blog team should be able to help you make the leap to what kinds of information could both aid the buy cycle and become a citable element on the page. Ask yourself:

- What specific tasks does the product or service on this page enable practitioners to accomplish? List as many as you have time for. These are sort of benefits, but not quite—you're looking for specific tasks completed as a direct result of a purchase.
- Are these beginner or advanced tasks?
- In a given day's cycle of work, where does this task typically fall?
- How do folks feel about these tasks? Are they self-selected tasks? Are they required by law or by standards of practice?
- Are these standard tasks or only for emergencies or edge/extreme cases?
- What issues or problems do folks typically have with this task array—even outside of the context of your product or service?
- The practitioner has an "object of practice" (e.g., the gardener works in their "object of practice"—the garden). What traits of the "object of practice" does your product or service control?
- Where exactly do your practitioners do their work? Not just geographically, but in what specific work settings or environments? We call this array of settings the "theater of practice." List as many as you can think of, and they can give some surprising turns to your citable-element brainstorm.

- Are there any common practitioner conditions to take into consideration (super sleepy parents of newborns, stressed groom to be, physically disabled gardener, hungry small-business owner)?

The point of all these questions is to create enough task- and practice-specific detail to spark you or your writing team on elements that could really assist the practitioner in the action cycle, not just the buy cycle you want them to have on your page. Because when you know and knowingly support the practitioner in their assault on task mountain, you also support the off-site how-to writer. That's their job, too, you see— knowing and supporting the practitioner as they encounter and plan for tackling their task lists for the day. Additionally, it is important to translate your keywords to your targeted audience.

KNOW YOUR AUDIENCE'S NAME

It's increasingly common to speak with link builders who target a specific audience. That said, most have specific keywords in mind that they want to rank for, and most use those keywords for discovering opportunities. To best gauge the viability of a guest placement campaign, you must first translate your target keywords into a target audience. Let's say your client wants to rank for web hosting, and they specialize in hosting for small, online business owners. Starting from their target of "small online business owners," you can parse out some potential audiences. This can be done in part by "thinking like a directory" and determining which categories a resource for "small online business owners" could fit into. It's well worth visiting a directory to help the brainstorming process.

For example:

- small business
- online business
- ecommerce
- web design

Also, take a pass at your audience keywords with the Ubersuggest tool mentioned on page 70. Once you have your audience keywords figured out, it's time to run a quick viability check.

QUICK VIABILITY CHECK—"[TARGET AUDIENCE]" + INTITLE: "WRITE FOR US"

Take your target audiences and combine them with the command intitle:"write for us." Pages that have "write for us" in the title tag indicate a demand for content.

Assuming you have effectively named your target audience, the quantity of results generated with this query along with the number of viable prospects in the top 10 to 20 results will give you a sense of whether a guest placement campaign is viable and at what scale.

If you see 2 to 300 results for each query, with 3 to 5 definite opportunities in the top 10, you can reasonably estimate 10 guest-post placements per query run (based on a 20 percent conversion). This quick test will let you know whether you need to really conduct a full inventory, or if you need to go back and think a bit further about your target audience.

You may find that there isn't significant volume and quality of opportunities for SERP impact at all, or you may recognize that you need to supplement with other higher-volume opportunity types. The very presence of write-for-us pages indicates that the keyword used will deliver prospects—and could be useful in prospecting for other tactics (see Figure 18–1).

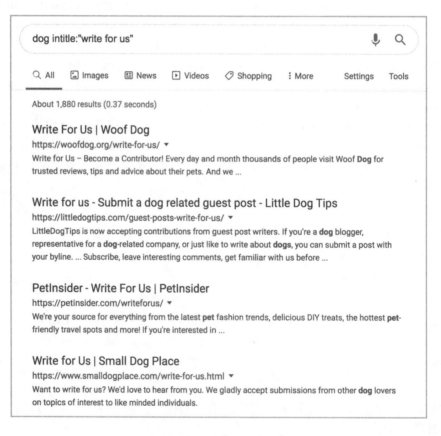

FIGURE 18–1. Intitle: Write for Us

IDENTIFY THE VOLUME OF PLACEMENT/POSTING OPPORTUNITIES

If you're seeing strong signs of content demand, you can start to expand your querying into a full-blown inventory—or at least set up the queries for someone else to do the prospecting for you.

Here is an excellent rundown of queries for thoroughly prospecting for guest publication opportunities. Remember to keep your eyes peeled for the footprints of prolific guest posters in your vertical—they will lead you to other opportunities. If you find guest posters with footprints across hundreds of sites, then set those aside for high-volume, low-value placement opportunities. They're out there, and you can get to a larger scale with them.

By measuring the volume of opportunity, you will know how many writers you'll need to cover all the available opportunities.

GAUGE THE QUALITY OF PLACEMENT OPPORTUNITIES

Quantity isn't all you need to look at, especially if you have your eyes on branding and reach. Here are some thoughts on gauging the value of a guest-posting opportunity:

- Copy and paste the title of a two-week-old article and search for it in quotes. Where does it appear? Are there scrapers, is the title in Twitter, does the site syndicate their RSS feed, etc.? This will give you a bit of insight into how wide the reach is for a given publication.

- Check how many tweets, shares, and articles get on a site—this will show you the social reach that the publication has developed.

- Check the quality and quantity of comments to get a sense of the community surrounding the site.

- Does the publisher aggressively link from within the article to their own pages? Check for it—it's common and could affect the SERP impact of your efforts.

- Scan their backlinks—are any recognizable sites linking in? This will give you a sense of who's reading and linking to the publisher.

- Are guest posters using exact match anchors or brand names? This can be an indicator of site policies.

- Do they require/request an ongoing content commitment? This can indicate a strong editorial hand, which usually means a higher-quality publication.

In investigating these items, you will get a sense of the characteristics your content will need to have to make it "placeable."

QUANTIFY THE LEVEL OF EXPERTISE IN EXISTING GUEST-PUBLISHED CONTENT

Now that you have your targets, it's time to figure out what level of subject matter expertise you'll need to meet your audience's information needs. Find out how readily available subject matter expertise is—are there forums, books, PDFs, etc., that you can use for research? Often when there's strong content demand, as exhibited by the presence of "write for us" pages, there's a ready availability of prepackaged expertise you can research and cite. If you're planning to "go big," it's also worth investigating how much or how little tip-based content exists. Note that you can use your audience keywords in your tip research as well.

GENTLY CROSS-EXAMINE THE CLIENT BEFORE SIGNING THAT CONTRACT

Guest placements certainly build links, and that's often what gets SEOs interested in the first place. However, if you're publishing on the right sites, with the right content, you can begin establishing expertise within a given category. To really deliver for your client on this expertise building, you'll have to get access to the client organization's subject-matter experts and get buy-in and sign-off. Here are some questions to ask before you get that contract with a new client signed:

- Is perceived brand expertise really a factor in the purchase decision?
- How involved can the client be in content ideation?
- Are there experts available for interviews?
- Does the client have published expertise (tools, PDFs, presentations, videos) that's suitable for promoting within guest placements?
- Is there unique data available relative to the client's market (that can be published)?
- Who has to approve content in the client's organization?
- How active is the client in social media channels, and do they intend to increase this activity?
- Can you get an @client.com email address (in under three months)?
- Whose name will be on the placements?
- Are there any do-not-contact publishers operating in your prospective client's MDKW space?

If it seems that the client is unable or unwilling to demonstrate expertise and build credibility, then guest placements (especially at high- and mid-quality publishers) are probably not a great direction and may not be suitable for inclusion in the overall link-building campaign design. If the client can see the value—the publicity, branding, and reach—of guest placements and is eager to share their expertise with the market, then you should see fantastic results.

Going big in guest posting requires careful planning at every stage, from viability analysis and prospect discovery to effective content design. Many sites offer guest blog posting tips and advice, like the example in Figure 18–2, below.

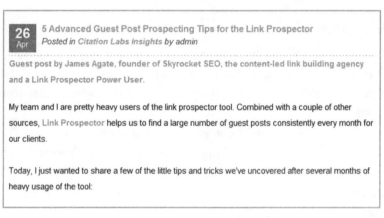

FIGURE 18–2. Guest Posting Tips

Note: This is outreach advice for campaigns in which all the content is written prior to placement. Some guest posters get content ideas approved by the publisher prior to writing anything. Getting publisher buy-in is fantastic and is much faster at the outreach stage. However, it slows the overall process and isn't advisable at a larger scale, especially when client approval of the content is required.

TRACKING THE OUTREACH PHASE'S "MOVING PARTS"

Outreach has many "moving parts" and a great deal to track in order to remain effective, efficient, and protective of the brand. Before digging into specific advice, here are several core elements to track in your campaign (these items also happen to make good columns for a spreadsheet).

Outreach Tracking Sheet 1

1. *List of outreach prospects*. At the beginning of any campaign, I prospect and project on 10 percent conversions, but usually get around 30 percent. If you have 10 posts, expect to need 100 different guest placement prospects.
2. *Specific niche focus*. This is vital so that you can be sure you're pitching the right "flavor" of article to the appropriate blogger within a topic area (e.g., while email

and SEO are two marketing methods, you shouldn't pitch your email marketing tips article to the SEO blog).

3. *Prospect contact information and/or contact URL*
4. *Anchor text/promotional link target*
5. *Notes*. These include any tips or guidance to help your outreacher when they're neck-deep in the inbox and convoluted spreadsheet you sent them.

Content Details Sheet 2

1. *List of completed content titles*. This is your master list of guest content inventory. This is what you're selling with your outreach emails.
2. *Specific niche focus of piece*. This will help you pitch the right titles to the right publishers.
3. *Content "status" for individual articles*. Use terms such as "written," "in consideration," "pending," and "placed" to track content status. *Written* needs promotion; *in consideration* means a publisher expressed interest and has it in their inbox; *pending* means the publisher said yes but hasn't published; and *placed* means it's live on their site.
4. *Domain of prospective publisher*. Replace with final published URL.
5. *Date of initial contact*. Use this to track to which sites you have already outreached.

OUTREACH: WHAT'S TEMPLATABLE, WHAT'S NOT

There are continual template/no template debates that go on in link outreach. Our experience is the more work you do in targeted prospecting and content design, the more templates you can use in your outreach. That's because you've done your homework and lined up the needs of your publishers with what you're pitching. This ensures obvious benefit to the publisher.

Using a "templating" approach can be as simple as using a single notepad application window and making alterations there or as complex as a merge macro in a word processing application.

Not Templatable

Here's what will need to be unique in every email you send:

1. *Establish initial rapport in the first sentence*. Don't overdo it though—they are publishers and very busy. Plus, you're offering them free content. It's not like you're begging for a link or anything. Primarily, you're establishing how you identify with the target audience. For example, "I'm a busy mom of multiples who somehow finds time for freelance writing!"

2. *Prove you read their guest submission requirements.* Assuming guest publishing requirements exist—and about 20 percent of the time, they do—poke around and make sure what you're sending in fits.

3. *Two to three titles you're pitching.* Keep this number small. You don't want to give the sense that your email is part of a large, well-oiled campaign. Also, having fewer choices can make for a speedier response time.

4. *Benefits of pitched pieces to publisher's audience.* Usually the title of the piece needs to make the benefit clear. However, it never hurts to explain a bit about who the article helps and how.

Templatable

These are things you can reuse quite a bit. It's OK if you find yourself altering core aspects of templates as you go along for clarity, readability, and believability. Also, omit needless words.

1. *Who you are, who you're with, why you're writing.* Keep it cordial, brief, and easily alterable. (This is your first sentence, which you will tailor per site.)

2. *Relevant accolades that could help them say yes more quickly.* Are you or is your writer or brand known for anything laudable? Mention it!

3. *Two or three most notable prior publications.* This helps demonstrate that you or your alias has content that others consider publishable. Also, publishers can read your previous work.

4. *Numbers of tweets, shares, and links received by your guest publications.* This can be a deal-sealer if you can throw around some high numbers.

5. *How you will promote it once the post is up.* Tweet, share, link to it, email newsletter, etc.

6. *Your eagerness to make any changes they require.* Demonstrate that you're willing to work with them, and make sure your content is a good fit for their audience.

P.S. The Piggyback Pitch

You've done all that prospecting, and you may as well piggyback another request or two into your outreach. Here are a few thoughts on an "Oh, and by the way" section of your outreach emails.

1. *New, high-utility content you're promoting for their roundups, Twitter followers, etc.* Pitch your infographics, widgets, videos, new articles, etc.

2. *Ask if they accept items for contests/giveaways.* Many sites conduct giveaways for their readers. Do you have anything to offer?

3. *Ask if they will answer interview/survey questions.*

OUTREACH EXECUTION ADVICE

The best advice we can give you on outreach execution is to just dive in there and do it. It's the best way to learn. Here are some additional, tried-and-true tips for outreach execution:

1. *Send 10 to 20 emails and wait one or two days.* It takes a while for publishers to respond. Plus, you're pitching unique content and don't want to overpromise a piece.

2. *Pitch titles; don't send or pitch pieces as complete.* Give the publishers the sense that you're writing pieces "on the fly." This will help reduce suspicion that you're pitching already-published content.

3. *Have "placed" folders on your hard drive so you don't double publish.* Oops! You sent two people the same content and they both published it? When a piece gets placed, move it or delete it so you never, ever attach it to another email and send it.

4. *Your spreadsheet doubles as a reporting sheet and prospect approval sheet.* Use your spreadsheet for project management, client reporting, and input. Centralize!

5. *Published-piece tracking and contact information helps you build a master sheet for repurposing down the road.* One of the biggest values you're building for your organization is a list of sites you can go back to with new content that supports new initiatives (and targets new keywords). Guest posts work great as off-site satellites promoting a flagship piece of content on your site.

In the next chapter, we will cover targeting website's outbound links that are no longer active and creating campaigns for a tactic known as broken link building.

Chapter 19

Creating Broken Link-Building Campaigns

Broken link building (BLB) is one of only a handful of highly scalable *and* white-hat link-building tactics. With this tactic, you check your target website's outbound links to see if they're still up. If your target site links to a competitor's information page that's dead, you then email the target site and suggest they link to you instead. As Russ Jones, CTO of Virante describes broken link building: "The success of the campaign is directly proportional to how much good you do for the web."

The process described in this chapter is not elegant, but it does help you cover a lot of ground—you can find and analyze thousands of resources and root out the dead pages and sites quite quickly. It is possible to build more than 40 links a month with this method while selling BLB prospecting as a service to others. As we have said before, link rot is your friend. In this chapter, we'll cover the process and the tools we use and recommend to get the job done.

SEARCH FOR LINKS PAGES

You guessed it—use your link prospector for this, prospecting phrases that categorically represent the topic area you're promoting and plug those right into the tool. If you don't use the link prospector, you could try the prospecting queries mentioned here, as well as tildes, lots of tildes!

What you're looking for are curated links pages where your content could fit—with light scrutiny—whether you found a broken link or not. This, of course, presupposes you're promoting good-quality, long-form content for which there are hundreds of "curators." If you search, and each of the top ten pages are good prospects, then you're in a good space for this effort.

SEOs used to go through hundreds of pages and pick only those they thought had the highest relevance. Now, they rarely spend much time "qualifying" links pages. They rely on our tools and common sense and just pass a big ol' batch of links pages right on over to . . . the next step.

SCRAPE OUTBOUND LINKS FROM THE PAGES

Next, using an outbound link scraper (one of the four tools in our scraper suite), scrape the outbound links from the batch of links pages you've found. You can see an example of this in Figure 19–1.

FIGURE 19–1. Outbound Link Scraper

CHECK THE STATUS OF EACH OUTBOUND LINK

Once you've completed extracting outbound links from the resource pages, it's time to check the status. And, yup, we've got a tool for that in the scraper suite—the URL Status Checker (which you can see an example of in Figure 19–2, on page 183). This tool checks and reports on the status of each URL, just as the name suggests. The tool does split large sets up into batches of 1,000. This means your 12,000-plus-URL project

FIGURE 19–2. URL Status Checker

will be in 12 separate comma-separated value documents (CSVs). Yes, that's a pain, but that's the row you've chosen to hoe here, so put your back into it. Merge the CSVs from this tool and sort them to isolate the dead and nonresponding pages from your set. This obviously can take some time.

And then . . .

RECHECK THE STATUS OF EACH DEAD LINK FOR FINAL VERIFICATION

Recheck, because the tool's not 100 percent accurate, and it's heartbreaking further on in the process to think a site with 30,000 unique linking domains is dead when really it's just responding slowly. So, recheck everything that the tool reports as dead. Some people, whom we'll refrain from naming, check three times when feeling especially obsessive.

GATHER METRICS FOR THE DEAD/UNRESPONSIVE PAGES

We use Majestic SEO's bulk backlink checker for learning which dead URLs have the most linking domains, though they limit you to checking only 300 rows at a time. Simply copy and paste in 300 of your dead URLs, sort by the number of inbound linking domains, and you'll have a good idea of where to start your deeper investigations. You can see Figure 19–3, on page 184, for an example of a bulk backlink checker.

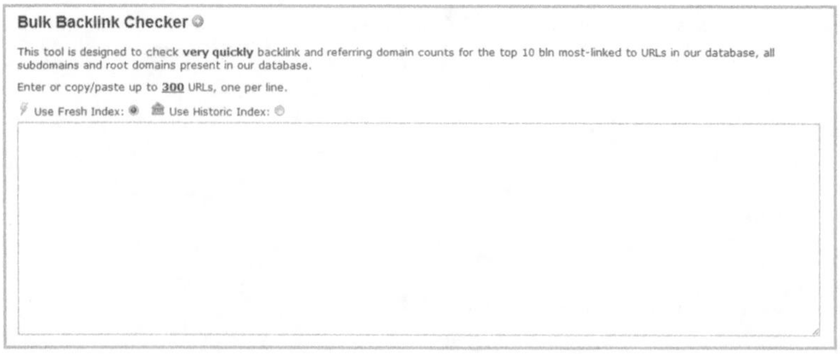

FIGURE 19–3. Bulk Backlink Checker

REVIEW DEAD PAGES BY HAND

Here's where the intuition starts, and the slow combing through URLs. And yes, this is where automation falls apart, at least at our current levels of coding and expertise. So, first things first, sort that list by number of inbound links to the page. This will give you a sense of the opportunities with the most links. You'll need to add some columns to your spreadsheet, so here are my thoughts on columns that will help your review:

- *How is it "dead"?* For many .gov sites, for example, the non-www doesn't redirect to the www subdomain. And yet they sometimes have hundreds of linking domains pointed to the non-www. Other times the site is a parked domain now. Still other times it's just plain gone. All this information is important for further on when you're writing your outreach emails.

- *Topic.* What is this dead page about, according to Archive.org? Does the site or page have anything to do with the site I'm promoting? I use Majestic SEO at this point also to check out anchor text as that gives a good clue if Archive.org doesn't have info.

- *How big is the opportunity?* Is the whole site dead? Just one section? Just one page? All this needs to be recorded so you can figure out how to best pull backlinks for the opportunity.

- *What are you promoting?* Is this a one-to-one replacement opportunity? (These are the best, whether you write it as you find it dead or already have something written.) Is it a fix suggestion and similar-resource link request?

Be sure to save any and all dead sites you find with 100 or more links—even if you can't use them now. You can always come back later or possibly come up with an angle down the road.

PULL AND QUALIFY DEAD BACKLINKS

With our metrics tool, you can also pull backlinks for the dead links you'd like to pursue. Ah, but we wish we could tell you it was as easy as taking all the links and heading over to the contact finder (one of the tools in our scraper suite). Nope—you've got to scrub this data, or you'll end up wasting your time.

First and foremost, do not get excited about apparently large lists of opportunities. It's quite common to start with 16,000 unique linking domains and boil those down to 50 actual opportunities for outreach. So don't tell clients how many ops you have for them until you've done your distilling—you will end up profoundly overselling what you have.

You can use Citation Labs' metrics suite for Linkscape data if you like and input each URL you'd like backlinks for. You then designate how many backlinks you want us to pull and pay per backlink (one backlink—one row in a spreadsheet). I like to use Majestic SEO for this, too as they seem quite a bit fresher and more comprehensive. That said, Majestic SEO's comprehensiveness comes with a great deal more "scrubbing" required. Whether you use Linkscape data sourced through our metrics suite or Majestic SEO, you can use our scraper suite tools for boiling them down further:

- *URL Filter Tool.* I use this to isolate the links and resource pages as these are often the best opportunities for what I promote. Input your backlinks into the input field, then add this string: resources?|links?|faqs|(web([^/]*)?)sites?|references? to the "Match Any" box. This will extract URLs that are most likely to be links pages.
- *One URL per Domain.* Once you have your probable links and resource pages, you should double-check that you have one per domain. Rarely is it "good form" to send two separate emails to a webmaster requesting links on two separate pages with broken links.
- *Backlink Checker.* Especially when using Majestic SEO's data, double-check that the pages still exist and that the links you're suggesting be changed are still actually on the pages. You can do this with the backlink checker that's a part of the scraper suite. Just copy in the domain of the dead page and paste in your list of suspects. The tool will show you on which pages the link still lives on.

Wow! That's right. Your list of prospects is now significantly diminished. You should be pretty happy when you still have between 50 and 80 real linking prospects to a now-dead resource. We have found upwards into the 1,200s in the past. But even so, we're not ready to outreach; we still have to . . .

Pull Contact Info

Yes, the scraper suite does have a contact finder, but it won't solve all your problems. In fact, you may find it only around 25 to 30 percent accurate for contact info on links and resource pages (much better than nothing, for sure). It's great for blog contact finding, but the old, custom-CMS kinds of sites where links pages are commonly published don't always have standard ways of displaying contact info. There can even be tens or even hundreds of email addresses discovered with the tool for a given domain. This is why we have contractors whose sole job is to process the contact finder reports. They have to select the best email address or contact page and, when the tool doesn't find anything, go onsite to look for contact information. Last, they deliver a spreadsheet with two columns: URL where the dead link appears and contact information.

BROKEN-LINK OUTREACH

Much has been written about broken-link building, so let's keep things short and sweet. Tell your contact where the broken link is and provide code for fixing it. Mention only one dead link on the page. If you're affiliated, say as much, though often assert that the person had some hand in writing the content.

As for conversions, be pleased with a 5 percent conversion rate but expect/plan/ prospect for a 2 percent conversion. I got 15 percent conversion once on a small-run, exact one-to-one replacement campaign in which the dead site had gotten parked. My outreach email told webmasters they were linking to a spam site. This is quite rare, but do note that the closer you can get to a one-to-one replacement, the better your results will be. Content recreation as a service is an interesting proposition but goes beyond the scope of this book on link building.

LINK EQUITY SALVAGE CAMPAIGNS

Link equity salvage is the process of finding and redirecting your site's dead pages, folders, and subdomains that still have links—sort of the reverse of the previous section on broken-link building. These are the old and misredirected, unredirected, or simply deleted sections of your site that webmaster tools don't know about since the URLs got axed more than 35 days ago.

We're talking about pages that even site crawlers aren't finding, presumably because they don't have any links from the visible pages of your site. And remember, link salvagers, you're not only recovering lost link equity here, but blocking competitive off-site link salvage experts from capitalizing on your squandered links.

You don't necessarily need to rush off hunting for onsite link salvage opportunities, though—especially if your site's only a couple of years old and never had a redesign. If you can say "yes" to one or more of these criteria, then definitely keep reading:

- Your site is more than five years old.
- Your content naturally earns editorial links.
- You've had one or more migrations from one content management system to another.
- You've had several major site redesigns over the years.
- You know of at least one mismanaged site redesign.
- You have a 10,000-page site.
- You aren't seeking targeted keyword ranking increases.

The link equity salvage process can typically be accomplished in four steps: compiling, status checking, link checking a comprehensive-as-possible list of your site's URLs, and then redirecting them. The majority of the tools here are for compiling that critical master list of URLs, which is the biggest hurdle of the process. We'll also cover a few tools for link and status checking.

Majestic SEO's Historic Index

Some folks complain of Majestic SEO's large quantity of dead links and pages. Don't be one of them.

- Look for quick wins. Place your root domain (no www) into Majestic's Site Explorer.
- Click the Historic Index Radial. Then click Explore.
- Download your Top Links (shows highest-value links and the pages on your site they point to) and Top Pages CSVs.
- From both of these reports extract your site's URLs.

You now have a big list of the most important pages on your site, according to Majestic. You could also run a full-site report with Majestic and get all your site's URLs that Majestic shows has an Citation Flow of 1 or higher. This costs more resources but provides a more thorough list.

Xenu's Link Sleuth

Xenu is a relentless beast of URL discovery, and it even status checks the URLs for you. It won't find every last URL, at least it hasn't in our tests, and it obviously can't find your legacy pages that still have links from off-site like Majestic SEO does. It finds only what's

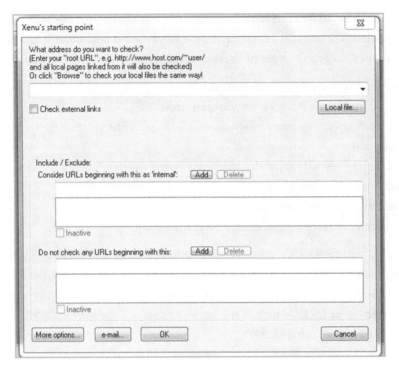

FIGURE 19–4. Xenu's Broken Link Checker

linked to onsite (as far as I understand how it works). Read "Checking Links with Xenu" for more information, and see Figure 19–4 for a peek at Xenu's broken link checker.

Xenu's Orphan Checker

We haven't used this on a client's site yet, only salivated at the opportunity to try it out and run a comparison to what can be found via Majestic SEO. Give Xenu's Orphan Checker FTP (File Transfer Protocol) access, and it looks for pages on your server that are not linked to any other pages on your own site.

Our guess is that the Orphan Checker isn't going to show you anything that's been flat-out deleted from your server, as can sometimes happen, so it's not a replacement for Majestic SEO. But if you're on an obsessive hunt for link equity, it's worth a check.

Check Links Pages, Old Directories, and Press Releases

If your site has been getting editorial links and publishing press releases for years, you could have links to now-dead pages from pages that Majestic may not have discovered. First you need to prospect for links pages and old press releases, then check those pages for your domain with a bulk link checker.

Use Google Queries to Find Legacy Subdomains

Not every salvage requires a dead page—it could be a long-forgotten initiative prompted by an executive long gone from your organization. These subdomain-discovery queries can help you find possibly abandoned subdomains:

- *.domain.com
- *.domain.com -inurl:www.
- site:*.domain.com
- site:*.domain.com -inurl:www.

Some of these queries work for some sites but not others. It depends on the size and/or configuration of the site.

URL Status Checkers

Once you've compiled your insanely large list of URLs, it's time to check, recheck, and re-recheck their status codes. Yup, we advise at least three checks of a URL list, no matter what tool you're using.

One-off URL status checkers abound. You're going to need something with a bit more capacity. We know and love the bulk URL status checker built into our scraper suite.

Whatever tool you choose, it needs to work in bulk—large bulk. If it's on your desktop, it could be tying up a machine for a few days. And remember—check your lists of failed URLs a couple more times. You'll always shake out more false positives.

Bulk Link Count Checkers

With your dead URLs in hand, it's time to separate the wheat from the chaff. This requires a bulk link checker—ideally one into which you can paste (potentially) thousands of dead URLs. We know of two. There are probably more, but these are the best known at the moment:

Majestic has a nifty "Bulk Backlink Checker" built in (with limits based on subscription level). If you've got 6,000 dead URLs to check, you could run it 20 times. Also, you can use our bulk backlink checker that accepts as many URLs as you can copy and paste in—it uses the Linkscape data set.

Once you get your data back from either tool, you can sort by number of referring domains and at last start the process of mapping and 301-redirecting your equity where it belongs.

When your broken-link building campaign is complete, it is time to start bulk outreach and test your link-building process. In the next chapter, we will outline our process for larger-scale outreach.

Chapter 20

Bulk Outreach and Link Building

Because we hand-build links at relatively large scale and always look for ways to go bigger, we continually test our link-building processes and beliefs. For example, when you have more than 80 guest posts to place in a month, you don't have the luxury to woo each and every prospect with commenting and tweeting (a common preciprocation warm-up tactic). To be sure, set aside a small handful of targets for relationship-based link building, then read this chapter on the principles of bulk outreach.

FROM LINK BUILDER TO EMAIL MARKETER

Link builder, it's time to think a bit differently. You are now an email marketer. Your task is not to build links, but rather to build lists, lists of relevant prospects and their contact information.

Then you must create an offer that will get these prospects to respond to you. Next you must lead them, often through further inbox dialogue, to take an action that will ultimately lead to a link, social distribution, and/ or content that can attract more links.

LISTS OF PROSPECTS ARE EVERYWHERE

Though we still scrape SERPs for link prospects, we learned to supplement this method by searching for and scraping lists of websites. Sometimes I even look for lists first, then brainstorm potential offers to make. Other times, I follow a hunch, such as "If I could find a list of hospitals, what could we offer them that could result in links?"

CREATE OFFERS THAT WORK AT SCALE

In bulk outreach, the ideal offer is one that's relatively unlimited. Guest posts—if you're pitching great content—are a bit limited. They can work, but they aren't ideal.

Free trials of web-based software? That's a bit less constrained. Widget installs? Ditto. Go to town! Ask experts to take a survey? Unlimited—you make one survey, then conduct outreach. Remember, you must be certain that your offer genuinely appeals to the prospect list you've built and that you'll get links in the process. Here are some examples of offers that scale:

- Free content (guest posting, infographics, widgets)
- Free products/services (for reviews and contests)
- Participation in expert surveys (they answer questions, you publish answers, they link/share)
- Timely analysis and/or access to expertise (pitching a hot, topical interview with your expert)
- Philanthropy and fundraising participation (ask to spread the word, ask to pitch in too)
- Help fix broken, rotted, and now-parked links
- Money (not our bag, though some of our best friends are link buyers)

WRITE POWERFUL PITCH TEMPLATES

An effective offer, tailored to your target prospects, is 99 percent of a great pitch. That said, there are some key ingredients that your pitch should contain:

- Make the benefits of your offer crystal clear.
- Make sure the pitch highlights benefits to the publisher and their audience.
- Flaunt your brand. (I like to lead with the brand in my first sentence if it's recognizable and OK with client.)
- Flaunt relevant success metrics. (My previous guest post got over 700 RTs! Our last fundraiser netted over $5,000! Our last group interview got linked from Time.com!)

■ Promote the page that contains your link. (I like offering to pay for traffic from StumbleUpon for guest posts.) And toss in a light dusting of your personality (This evolves for me over time, but it can give the more relational-type prospects. something to respond to.)

SIMPLIFY YOUR PROSPECT QUALIFIERS

If your lists are targeted and relevant to your offers, then you have far less qualification work to do. In fact, your biggest problem should be taking the cream off the top for high-touch engagement rather than cutting out the junk.

Part of the whole bulk outreach play is developing an offer that works across a spectrum of sites. For this reason, we propose that a principle qualifier for bulk outreach is whether you can scrape the contact information. With a contact finder tool, you can see anywhere from 25 to 80 percent availability of contact info for sites depending on the vertical and how contactable the site owners want to be.

SIMPLIFY YOUR CAMPAIGN SUCCESS METRICS

Besides links earned (which isn't always that simple, anyway), email response rates (# of responses/# of emails) are strong indicators for bulk outreach campaigns. This tells you if you've pitched the benefits clearly and if your template is personable enough and can give you a sense if you're even using the right offer.

We also recommend splitting your list and/or only sending to 5 to 10 percent of your list at first to allow for tune-ups. Make sure you have someone who's "good in the inbox" for closing the emails that do come back—they need to be personable, chatty, and laser-focused on making those links happen. All this comes out in the responses you get. Getting more responses helps you get more links.

EDUCATE YOURSELF ON CAN-SPAM

Can-Spam is the law that established rules for commercial email and messaging, giving recipients the right to no longer receive emails from businesses. Here are some of the basic tenets of Can-Spam:

■ Don't use false or misleading header information.
■ Don't use deceptive subject lines.
■ Tell recipients where you're located.
■ Tell recipients how to opt out of receiving future email from you.
■ Honor opt-out requests promptly.

■ Monitor what others are doing on your behalf.

Since so much of link building is email marketing, you'll want to learn more than just the basics and how they apply to your situation.

Here's the best resource: www.business.ftc.gov/documents/bus61-can-spam-act-compliance-guide-business. It's easily found by searching for Can-Spam compliance in Google.

In the next chapter, we will discuss local link building through sponsorships.

Chapter 21

Local Link Building with Sponsorships

This chapter is about how to build a local sponsorship program for visibility and links, whether for an enterprise campaign, an agency, or a small business. There isn't one right way to do sponsorships, but there are many approaches that can slow you down or cause snags along the way. As you'll see, we've interviewed brands from Whole Foods to Wells Fargo and have looked at local sponsorship data across the U.S. Just as with people, no two companies approach giving the same way. In this chapter, we'll walk you through ways you can build your local links with sponsorships.

The current formula for local sponsorships almost always puts the burden of outreach on the local organization that's seeking sponsors. They reach out to a brand, filling out an online form with a request, and are promised a response in a few weeks. In other models, agencies charge local nonprofits to find them sponsors.

The problem with the traditional local sponsorship model is that both entities—local organizations and potential sponsors—are often flying blind when it comes to partnerships.

Local organizers hit up brick and mortars and brands they've heard of, meaning your grocery store and your local bank receive hundreds or thousands of requests each month, while many online companies receive few non-industry requests. And brands often end up working with the local organizations that have the time and resources to approach them, instead of surveying target ZIP Codes at scale.

A local sponsorship program can serve many goals and using the internet to find opportunities means taking a broader picture of the local partnerships that are available.

SPONSORSHIPS: A HYPER-LOCAL MARKETING CHANNEL

Whether you're a local business looking for more walk-ins or a startup launching in select regions across the U.S., your marketing team needs to access people who live, work, eat, and play local to your target city. But the current leaders in local advertising are purely digital and almost entirely ad tech. We've found ways to target customers in their news feeds and via notifications. Banner ads may be intrusive, but they're increasingly creative and complex, with the capabilities to target highly specific local personas. But these mediums remain stuck behind a screen.

Sponsorships of events and nonprofits provide a way into a local community. They're personal and relaxed, and they're the ultimate silo-free marketing option, with potential SEO, PR, branding, networking, and social media benefits for sponsors.

In fact, in a 2015 BrandMuscle study, 80 percent of local marketers polled were satisfied with event sponsorships, and 71 percent felt the same about supporting local nonprofits. This is compared with a 65-percent satisfaction rate for traditional media and an average of 67 percent satisfaction with Facebook and Twitter. But like any endeavor that seems too good to be true, this intro hides a hidden cost: Local sponsorships can be a total time suck.

Many of BrandMuscle's respondents reported that in spite of their high satisfaction rating, very little of their overall marketing budget went toward events and organizations because these marketing vehicles were too time-consuming and costly.

It is easier to order an ad or place a blog post on Twitter than it is to coordinate local sponsorships, especially from another city. But there is a way to go local on a budget, or at least within measurable parameters.

HOW BIG BRANDS MEASURE SPONSORSHIP SUCCESS

Approximately one-third of sponsorships—of the 15,000 or so we've fully vetted—involve the sponsor's presence at the event, typically at a table or booth. That's a lot of employee time!

So, we spoke with some of the most frequent sponsors in the Raleigh/Durham, North Carolina, area to see how these prolific donors to local Little League teams, races, and holiday parades justified the money and employee hours that sponsorships often require.

We found there are three primary reasons large brands sponsor local organizations.

1. For Corporate Culture

One prominent brand explained that their organization's culture was so ingrained in the community that they had a "hard time saying no" to local sponsorship requests. (This brand declined to be named to protect their sponsorship strategies.)

Another local, Tim Huntley, founder of Centervention, told me that his online gaming company asks employees to choose charity opportunities; executives see sponsorships as a way for employees to feel personally empowered within the organization.

It's difficult to measure community goodwill or a happy work culture—both are closer to "you know it when you see it" on the scale of quantifiability. While this level of philanthropic giving is the most idealistic, it may not be possible for businesses with limited budgets.

2. For Local Branding

We spoke with a marketing metro team leader at Whole Foods Market, who said that the grocery chain's health and wellness mission is highlighted in the events and organizations his team chooses to sponsor.

We also spoke with the marketing manager of North Carolina's PDQ restaurants. Like Whole Foods Market, she told me that PDQ focuses on a target audience—in their case, families who live within a five-mile radius of their restaurants. But they leave sponsorship selections to local employees.

The marketing manager added that PDQ measures the ROI of their campaigns more on gut than on numbers. Employees notice if the Little League team they're sponsoring visits the restaurant after games, for example.

And the marketing manager recently signed a sponsorship agreement with the Carolina Hurricanes NHL team. PDQ wants more than just a logo on a sign, she said, which is why PDQ signed on to sponsor in-game entertainment for the fans.

Organizations such as these are stricter with their marketing budgets; choosing opportunities that fit their target market is a priority.

3. For Local Marketing

Remember those BrandMuscle respondents who said local events were too time consuming? Our research, while more anecdotal than scientific, aligns with those findings, especially for brands that try to measure the success of local marketing initiatives with direct sales.

There is another way.

The Whole Foods team added that the processes they built to take in sponsorship requests do measure potential organizations' ROI, particularly for sponsorships that aren't as closely aligned with health and fitness. They measure return based on sponsorship benefits. It is possible to measure the return, as long as you're not measuring immediate conversions. As multi-channel marketing becomes more the norm, the idea of attributing a sale to the "last touch" marketing source is increasingly outdated. To understand the true value of local sponsorships, it makes sense for brands to consider counting the equivalency of marketing benefits earned through the sponsorship instead of direct sales from the sponsorship source.

This is good news for local organizations, which often offer multiple messages to a highly targeted audience.

When choosing local sponsorships, consider the value your marketing department places on:

- a social media impression among your target market
- a local link in your target city
- an email impression among your target market
- a mention in local news
- a blogger mention
- a booth at a local event

To sell local sponsorships internally or to a client, create a formula based on the value of these impressions, and show how you'll measure potential opportunities against this rubric.

The Downtown Los Angeles Art Walk, for example, offers a project sponsorship package (outlined in Figure 21–1, on page 199) that offers a mention in the organization's press release and email newsletter (with distribution to 5,000 subscribers), as well as multiple social media mentions to 150,000 followers.

If your target customer is involved with the arts, and if your brand wants more attention in Los Angeles, then these offerings can be compared with other paid social shout-outs or PR efforts to determine whether $2,000 is a worthwhile spend. Ultimately, it may come down to your target audience.

WHO'S ALREADY DOING LOCAL SPONSORSHIPS AT SCALE?

At scale local sponsorships are a practice we've seen in large and small brands. But there are a few that stand out, which we've seen on thousands and thousands of "thank you to our sponsors" pages across the U.S. With goals that stem from employee connection to out-branding Amazon, these brands have incorporated local donations into their corporate strategy.

For the purposes of this research, we took the list of "sponsor thank you pages" scraped their outbound links, and counted the frequency of each domain. We removed social

---

PROJECT SPONSORSHIP

Project Sponsorships start at $2,000

- Brands wishing to reach a particular segment of our audience may be interested in sponsoring one of our programs, such as:

  ▸ **The Historic Core Mural Tour**: viewing the latest Street Art and murals created in Downtown Los Angeles.

  ▸ **The Kinder Walk**: an Art Walk Made specifically for undeserved children K-12, and/or High School students.

  ▸ **Gallery Tours** or **Collectors' Tours**: exclusive curated tours of the local galleries.

- Includes brand logo and mention in our press release and subscriber newsletter (5,000 distribution)

- Brand is marketed to fans on social media as the Presenting Sponsor of the project and mentioned in all project-related posts (brought to you by...)

- Brand placement on gift / swag materials for project participants, such as T-shirts, caps, or gift bags are available for an additional fee (material)

FIGURE 21–1. Sponsorship Example

networks and hosting sites from the list, as many organizations point to Facebook, Twitter, or WordPress from every page (including the sponsor thank you page). Additionally, there are other ways that sponsors are thanked on websites, such as via non-linked images or mentions, that we did not account for. However, it's our experience that there's no significant difference between organizations that link out to sponsors and those that don't, so we believe our cross section is still an accurate representation of the whole.

Finally, while we do work with organizations in every U.S. state, our database leans toward urban and suburban areas, so we may have missed, or underrepresented, companies that sponsor rural nonprofits. We also primarily work with nonreligious and nonovertly political organizations (we include environmental organizations, but not Green Party events, for example), so companies that focus their sponsorships on organizations with a strong religious or political bent may also be underrepresented.

The List: The Top 60 Brands Doing Sponsorships in the U.S.

The statistic next to each name indicates the percentage of organizations in the ZipSprout system sponsored by this brand (full disclosure: Garrett French owns ZipSprout, an agency focused on local links and lead gen via event and non-profit sponsorships). We found little evidence that these brands were "in it for the links," though we do expect to see an uptick in awareness at these brands regarding potential SEO impact they could realize.

1. Wells Fargo: 2.89 percent
2. Marriott: 1.63 percent
3. Dick's Sporting Goods: 1.39 percent
4. Whole Foods Market: 1.3 percent
5. State Farm: 1.07 percent
6. Pepsi: 0.98 percent
7. US Bank: 0.97 percent
8. Bank of America: 0.92 percent
9. Budweiser/Bud Light: 0.76 percent
10. Clif Bar: 0.74 percent
11. Coca-Cola: 0.72 percent
12. Edward Jones: 0.68 percent*
12. Walmart: 0.68 percent*
14. McDonalds: 0.67 percent
15. Kind Snacks: 0.66 percent
16. PNC Bank: 0.65 percent
17. Starbucks: 0.63 percent
18. AT&T: 0.58 percent*
18. Lagunitas: 0.58 percent*
20. IBM: 0.55 percent
21. Chick-fil-A: 0.48 percent*
21. Allstate: 0.48 percent*
23. Union Bank: 0.47 percent*
23. TD Bank: 0.47 percent*
23. Tito's Vodka: 0.47 percent*

26. Kroger: 0.46 percent
27. Chevron: 0.42 percent*
27. Delta: 0.42 percent*
27. Geico: 0.42 percent*
27. H-E-B Grocery: 0.42 percent*
31. Les Schwab Tires: 0.41 percent*
31. Trader Joe's: 0.41 percent*
31. Boeing: 0.41 percent*
34. Home Depot: 0.40 percent
35. Buffalo Wild Wings: 0.39 percent*
35. Gatorade: 0.39 percent*
37. Target: 0.38 percent*
37. PWC: 0.38 percent*
37. Toyota: 0.38 percent*
40. BB&T: 0.37 percent
41. Costco: 0.36 percent*
41. Southwest Airlines: 0.36 percent*
43. Capital One: 0.34 percent*
43. Cigna: 0.34 percent*
45. Walgreens: 0.33 percent*
45. Fred Meyer (owned by #26 Kroger): 0.33 percent*
47. Stella Artois (owned by #9 Budweiser): 0.32 percent*
47. Eastern Bank: 0.32 percent*
47. United Airlines: 0.32 percent*
50. Lyft: 0.31 percent*
50. Ace Hardware: 0.31 percent*
50. Cisco: 0.31 percent*
50. Publix: 0.31 percent*
50. Realtor.com:.031 percent*
55. RE/MAX—0.30 percent*
55. Nike: 0.30 percent*
57. Sam's Club (owned by #13 Walmart): 0.29 percent
57. Subway: 0.29 percent*
57. Dairy Queen: 0.29 percent*
60. Barefoot Wine: 0.28 percent*

two or more businesses are tied at this rank

Why Local Sponsorships? Clif Bar Says: Community Connection

Companies can have different reasons behind local donations, from branding to employee satisfaction. Michelle Ferguson, the EVP of food and innovation of Clif Bar (ranked #10), shared how her company came to embrace local giving in a recorded interview with a California business school:

> *"The premise for our marketing is centered around grassroots marketing, or building consumer relationships. Realizing that in every interaction we have a consumer we have the chance for that person to become an advocate, a friend, a supporter [to reach] someone who is upset with us as well; and also have a chance for us to learn something."*

(The presentation is about an hour long, but worth watching if local, on-the-ground marketing is of interest.)

Whole Foods Market Says: Mission Fulfillment

Other brands see local sponsorships as an opportunity to share their brand's mission. Regional marketing managers at Whole Foods Market (ranked #4) in Raleigh-Durham, told us in an interview that the grocery chain's health and wellness mission is reflected in the events and organizations the team chooses to sponsor. They explained that the processes their team built to take in sponsorship requests measures potential organizations' ROI, particularly for sponsorships that aren't as closely aligned with health and fitness.

Wells Fargo Says: Employee Engagement and Community Investment

Wells Fargo (ranked #1) gives $1,000 of discretionary donation funds to many of their local branches. Debbie Ragsdale, the Piedmont East sales and marketing director for Wells Fargo, told me: "Banks are dependent on the community being successful. We want to see our community grow and thrive. We have a passion about helping our communities. That's what gets at the local level."

Wells Fargo has some limitations on the organizations their employees select—it must be a 501(c)(3); it must not be an organization that regrants funds, and it must fit into Wells Fargo's focus areas, which include K-12 education, health and human services, arts and culture, or civic and environmental, says Wells Fargo's former community affairs officer Carrie Gray.

Your local campaign doesn't have to be as broad as a Fortune 100 brand's, but we like to share this list to provide inspiration beyond simply building links!

CAMPAIGN PREP: A FEW LAST-MINUTE SECRETS

So you've got buy-in and you're ready to launch a local sponsorship campaign. In this section, we'll let you in on a few final prep lessons we've learned along the way. Every item on this list is the result of "oops" moments we've had at ZipSprout, so learn from our mistakes and plan ahead with the tips below.

1. Know the Benefits of the Sponsorship You're Seeking

The list below is a pretty good roundup of the sponsorship benefits we typically see. Many (though not all!) local organizations have preset sponsorship packages, which are posted on their website or can be requested via email. And many (though not all!) of the packages are negotiable. If you want to forgo or add on benefits to a certain package, pricing can be customized. Know ahead of time what you're looking for. Here's our working list of benefits (shown in Figure 21–2):

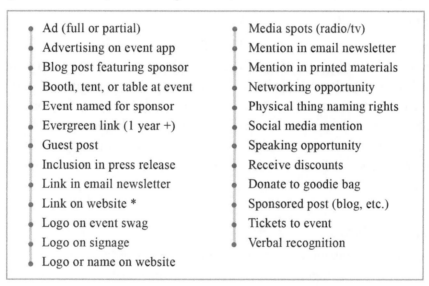

- Ad (full or partial)
- Advertising on event app
- Blog post featuring sponsor
- Booth, tent, or table at event
- Event named for sponsor
- Evergreen link (1 year +)
- Guest post
- Inclusion in press release
- Link in email newsletter
- Link on website *
- Logo on event swag
- Logo on signage
- Logo or name on website

- Media spots (radio/tv)
- Mention in email newsletter
- Mention in printed materials
- Networking opportunity
- Physical thing naming rights
- Social media mention
- Speaking opportunity
- Receive discounts
- Donate to goodie bag
- Sponsored post (blog, etc.)
- Tickets to event
- Verbal recognition

FIGURE 21–2. Sample Sponsorship Benefits

* Unless there's evidence that a sponsorship link lasts indefinitely, expect most links to be live for about a year.

2. Know Your Brand's Limitations

Is your brand OK associating with religious organizations? What about organizations with a political bent? It's best to get all these questions out of the way upfront, especially if you need approval to enact sponsorships.

3. Alert PR

We've had cases where local organizers have reached out to clients' PR teams to verify that they were, in fact, seeking local sponsorships. We don't necessarily need PR to be involved, but make sure that the team, as well as the social media team, is aware of the campaign. There will be a sudden influx of brand mentions once sponsorships start coming through, and we've learned that most marketing teams like to be aware of where their mentions are coming from.

4. Plan for Email Sending

If you're emailing multiple local organizations, using a template is a fine way to go for a first-touch outreach, but make sure you're still personalizing. If you have a favorite email-sending tool, such as BuzzStream, this may be the time to renew your subscription.

5. Plan for Phone Calls

A 15-minute conversation can mean the difference between a successful sponsorship and one that doesn't happen. But phone calls don't always scale. If you can incorporate calls with local organizations into your outreach plan, we highly recommend it (and we'll discuss this method more in the sponsorship outreach section). But for now, know they'll be a part of the process, so make sure you have a unique work phone number that's separate from your cell phone. We use Phone.com to manage work numbers on our cell phones and Calendly to avoid the burden of back-and-forth phone call scheduling.

6. Plan to Write Checks

We know many companies don't just hand over the checkbook to any marketing team member with a "highly urgent" request. You may have a company credit card, but getting a paper check takes six months, 57 emails, and a few batches of chocolate chip cookies. If this is your organization, or if you don't know the policy around check writing, now is the time to make a plan. Find out how you would send a check to local organizations, if you could write it yourself, or if someone in accounting or HR needs to disburse the funds. Also find out if your company requires 1099s from organizations you sponsor.

Some of the local organizations we work with only accept checks as a form of payment. If checks are possible, that means more opportunities. If they're not possible, it's good to find out early so you can seek only organizations that take credit cards or PayPal.

SPONSORSHIP PROSPECTING

At ZipSprout, before we had our own tool, we used the Citation Labs Link Prospector, an at-scale prospecting tool, but if you're doing a smaller search, it may be easier to browse on your own. Use advanced operators to find web pages indicating that a sponsorship is available.

We recommend starting with:

- intitle:"Our sponsors" + [CITY NAME]
- "Our sponsors" + [CITY NAME]
- thank you to our generous sponsors + [CITY NAME]
- "our donors" + [CITY NAME]
- "Our partners" + [CITY NAME]

Search for Sponsorships

Maybe we want to see all the sponsorship opportunities Denver has to offer. See Figure 21–3 for what a search for sponsorships in Denver looks like using this method.

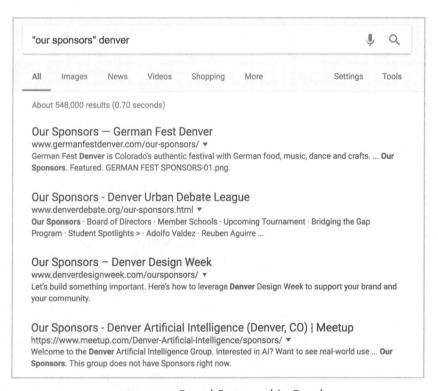

FIGURE 21–3. Broad Sponsorship Results

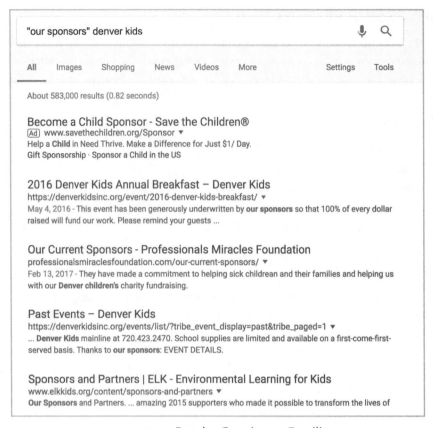

FIGURE 21–4. Results Catering to Families

Or maybe we only want to find events that cater to families in Denver. See Figure 21–4 for what that type of search looks like.

Maybe we want to find only sponsorship PDFs that include details of how to sponsor. This is recommended if you're in a hurry because you can find organizations that publish their pricing, which means you can make decisions more quickly. That said, you will miss out on opportunities if you only search this way. (See Figure 21–5, on page 207, for an example of what this type of search looks like.)

You can get more specific, such as *inurl:pta,* if you want (see Figure 21–6, on page 207).

We've also found that searching for upcoming seasonal events can be a way to quickly find relevant event sponsorships. For example, in July and August 2017, the ZipSprout team reached out to thousands of Fall Fests, Labor Day parades, and Halloween events across the U.S. We contacted these event organizers two to three months out from their event, when they were in prime sponsor-seeking mode. These organizations responded quickly, and they fulfilled sponsorships quickly, too, because we found them at the right time.

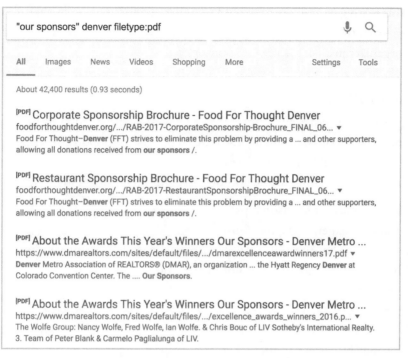

FIGURE 21–5. Sponsor PDFs Only

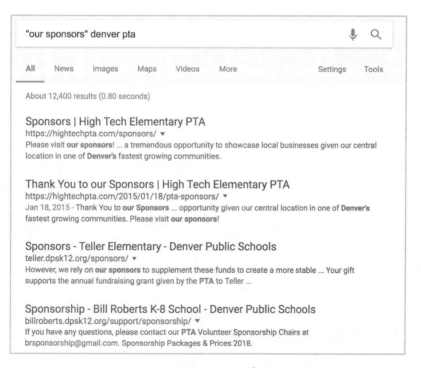

FIGURE 21–6. More Specific Results

For this reason, we don't recommend reaching out about an event that is more than six to seven months out. Sometimes these sponsorships work out, but more often than not, the organizer just isn't ready for sponsors yet.

A Word on Qualifying

Because we work at scale and prospected at scale, the ZipSprout team has spent a significant amount of time qualifying local sponsorship opportunities. As with any search query, there will be false positives.

With local sponsorships, these non-opportunities tend to fall into a few categories:

- Blogs that accept sponsorships
- Local newspaper/magazine websites
- Nonprofits that are not local and serve a national or international audience (they're still sponsorable, but not in our wheelhouse)
- Conferences
- Local events that last occurred over two to three years ago (they're *probably* inactive)
- Local clubs and associations that only accept sponsorships from local members (this may be perfect, though, if you're prospecting for a local business)

Again, depending on your goals, some of these false positives may work for your campaign. Conferences, for example, don't reach local audiences typically, but they can be a solid opportunity if you're targeting people who work in a particular industry. Sponsoring bloggers, or creating sponsored posts on popular blogs, is a great way to reach new audiences, but most bloggers are more niche-specific (beauty, fashion, cause-related, etc.) than location-focused.

Moving Forward

Once you have a list of local opportunities you're interested in sponsoring (and this list can be as small as five opportunities or as large as 500), you're ready to launch the outreach phase of the project.

We recommend, for time's sake, that you find at least five to ten local options in the prospecting phase, even if you only plan on doing one or two sponsorships. Not every local opportunity pans out, and it's better to have a few options as backups, instead of repeatedly wasting time by going back to prospecting.

LOCAL SPONSORSHIP OUTREACH

We started with San Diego. Now, many cities later, we've learned that San Diego is a relatively small and pricey market for local sponsorships, compared to other major

U.S. cities. But this region has been a consistent need among ZipSprout clients. There's something about Southern California that appeals to marketers. San Diego is sunny, beautiful, and wealthy, yet feels full of everyday people.

I spoke on the phone and emailed with hundreds of San Diego local organizations in December and January of 2015/2016. One relationship that still stands out is Miriam Raftery of *East County Magazine*. Miriam is a former journalist who would get frantic calls from East San Diego County residents every time a wildfire threatened the area. This was the early 2000s, so news was still TV- and radio-based. So, Miriam founded a texting service for fire alerts and evacuation routes, which turned into a simple website, then became a bigger website focused on local news in Eastern San Diego County.

I remember Miriam foremost because of her passion. She cares. She loves East County—its small towns and its rural feel, so different from the western region of San Diego, host to Comic-Con and the world-famous zoo. And I remember *East County Magazine* because it's the platonic ideal of a local organization. It's hyperlocal; it's a nonprofit that hosts local events, and it reaches a highly specific audience.

It was after about a month of conversations with people like Miriam that we began to see ZipSprout as bigger than a side project, which needed a team bigger than me. Local visibility begins with local relationships. And building relationships with local organizations is simultaneously common-sense easy and highly complex.

Local event and nonprofit organizers are generally warm and simple to work with. Founders and development directors want to talk about their organization's accomplishments, and many want to hop on the phone and get to know their potential donor. Many are happy to customize sponsorship levels to find options that work for themselves and potential donors.

That said, local organizers are also highly scrutinizing. They want to know about the company that's donating to them and understandably so. Many won't take donations without a phone call or two. And some organizations will say no to money if the donor's brand doesn't align with their values or their ideal type of sponsor. It's rare, but it happens. Various clients have been rejected because they weren't on-brand enough, due to their online reviews or their CEO's affiliation with other politically leaning organizations. At other times, we've had to ask about clients' environmental policies to secure a sponsorship.

Follow the four steps below to launch your outreach strategy:

1. Determine Your Sponsorship Goals

How many local events do you need to support your link building goals—what about your local impressions target? What's your total budget—what's your max budget for a single organization? What types of audiences are you hoping to reach? How much information will your team need from a local organization before making a decision?

2. Decide on an Outreach Strategy

If your team is hoping to secure multiple sponsorships in a short period of time, then an initial contact by email may be your best bet. But if you're working against a tight deadline or just around the corner from a holiday, we've found that phone calls can work well for building a rapport more quickly. Here are our best practices for handling three types of outreach:

- *Email outreach.* Introduce yourself and your organization, but keep it short and sweet. Simpler and more concise emails almost always win out against introductions that take a paragraph or two. And keep your "ask" simple, too—you're just starting a dialogue after all.

  If you're curious about pricing for a particular sponsorship, ask for a sponsorship packet or PDF. If you'd like information about multiple sponsorship opportunities, let the organizer know you're flexible, and you'd like to learn more and find a good fit. See Figure 21-7 for an example of an email outreach.

  Don't over-email. If someone doesn't respond after a single outreach and a follow-up email, they're likely not interested in a partnership—or worse, they're disorganized and would make a potentially bad partner.

- *Phone call outreach.* The email guidelines apply to phone calls as well. Introduce yourself, and ask a question about sponsorships. In our experience, phone calls with local organizations can take 10 to 20 minutes, depending on how much information is needed from both parties, so be sure to budget enough time for these calls.

  You should generally reserve outreach phone calls for local organizations you think could be a particularly good client fit. It's also easier to develop modified sponsorship packages over the phone. We've found that many local organizers are happy to alter the costs and benefits of a sponsorship package to fit a donor's

FIGURE 21–7. Sample Email Outreach

needs. However, this is not always the case, so we don't recommend assuming that sponsorship modification is a given with each organization. It might get awkward.

■ *Email and phone call.* Voicemails, in our experience, are not as effective as a phone conversation. I won't even pretend to understand this trend, but it's consistent across ZipSprout matchmakers. However, a voicemail plus a follow-up email results in a response more frequently. So, if there's a local organization you're particularly interested in, pick up the phone, then follow up with email.

3. Collect Data

You'll want to use a spreadsheet or a customer relationship management tool to keep track of the various organizations you reach out to. And if you're working at scale, with more than a few hundred local organizations, you'll want to find a good CRM. At ZipSprout, we developed a customized tool to help us keep track of individual conversations and relationships with local organizers. But if you're just starting out, an Excel or Google Doc spreadsheet should work fine (that's what we started with—now our database has over 55,000 sponsorable organizations).

Here are some column headers we recommend for your tracking spreadsheet:

■ Unique number or ID—for easier identifying later
■ Organization name
■ Keywords—you may want to come up with your own list, or feel free to use ours; they're an easy way to identify what an organization is all about
■ URL of organization
■ Location
■ Email address
■ Phone number
■ Contact first and last name
■ Domain authority
■ Cost of sponsorship level with our target benefits
■ List of benefits we'd receive
■ Link to sponsors' page
■ Link to sponsorship PDF
■ Notes
■ Status

Oftentimes, you'll hear back from an outreach email within 24 hours. But there are times when local organizers have responded weeks, even months later. We recommend giving about two weeks to gather all responses before moving on to sponsorship selection.

SELECTING SPONSORSHIPS

Recently, when looking over a list of sponsorship opportunities with a client, they asked, "How should I be evaluating these? What metrics do I go by?" When building a list of potential sponsorship opportunities, you're going to end up with a lot of data. It can be difficult to parse out spreadsheet rows and columns after a while. In this section, we've listed a few factors beyond cost to consider when selecting sponsorships. When you find organizations that are a great match in one or more areas, find a way to mark them as a "favorite." It will be a lot easier to scan for favorites later than to grind through rows of data at the end of the project.

Benefits

This is the time to go back to your goals. What is the purpose of this campaign, and how are you measuring success? We've seen clients use sponsorships to build buzz for an event. Others use it as a link-building tactic. Others engage in sponsorships as an employee reward system. Still others use them simply for connecting their brand ambassadors with local populations at scale. Your goals should be the primary driver of your sponsorship selection. Here are some example goals:

- *Building buzz for an upcoming event.* Seek sponsorships with a large reach (see below) and high engagement in the organizations' email newsletters and social feeds. It's also a good idea to find sponsorable events where you can hand out invites for your event in goody bags or at the door.
- *Local leads, by any means.* Seek sponsorships with benefits that include customized social media email newsletters and website posts. Create a coupon or an affiliate incentive for the organizations' members, and ensure the coupon code is included in all postings.
- *Local leads, via event marketing.* Seek sponsorships with the opportunity to have a booth or table at an event. Bring swag and coupons so you can meet and greet and track conversions later.
- *Local link building.* Seek sponsorships that offer links from their sponsors' page to your website. Make sure to provide your local landing page URL and a proper logo. You may also want to seek out organizations with blogs and see if your team can provide a blog post or interview in an article that links back to your site.
- *Employee engagement/rewards.* Seek sponsorships that offer booths; tickets to events, such as arts performances or golf tournaments; and/or networking opportunities. You may also want to sponsor local associations or alliances, where your employees can get a foot in the door to meet others in their industry and show off your brand as a local leader in your sector.

Reach

Reach is our version of "impressions" for local sponsorships. Let's say a sponsorship's benefits include a social media post and an email newsletter shout-out. Is the shout-out going to 150 followers, or 1,500? Is that email newsletter audience just friends and family, or is it a larger network? If you're able to quantify audience size for all sponsorship benefits, you can compare same-city opportunities. But reach is not always obvious at face value.

We once partnered with an organization, The Loft Artists Association, which serves a moderately sized community of children via summer art classes, but markets themselves, and their sponsors, with end-of-school-year flyers in 40,000 local kids' backpacks. For a brand targeting families of elementary school students, that's reach.

At ZipSprout, we've developed a "Reach Score" for each organization we partner with, which factors in:

- Event attendance
- Website domain authority
- Facebook following
- Twitter following
- Email newsletter sign-ups

All measurements are relative to other organizations in that city. You can calculate the reach score of any local organization at zipsprout.com/reach-score.

Demographics

Demographics are obvious when we're talking Little League or beer fests. But what about local nonprofits? Your target audience may be community members who are homeowners or who have a target income level. Does this limit your donations to local museums? Not necessarily. When it comes to local nonprofits, consider the demographics of the local, private donors. An organization that raises funds for underserved populations may have galas, meetings, or other events, where your team can meet and mingle with other local sponsors and charitable donors.

Additionally, demographics can play a larger or smaller role depending on the benefits of sponsorship you're seeking. For link-building campaigns, they may be less of a factor. But if you're seeking local leads, or event attendees, it matters. In our experience, most clients either don't limit their sponsorships by demographics, or they use highly strict limitations. We'd recommend a middle-of-the-road approach. You may find only one or two opportunities where every event attendee is a member of your target audience, such as the Loft Artists Association example above. But a business targeting local families of elementary school children will likely find many target audience members at a local parade or festival.

Mission

Mission can be, but does not have to be, a corollary of demographics. Mission is your brand's backbone—what you stand for.

When we talk about branded mission, one of our favorite examples is Stella Artois. Since the 1980s Stella has sponsored film festivals across the U.S. and internationally. For Stella, film festivals support it's mission within it's brand-building strategy. A relatively mainstream beer, Stella is advertised as a drink to be sipped from a chalice by a man in a suit. Stella's marketing team topped the chalice and film star-focused campaign with the slogan "reassuringly expensive," and the brand has the budget to pull this image off. Film festivals provide the perfect opportunity to extend this branding to on-the-ground sponsorships.

An unbranded, or brand adjacent, mission is no less impactful. Tito's Vodka, for example, sponsors local dog shelters across the U.S. Tito's site has a landing page explaining the team's love for their four-legged friends, and they even sell Tito's branded canine merchandise, whose proceeds go to a pet charity. The connection between dogs, dog-lovers, and Vodka consumption is not strong, but to the Tito's team, caring for dogs is a passion area; it's part of their brand because they made it part of their brand.

Timing

Timing is an often-overlooked component of local sponsorship development. For general organization donations, it isn't a factor, but for events, you want to be one to five months out from the event date to make sure there's enough time for details to get in line, but not so much time that fulfillment is a long, drawn out process.

Additionally, some events fulfill sponsorship benefits in the months leading up to the big day; others wait until the days just before or after the event. It can be difficult to determine which organizations fulfill when ahead of time. Depending on how quickly your team or client expects results, you'll want to select events whose dates are no more than a few months out.

Cost

Of course, we can't talk about sponsorships without talking about pricing. In our experience, you'll want to expect to pay on average approximately $500 per sponsorship, give or take $200, depending on your location. We've found Chicago and Atlanta to be less expensive than New York or Miami, and Hawaii is one of the most expensive markets we've worked in.

SPONSORSHIP FULFILLMENT

One of the biggest surprises for the ZipSprout team was that the fulfillment process could be almost as involved as selecting and matching sponsorships. Who's going to say no to money, right? Turns out, local organizations do say no for a variety of reasons, including:

- The timing is poor. Maybe the event is eight months out, and the organizer is too busy with other obligations to accept sponsors.
- The organization leaders disagree with the sponsor's business ethics.
- The organization only accepts hyper-local businesses as sponsors.
- The organization or event is temporarily or permanently on hiatus. This is especially a risk with extremely inexpensive, almost "too good to be true" sponsorships. Unfortunately, it's the smallest organizations that are the most vulnerable.

To make fulfillment as simple as possible, we recommend developing a process similar to the initial outreach plan.

Pre-Notifications

We work with clients who need to approve every sponsorship, so if a local organization later rejects a client or falls off the grid, we're in a bit of a pickle. We then have to find a replacement sponsorship, send it back to the client for approval, and cross our fingers that this one works out.

We've learned that it's much more efficient to give the organization a heads up. We've developed emails we call pre-notifications, explaining to the organization that we're recommending a particular organization to [*Client Name*] at the $XXX level, then reconfirm the benefits of sponsorship at that level, and the duration of a live link or newsletter/email campaign. We send these out and wait to hear back before we recommend sponsorships to the client. This way, we avoid replacing opportunities post-client approval.

Benefit Checks and Email Follow-Ups

With some sponsorship benefits, such as booths or sending swag, redeeming the benefit will be part of the process. With others, such as digital posts or link placements, it's best to ask the local organization their anticipated timing for placement so your team knows when to check back in and when to engage with social media posts.

Timing

A couple of years ago, the average ZipSprout sponsorship took about 25 business days from client approval to fulfillment. By embracing pre-notification and better tracking practices, we've lowered this turnaround period to less than 10 business days. Your fulfillment time will vary, depending on how many resources you're able to dedicate to this part of the sponsorship process.

Your Assets: Logos, Coupons, Ads, Etc.

Local sponsorships are not yet scalable in the same vein as, say, paid search. There are no networks where businesses can bid on sponsorships for ice cream socials in Schenectady or Little League teams in Tallahassee. Plus, based on our experience with local nonprofit leaders, organizations aren't eager for such a platform; nonprofits often want to interact with their potential donors before establishing a more formal relationship.

And yet the lack of a communal system does not mean that some standards wouldn't be welcomed. At ZipSprout, we see firsthand the back-and-forth when it comes to asset exchanges. Prepping assets before launching a local sponsorship campaign will save your team time and hassle later on.

Below you'll find a checklist of commonly requested assets for local sponsorship campaigns.

Logo

A logo for a white background in png format should be at least 500 by 500 pixels, while one for a dark background in png format should be at least 500 by 500 pixels.

If your standard logo is not square—if it's more horizontal or vertical—it's advised to provide a secondary square logo for organizations that cannot use a heavily horizontal or vertical asset for every content piece.

Coupon Codes

If your business can generate and accept coupon codes, we recommend creating unique codes for each local organization, and asking them to share codes with their email subscribers and social media followers. This is a great way to further incentivize an organization's organic audience to engage with your product, and it also helps attribution afterward. Attending the event or have the option to send swag? Create postcards with coupon codes to hand out (see an example can be in Figure 21–8, on page 217).

Other Art-Based Assets

Below are some additional art assets you might want to consider:

- Square ad (500 by 500 pixels), which includes copy and business URL
- Vertical ad (300 by 600 pixels), which includes copy and business URL
- Horizontal ad (1,200 by 628 pixels), which includes copy and business URL; also perfect for a Facebook post

FIGURE 21–8. Create Unique Coupon Codes

- Horizontal photo (1,200 by 628 pixels), which includes a logo or URL, but no copy

Print-Ready Ads

Some local organizations offer the opportunity for a business ad in a print program or newsletter. Ad specs for these placements can vary widely, so we recommend having horizontal and vertical print ads on hand, with a space for editable coupon codes, which can be easily resized.

Business-card-sized ads are a common standard: 3.5 by 2 inches, with an 1/8-inch bleed.

For print, convert color to CMYK, deliver via jpg, eps, psd and/or pdf.

URLS

Many organizations link out to sponsors from their web pages and/or social media pages. We recommend, at least, providing the correct link to the homepage of your business to every organization you sponsor. But better yet—go local!

- If your site has city-specific pages, have those links on hand and geographically organized to send out to organizations.
- For tracking, include UTM codes* unique to each organization, accompanied by a one sentence company description for social media and newsletter posts.

A UTM Code (Urchin Tracking Module) is a code that you can attach to a custom URL which allows you to track where specific web traffic is coming from.

Custom Content

Some assets cannot be standardized. Businesses who want to get personal may have custom social media messages or blog posts for each local organization. And while the content cannot be created ahead of time, the process can be. If you know that your team wants to customize each local organization's campaign, make sure to work with an in-house copywriter to ensure they make time for custom content creation.

Common examples of custom content:

- Custom Facebook posts or tweets, directed at each local organization's audience and posted by your business
- Custom Facebook posts or tweets, directed at each local organization's audience, sent to the local organization, and posted by them
- Guest blog post about your business or unique features of your company, posted on the local organization's website
- Blog posts featuring the mission and purpose of each local organization—or select key organizations—in a campaign posted on your business's website

MAXIMIZE THE BENEFITS OF LOCAL SPONSORSHIP

You can bump up the effects of your local sponsorships in a variety of low-to-no budget ways that are reliable, fast, and relatively easy. Here are a few suggestions.

Boost Social Media Mentions

If you're already engaging in Facebook ads, experiment with boosting local organizations' social media posts that mention your sponsorship and theirs to your audience. To accomplish this, the page's admin will need to set someone on your team up as an advertiser.

Write Stories on Your Local Sponsorships

Sponsorships are blog fodder. Phone interviews with local organizations that your brand sponsors give extra context to the relationship, and it will provide an additional moment of promotion from the local brand (and maybe another link if they mention you on their press page). In fact, the more you can mention the relationship with local organizations onsite or on social media, the more the stories will be shared, which will direct their audience attention back to you.

Add Messaging to Email Newsletter Copy and Social Media

Ask organizations if you can send them custom content for digital posts. Possibilities for custom content include a coupon code, a link to a locally oriented blog post, or unique messaging for that organization's audience. Developing and distributing local content at scale is a challenge for large and small teams, but local sponsorships are an organic vehicle for a local strategy.

Send Local Customers to Events

Many local sponsorships come with complimentary tickets. If your team isn't local, we recommend having a list, or even a listserv, of local top customers who would be willing to accept local ticket perks. This can be a great reward for a base of top customers, and it will show the organization that you care enough to make sure their event attendance is strong.

LOCAL SPONSORSHIP MEASUREMENT

Various brands have their own goals for going local. Some are OK with a pure branding play; others want more concrete results. In general, online ads are pushing the entire market further in the direction of direct attribution. Here are some ways you can measure your local sponsorship game.

Direct Attribution Measurements

We like to use two direct attribution measurements: coupon codes and affiliate links.

Using custom coupon codes for each local organization has two great benefits:

1. They provide an extra incentive for locals to sign up for the tool or service.
2. They allow a brand to monitor coupon code uses to decide if the sponsorship hit an interested demographic.

Some ride-sharing companies like Lyft already employ programs that allow local businesses or events to sign up for a unique coupon code to distribute. Affiliate links and local events/organizations can work well together in a couple of ways. First, there's the Amazon Smile model, where Amazon donates to nonprofits whose members shop on Amazon from a unique affiliate link on the organizations' websites. Some see this program as doing more harm than good, but it is an option for companies who like to give back.

But you don't have to promise a percentage of your profits to local organizations to use affiliate links. Simply request that local organizations use a unique link when mentioning your brand on their website, in email newsletters, and in social media.

The latter option means an upfront sponsorship, but local organizations may be more amenable to this traditional type of donation.

Measure Brand Awareness Growth with Sponsorship Google Trends

Google Trends was recommended to us by Professor Maps himself, Mike Blumenthal, founding partner of GatherUp, and it's one of the few tools we know of that provides a reflection of local branding within a given geographical area.

By searching for the Swedish furniture store, Ikea, for example, we see that Ikea's branding is strongest in the Pacific Northwest, but it also looks like a store just opened in Fishers, Indiana, based on the dramatic increase of Ikea searches in that area. You can see this change in Figure 21–9.

A lift in branded organic searches is more likely in campaigns that focus on reach and messaging. Link-focused campaigns may not see much lift in this area.

FIGURE 21–9. Ikea Growth in Fishers, Indiana

SERP Ranking

The search engine results pages are a messy playground, but they can be measured. If you're sponsoring local organizations in a few key cities, we recommend comparing rankings with a few similarly sized cities where you're not sponsoring.

At ZipSprout, we use Whitespark, but you can also use Moz Local or BrightLocal to monitor rankings in key markets.

SERP results will vary depending on your location and industry. For some, five sponsorships with links will lead to a rise in results. For others, even 20 sponsorships may not be enough to move the needle. If link building is a primary focus, we recommend starting with a competitive analysis on your local pages. Check out your competitors backlinks in Ahrefs, and look at their successes with other ranking factors to determine the investment you'll need to make a measurable impact on revenue.

KNOW YOUR LOCAL BRANDING LIMITS

Local branding isn't for everyone. An orthotic shoe brand may see benefit from sponsoring a podiatrist conference, but they're not going to gain too many customers by scaling Little League donations.

And just like a good orthotic shoe, marketing is not one-size-fits-all. (Did we really just make that analogy?). Yet we live at a time when Google Ads or some equivalent form of ad tech is often the first stop for marketers. The idea that customers are out there, searching or scrolling for you, is appealing.

If your product is an item that is not frequently repurchased by the same customer, such as a tech-savvy suitcase or a sports watch, then selling your product via an online ad is probably going to generate the most ROI.

On the other hand, if you provide a service, such as a babysitting app, a restaurant, or home cleaning; if you're a lifestyle brand or a consumable; if your product is a high-cost item that requires consideration; or if you have local stores or agents who need to network to gain clients and business, you want to be top of mind beyond banner ads. Sure, ads work, but branding makes people feel good about spending their money with you.

Local sponsorships give potential customers the opportunity to experience your brand right in their backyard.

LOCAL BLOG ENGAGEMENT FOR LOCAL LINKS AND VISIBILITY

In addition to local sponsorships, we've also found local blogs to be a scalable publisher-type for hyper-local visibility and link-building campaigns.

This section details what you need to know about local blog engagement based on how we've grown our program over the past few years to build hundreds of city-specific links per month. The points below should help demonstrate a link-building path for both enterprise teams seeking scaled local links to city-specific pages across the country and small businesses with just one or a few locations.

1. Local Blogs Defined: The Local blog "Universe"

We group publishers—local and otherwise—into the following two categories: ad-supported and visibility-supported. Here's how we characterize these two types:

- Ad-Supported Publishers (aka The 1 Percent of Publishers)
  - local news sites
  - lifestyle magazines (usually print-first legacy publishers with a token web nod)
  - donation-supported independent local news publishers (small but growing publishing type)
  - high-profile local bloggers (usually end up working for newspapers)
  - frequently have subscribers, either paid or newsletter, etc.
  - often have "print" reach
  - strong social reach
  - audience-first (usually) in publishing choices

- Visibility-Supported Publishers (aka The 99 Percent of Publishers) local organizations such as:
  - specialty stores/product manufacturers
  - services (e.g., health/home services/tourism)
  - local noncommercial, community-centric organizations
  - "less visible" local lifestyle bloggers (parents, foodies, fashion, nightlife, etc.)
  - rarely have subscribers, social or otherwise
  - make publishing decisions based on attracting new customers with content as opposed to ad revenue

As an agency, we primarily concentrate on the "visibility-supported" publishers. We've never really tried that hard going after the ad-supported publishers, though we have heard of the "Top 10 Cities for XYZ Demographic" campaigns that seemed to play well circa 2015. So, it's definitely possible to target top-tier local publishers, though, of course, you'd be hard pressed to build direct links to your site's local city pages (in other words, sales pages) with that publisher type.

2. Local Blog Discovery

Local blogs are out there, and the largest body of them are visibility-supported, meaning they're local businesses and entrepreneurs who publish content in an effort to attract customers. They're content marketers at the local level. The question is, for your target location, which types of businesses and organizations have really bought into web publishing? Those are the verticals you'll have to figure out how to connect with, earn the trust of their editors, and ultimately reach their audiences.

So, your first step really is to learn which types of organizations are your local visibility-supported publishers.

Here's how.

First collect the following information about your target city:

- county name + state abbreviation
- city name + state abbreviation
- two prominent neighborhood names + city name
- three random zip codes

Combine each one with inurl:blog and query them in your favorite search engine, then observe the organization types.

For example, I'm in Louisville, KY. Here's what my collection of queries could look like:

- Jefferson County, KY inurl:blog
- Louisville, KY inurl:blog
- Highlands Louisville inurl:blog
- 40202 inurl:blog
- 40213 inurl:blog
- 40258 inurl:blog

So now I can run each query and get a sense of which local organization types are publishing content. I could also set my time-range delimiter to only show results from the past month, which helps me further narrow the set to publishers who have published in the past month. Why would we care to see that? It shows us active publishers who still invest time and effort in visibility.

Comb through the results. What kinds of organization types are you seeing quite a few of? Which organizations could you start imagining an email pitch they might say "yes" to?

3. Local Blog Engagement Strategies

Since we don't really go after the ad-supported publishers, in this section we'll examine some engagement approaches for all those visibility-supported hyper-local publishers out there. Then in the next section, we'll dig into quick tests for what types of organizations have blogs in your target location.

Before speculating on engagement approaches we haven't mastered, I'll share what we currently do. Nothing crazy here; it's a pure execution play.

We pitch helpful, how-to content titles—usually topics unrelated or lightly related to location—and hope publishers will be open to adding them to their sites. Conversions vary based on the quality of our topic pitch and how well we've lined up topics with our prospective publishers. This has worked, but I'd caution other marketers that it's an uphill approach and we're seeing declining returns. Luckily there's no shortage of ideas to try!

Here are several other approaches you could test, some of which we've actually seen in the wild. Some we've tried but not really gotten to work as efficiently at scale as topic pitches.

Local Blog Engagement Strategies

- *Group interviews with local service experts adjacent to publisher.* If you've got a list of dog-boarding sites that have blogs, you could interview local dog walkers to find the best places to walk dogs. In theory, the dog-boarding folks, so long as they don't compete with the dog walkers, won't begrudge some visibility for non-competing service providers who can help their site visitors learn some great places to walk dogs. How does your link fit? It depends on what pages you want links to, of course, but if you're a real estate service, you could add a dog parks section to your city page and link there.

- *Coupon/savings roundups of adjacent and related products/services.* Like the example above, we approach audience- or market-adjacent businesses to hopefully entice them to publish their promotional coupon along with other non-competing businesses that also target their demographic. Here's how it works: You approach a local yoga studio with a collection of local yoga-related coupons and deals that you've aggregated. Think acupuncture, massage, meditation, health food etc. The yoga studio gets some great offers for their audience, and you can earn a place for your brand as well.

- *Upcoming events of interest to target audiences.* General contractors and home builders with blogs might be open to write-ups about upcoming home-related events. Interview someone from the event to increase your likelihood of getting published. How does your link fit in here? Maybe it doesn't, so try the local pediatricians' offices and showcase upcoming educational events for parents. How about upcoming bridal shows for the wedding photographers in your city? You may have to run through quite a few to find a fit, but there's probably one out there, right? Lastly, if you're investing in staffing booths at local events, then you should definitely be taking pictures and creating content from your time at the event that could fit both on your blog, the blog of the event itself, and with other publishers in your area.

- *Spotlight on mover and shaker types.* Perhaps not too far removed from the group interview concept above, what about profile interviews with local artists placed on the blogs of local art galleries? Honestly that's probably a bit far-fetched—who knows if the modern gallery would want an interview with the wacky folk artist. So, what about entrepreneur profiles at the local credit union—something to get their readers fired up to borrow some money? How does your link fit, though? Maybe just as the author? How can your content enable these local movers and shakers?

- *Spotlight on local hot spots of interest to audience.* As you're interviewing folks, be sure to learn about the best places for X, Y, or Z in their location. Then when the local farmer's market says yes to your guest post, you have a good listing of all the local community gardens. And the day cares with blogs also say yes to your listing of local kid-friendly breweries. Ok, no they probably won't, so don't try that one. But the local tourism websites might, as would the local bed and breakfasts that have blogs.

   Almost all our examples above involve an interview angle—mostly because we lack localized knowledge about the cities, neighborhoods, and zip codes where we're supposed to know enough about to earn placements. The more you know—local people, places, and facts—the better. You can't go wrong if you stay positive and look for ways to make everyone involved look as good as possible!

4. Citation-Justified Relevance

Just because there's a local education nonprofit with a blog doesn't mean you can land a guest placement with them. As you're reviewing the array of local organizations, you have to stay mindful of either generating or qualifying your engagement strategy (see the previous point on "Local Blog Engagement Strategies" if you happened to have blown past it). Additionally, with an engagement strategy in mind, you're still asking yourself— as pointedly as you can bear—what content on my site (existing or to-be-created) snaps justifiably into a citation for this publisher's audience. That's not so simple, especially if you're just starting out. That said, it's also painfully commonsensical. If you want a link, you must figure out how to create off-site value for your target publisher's audience. For longer-form articulation, read these sections: "Citation Justification" and "Building Links to Sales Pages."

5. Scaled Local Blog Engagement

You've got your city selected, and you've got an engagement strategy that could work with your target organization type. Further you've thought through your citation- justified content that you hope your editor will keep the link to when and if they actually publish. So, let's put that together in more concrete terms.

Let's say you're building local links for a national-facing personal-trainer marketplace (personal training lead gen). You want links built to your "Personal Trainers in Louisville" page, and you'd like those links from local websites. You've already sponsored several fun runs in the area (and included a coupon for the first training session free—smart!). Now you'd like to try some links from local blogs.

You did your initial discovery (see the "Citation-Justified Relevance" section, on page 225) and decided to target local fitness-related businesses—namely yoga studios and fitness centers. You're getting into tricky territory, though. You essentially compete with these organizations for fitness dollars. You'll have to get super creative with your citation justification, something the publishers won't see and decide to just remove your link (for example, don't include a link like: find a personal trainer near you!).

You have to make it fit well, so what about surveying the personal trainers in your database and asking them where they go locally for healthy food? From groceries to restaurants to organic supplements—where are the hidden gems? Get this information and include it on your city page. Then you have a great citation you can make from local fitness-related blogs: "The Physical Trainer's Guide to the Healthiest Foods in Louisville."

No good? You don't want your "Physical Therapist" pages to have food information on them? Well, OK, you could also ask the physical trainers for the friendliest gyms in the area, or the nicest places to go jogging, or the top reasons they see for people quitting their personal training regimen (this last one doesn't have as much of a local angle, though).

The majority of your work is finessing this relationship between the on-page citable element and the target publisher audiences—they have to be lined up, or links won't happen.

Once you're certain you've got a pitch and citable element that you're fairly sure publishers will say yes to, you've got to go out and find all the publishers. *All* of them, ideally. Here's how.

Gather the following information:

- county name
- city name
- all known neighborhood names
- all ZIP codes for the city

Combine the above information with the organization type you're after. For the above campaign, for example, I'd suggest combining all location data with the following terms:

- fitness
- yoga studio
- fitness center

Now you've probably got a hundred or more queries to run, but you're not done. You've got to add:

- inurl:blog
- blog

You can skip just the word "blog" if you don't need to dig extra deep, or you don't have a team for qualifying opportunities. Just including the word "blog" provides a wider range of publishers, since it's not quite as restrictive.

Then run all your queries through a tool like the Link Prospector. Dig 20 deep or so, and be sure to set the date range to the past year so you'll only see publishers who are a bit more active. You'll still have a great deal of qualifying left to do, but the output will be a list of local websites in the fitness vertical that also operate blogs.

All that's left is sending emails and possibly getting on the phone, and trying to convert those fine publishers into content placements. If you've done your homework on the engagement and justification side, then you have positioned yourself to move on to the final phase: learning if your outreach opens the doors to publishers' hearts and audiences.

THE GUIDE TO LOCAL LINK BUILDING VIA EXISTING RELATIONSHIPS

One of the most commonly cited—but rarely explained—pieces of link building advice is to "take advantage of existing relationships" or to "reach out to your contacts." This is not a sensational claim: We have confirmed, after auditing and analyzing the most commonly cited link-building advice, that this oft-cited suggestion has never received the deep dive it deserves.

The idea behind this advice makes sense, until it comes time to put it into action. Reach out to your existing contacts and say what, exactly? "Hey, do you want to help my business by linking to me please?"

Such an approach will not work. Let's consider what will work. The solution is not to blindly send emails to your friends and business contacts that make you look foolish or unprepared.

Fear not. We have detailed an easy-to-follow seven-step process, accompanied by a straightforward spreadsheet, that will keep you focused and on track.

Step One: Identify Who You Know Who Can Link to Your Website

It's important that you use both your time and the time of your contacts in a valuable manner. You don't want your time wasted and neither do they. As you ask the questions below, remember to fill out the spreadsheet to keep track of this information.

Consider some of the following factors when launching your outreach:

- *Who do you know who could potentially link to your website?* This does not necessarily need to be a business contact. It can be your dentist, your lawyer, your cousin, or your former boss. It could even be your childhood friend who now runs a mommy blog. What matters is that you consider everyone you know who is in a position where they might be able to help with this effort.

- *Do they have a website?* The reality is that many of your existing relationships don't have their own websites. At the same time, there are plenty of people you know who do have their own websites and who, if properly motivated, would happily send a link toward your website from their own.

- *If they don't have a website, what do they have?* What is their social media presence? Are they active enough on Facebook to warrant an effort, despite no website? Do they have significant social media followings? Remember that social media can be an impactful channel for short-term promotions or announcing new services or products. If you cannot get a link from their website, there might still be a media opportunity, including traceable promotional codes or word-of-mouth.

- *Who makes the decisions regarding the website?* This won't necessarily disqualify many contacts, but it is crucial to consider whether you are being realistic. Even if you know someone on Walmart's ecommerce team, it's unlikely they're going to be able to kick a link your way.

- *How strong is the relationship? How well do you know this person?* Are they a friend? A business contact? Rate each contact on a scale, with 1 being the most distant and 5 being the strongest.

- *Ask your employees and colleagues what opportunities you might be missing?* Are you sponsoring things? Are you involved in the community? Consider both your business and social relationships. Reach out to your accountant and ask if there are any other business relationships you may not be considering.

This is a lot to keep track of. Remember to use the spreadsheet to keep it all in order. Begin with an ambitious list of at least 20—as you go, you'll find the number both grows and shrinks, as you determine that some contacts are poor fits while discovering new opportunities that you did not originally consider.

Step Two: Determine What Kind of Online Asset Will Appeal to Each Individual

Now that you've determined who you are going to reach out to, you must determine what you will offer them. Ask yourself: What can I create that my contacts will genuinely want to publish?

- *A testimonial.* The art of testimonial link building has been around for decades. It can be extraordinarily simple: You provide a testimonial (e.g., a simple review) to someone you have worked with before. This can be an ideal option for someone with whom you have worked for or would like to build a stronger relationship with. You may opt to make this testimonial as simple as a one-sentence quip or as involved as an impressive infographic. What matters is that you share something that genuinely compliments and thanks your local contacts in a way that they cannot resist sharing on their website.

- *Images you have related to their location or product.* Consider how many photographs you have of the places you go, food you eat, services you've paid for, and products you've purchased. If you have some that are high quality, consider providing those directly.

- *A preferred vendor badge.* See the images in Figure 21-10 for examples. This is a simple thing you can provide to anyone you work with that immediately gets you more publicity, a stronger relationship, and a new link.

- *Sponsorships.* This is a similar concept to the preferred vendor badge but used specifically for local non-profits or other organizations you are sponsoring.

- *An interview or dialogue with your contact.* This is a concept we could explore much deeper, but at its simplest, it's a conversation between you and your contact, one that you will ultimately host on your website or will provide to them to host on theirs.

- *Unlinked mentions.* A classic move for earning links—and one made even easier when reaching out to an individual you already know. This can be as simple as vetting the websites in the spreadsheet to see if they already mention you.

FIGURE 21–10. Preferred Vendor Badge Examples

- *Unmentioned collaborations.* In some cases, you might have an ongoing business relationship or endeavor that does not have any mention online yet. In these scenarios, work with these individuals identified to create some kind of content that mentions your business on their website.
- *Content marketing with a local focus.* This typically takes more work but has a potential for major gains. It can be daunting, although it does not have to be. Quality content marketing can be as simple as a blog post that speaks to a niche audience with information they aren't used to hearing.
- *A press release.* Like content marketing, this can require a more advanced and structured approach. If you have several contacts in the world of local news or blogging, a press release is ideal. Remember that you are doing them a favor by giving them something they can easily turn into quality content on their website.

Before you start going down the wrong path, let's pump the brakes on something right away: We aren't recommending you incentivize them with anything other than quality content. This is not a guide to sponsored content, native content, or, worst of all, paid links.

Return to the spreadsheet, and under the column marked "Strategy," keep track of what kind of content fits your situation the best.

Step Three: Reach Out to Every Individual about the Asset You Can Provide

At this point, it can be easy to become overwhelmed. *Start with your strongest opportunities first.* Note that the spreadsheet gives you two different ways to rank every individual:

1. *Relationship Strength:* How well do you know this individual? Are they a friend of a friend? Do they owe you for a recent professional favor or positive business interaction?
2. *Ease Level*: This refers to how hard the ask is to complete. If you are asking for them to turn an unlinked mention into a link, it's a straightforward ask with a straightforward solution. If you're providing them with a press release, that's going to take more on their end. Consider this: Which of these are the easiest to get out the door?

The reaching out can seem daunting. But it does not have to be.

Step Four: Create the Appropriate Asset

In a vacuum, this would be the most difficult task in this list. However, if you have followed the three steps—with attention to detail and the spreadsheet—then this should become your easiest, most straightforward task. Create the best asset you can for each interested contact.

Step Five: Send the Asset, Tailored to Each Contact

This is the big moment—time to provide your contact with the asset you promised. We recommend using a professional email that includes a link to the content.

You should revise and tweak any sample you refer to for your own uses and to match your style of writing, as appropriate.

Step Six: Follow Up and Ensure They Have What They Need

You've made it through the hard part! At this point, you have to keep communicating. Remember, if you approached this correctly and used the spreadsheet throughout, these aren't strangers you've been cold calling. They're people you know. You should ensure they have what they need to link to your site while improving their own site in the process.

A few aspects of quality assurance to consider:

- Did they understand the ask?
- Did they implement the link correctly?
- Is the link nofollow? (Unfortunately, this might not be something you have any control over—but it's still worth checking.)

It's important to be professional throughout this process. You want to maintain and build relationships throughout this process, not burn any bridges.

Step Seven: Send a Formal Thank You

Once it's live, it's time for a thank you. Don't overdo it, of course. We aren't talking cheese plate and bottle of Scotch. A handwritten note goes a long way. Another simple option is to buy them a cup of coffee. Just make sure you do something simple and thoughtful to show your appreciation.

And finally, remember: Local relationships are cost effective and extra value to any marketing strategy.

In the next chapter, we feature an article by a link-building peer that covers the guidelines to follow for link buying.

Chapter 22

The Link Buying Guide

by Julie Joyce, owner of Link Fish Media

L et's get started with a cold, hard fact. Google does not want you to buy links. If you do buy links, you should add a nofollow attribute to the link, or you'll be in violation of their guidelines and subject to ranking penalties or even deindexing (complete removal of your website from Google's results). Despite this very clear rule and stiff penalties, links are still bought and sold all the time. For this chapter, I'll assume that, for whatever reason, you have decided to buy links.

WHY BUY LINKS?

My personal reason for buying links is that you get what you pay for. If you want specific anchor text or a link pointing to a specific page, you can get it. Clients want to buy links for many different reasons:

- They're convinced their competitors are buying links, and they want to keep up.
- They're in a boring industry and don't have great content or a lot of linkable assets, etc.
- They're unable to naturally attract links.
- They need links to specific pages that don't get many links.

There is also the assumption that a paid link is a bad link, and I don't believe that at all. There are bad paid links just as there are bad free links. If you take shortcuts and buy every link you can, of course, that's going to go poorly. If you approach link buying with the same care you'd take if you were performing outreach in order to get good free links, then you'll get good links.

Everyone from big international brands to your local mom and pop shop buys links. Over the years we have been contacted by people working in almost every industry you can think of.

Staying Safe as Possible

The most critical aspect of participating in the link buying process is staying as safe as possible. While there are no guarantees that you won't be penalized, there are no guarantees that if you follow Google's guidelines you'll enjoy amazing success. There are other types of penalties that can be applied, and many clients choose to risk link buys as it can be very difficult to determine whether a well-executed paid link was indeed one that was purchased.

The absolute first thing you need to do is make sure that clients know exactly what you're doing and how dangerous it can be. You're definitely playing with fire here, so make sure the client knows the risks. It's not enough to say that paid links violate Google's guidelines. You need to lay out what can happen, how likely that is, and have the client make the choice. Never talk anyone into buying links. In fact, I have talked probably 50 potential clients out of it because I personally didn't like the risk.

In all our contracts, there is a statement about the client acknowledging and understanding the risks of paid links. I realize that some of them would still throw me under the bus if they got caught, but at least I have that on record.

My personal philosophy is that if someone is coming to you with an offer to sell you a link on their site, you should run. If they are approaching you, they're approaching 1,000 or more other people. What you want to do is find a site that you have to pursue, rather than the other way around. I always try to look for sites that don't look like they were built to sell links and sites that aren't overrun with links, paid or editorial. As more and more webmasters realize that they can make a lot of money selling links, this becomes more and more difficult.

I'll discuss what I call due diligence below, but I think you can just look at a site and get a good feel for whether or not it would be a good linking partner.

One thing to consider when you're reading this chapter: I'm talking about buying links from bloggers, not from journalists or news sites. I'm not talking about buying a $2,000 link to get your client into *Entrepreneur* magazine. I'm talking about finding a blogger who's been writing a personal blog about their financial journey through their 20s. I'm talking about finding a hobbyist who's obsessed with DIY. I'm also not at all advocating that you seek any sort of endorsement. I never try to get a link where someone is recommending a site or a product. These links are secured as resources, usually where other competing resources exist.

Today, I don't see as much outing of link buying and selling as I did years ago. Still, I proceed with the notion that it could happen and I need to protect my client as much as possible. For that reason, I recommend not mentioning the client until the webmaster has expressed interest in working together on a paid link. It may take you one extra email, but in my opinion, it's a good strategy. You don't want a webmaster tweeting that ABC client just approached them to buy links. Once I feel like a webmaster is willing to work with me, I feel like they are in this with me.

Now let me say a few words about aliases. I personally like alias email accounts. Others think they're a bad idea, but over the years, my link builders have built almost all our links using aliases. I don't want them to use their real names due to the nature of our work. Alias accounts can also be very useful to craft with regards to the demographics for the site you're working with. To give you an example, when working on financial brands, a male alias tends to get more links whereas a female alias gets more links on a beauty brand. Like it or not, that's the way I've seen it work.

Female aliases do tend to get more responses than male ones overall for us. That can vary depending on the industry, of course, but in your case, we'd suggest using (or at least starting out with) female aliases. Depending on how well your link builders can communicate in whatever language they're writing in, you should try and use an alias that seems like it could be a real person. For example, if you are writing in English and targeting webmasters in the U.S., you might use an alias like Lori Martin or Lisa Evans. Webmasters are notoriously suspicious of names that sound "foreign" to them as it makes them think the work has been outsourced.

When buying links most clients aren't too keen on giving you a company email address. I don't blame them for it either. My link builders use a few different types of email accounts: Some use Gmail, some use an email on an alias domain, some do a mix of both. I've read that Gmail accounts look unprofessional and won't get you any links, but that has never been my experience.

When looking over a site that you wish to contact, always check their pages (especially their advertising page) to see if it looks like they list a policy stating that they do not sell text links. You are taking a big "outing" risk by contacting someone who specifically says they do not sell links. We keep a database of these sites and always check against it before contacting a site when we are doing discovery. You can easily find this information by typing "site:url.com text link" into Google. Never contact a site that says they do not sell links, and they do not wish to be contacted. If anyone responds to your outreach saying they do not sell links or do not want to be bothered, always add them to your "no contact" database.

Link Brokers

Ideally, you should avoid link brokers. However, it's the reality that there are some brokers who have multiple sites that aren't connected and are actually really good sites. In some industries, particularly finance, many good sites are now owned by a handful of brokers. We have had many, many occurrences of approaching a site for a link only to find out that the new owner is, in fact, a link broker. Should you turn that opportunity down for that reason? I'd say it depends.

You don't want to buy into some crazy network of templated sites that have spun content. You don't want to see that all these sites are connected by footer or sidebar links. You don't want to work with sites that don't look like good sites, period. You absolutely need to do your due diligence here. If the site is good and not obviously part of a spammy network, I won't usually pass up that opportunity.

Extra Safety Precautions

When we first started buying links, we set up a few alias domains to use. In many cases, ourselves included, paid links were not the only links being pursued, and we did not want to have our company name associated with the paid link process in case it somehow harmed our clients, especially the ones who were not using paid links. You may remember the outings of years ago when everyone loved to call someone out for trying to buy or sell links. Webmasters (and SEOs) seemed to delight in threatening to turn people in to the almighty Google. This practice of using alias domains was born during that era, and to be honest, it was a huge selling point as clients felt like we were doing things as safely as possible. I also liked the alias domains as they gave us alias emails that would not personally impact our employees.

In writing it down, I do think it sounds very sketchy, and if I hadn't done it firsthand, I am not sure what I'd think about it. I've likened link buying to giving out clean needles before. People are going to participate in certain activities no matter what, so why not make things as safe as possible? Paid links are not illegal, of course, and they seem to be more of an issue related to people's ethics than anything else. I understand that point of view. I just also understand what has worked for us and for our clients for over a decade.

We have had to burn an alias domain before. A very inquisitive webmaster decided to play one of our link builders and pretend that they were willing to work with us. As soon as we named the client, they got on a few forums and told everyone that X client was buying links from a certain alias domain. We had a few other ones, so we just moved to another one.

You can also set up a PayPal account to make the link payments. While I'm advising you to stay as safe as you can and protect your clients as much as possible, I'll advise you to connect this account with one of your alias domains. There are various ways of doing that, so just do it however you like.

You will also want to set up alerts (I use both Google and Talkwalker) for your alias domains and email addresses. If someone is talking about your aliases, you need to take a look.

Last but not least, I'd stay away from sitewide links like footer and blogroll links.

WHEN THE MONEY CHANGES HANDS

I have a personal limit to how much a link is worth, and that is and has been $150. That doesn't include whatever you're charging for labor, of course. I have well over ten years of experience that tells me this is 100 percent possible. There have been occasions where I might go to $175 if the link is amazing and the client agrees with me and authorizes the extra money, but those are rare. Usually we get the webmaster's PayPal information and make the payments, but some webmasters prefer to invoice us. That's the only payment method we use.

Here's how the payment negotiations tend to go:

1. We make an offer that is lower than our maximum of $150.
2. The webmaster says, "This is my most popular page, shows you their stats, and says they can't possibly go below $1,000."
3. We say, "Sorry we don't have that budget, but thanks very much for your time."
4. Webmaster either doesn't respond or responds to say that they have thought about it, and for just this one time, they can indeed accept our offer.

Always offer a lower amount than your maximum so you have wiggle room. We sometimes are able to push slow webmasters to get the links up quicker if we can add on some extra cash, so it's good to have that leverage.

Years ago we ran into issues with webmasters nofollowing or removing the links right after we'd paid them. That hasn't been a problem in a long time, but there are going to be cases where this happens. If we see a link go down, we will contact the webmaster, and nine times out of ten, it was something like a site back-up from six months ago had to be put in place for some reason, or they moved a page and didn't get all the links in. I've learned to give webmasters the benefit of the doubt as it's been years since anyone has just taken our money and run.

TIME LIMITS AND LINK RENTALS

Our goal is to have a permanent link up. However, webmasters know that they can get yearly payments, so I tell clients to expect that maybe 50 percent of them will be back in touch with us for more money. The other half seem to just forget the links and leave them up. Sometimes the sites go way downhill in a year. Sometimes they improve, but most stay the same. In a way I like the opportunity to easily remove a link if the site gets penalized, and a lot of clients seem to like the yearly ability to change the links to point to a newer page or do something different.

DISCOVERY PHASE: FINDING GOOD LINK PARTNERS

I'd say there has been a 50/50 split in all our link builders with half loving the discovery phase and half despising it. Discovery is the process of finding good sites to contact, no matter how you do that whether it's by searching the web, rummaging through a database, seeing a site on social media, or any other method you have. Sometimes you can spend an hour searching and finding nothing usable. Sometimes you hit upon a great search query, and within an hour, you have 20 sites to contact. From my experience, finding those good sites is only getting harder.

There are many useful advanced search operators available, but there is also a danger in tightening up a query to the extent that almost nothing is returned. Many operators can be combined. I'll go over a few quick and easy ones that I've personally found useful, but the best references are found on the web by searching for advanced search operators.

1. Allinanchor: This operator returns only pages where the anchor text of the links to the pages on a site contain the words specified.
2. Allintext: This returns only pages containing the query words used somewhere in the text of those pages.
3. -: This excludes terms from the results. It can be nicely used with other operators.
4. *: This is a wild card which can be used to perform searches using many different variables.

Below are a few sample queries to get you started:

- allinanchor:kids money
- allintext:teaching kids about finance
- educate children about saving money -inurl:bank
- teaching * about saving money

DUE DILIGENCE

To me, it's much more valuable to spend a lot of upfront time researching your target sites. When we first started our company, we let the link builders do things in two ways:

1. *Cast a wide net.* Email everyone, and if you get a response, then look over the site and do your due diligence.
2. *Home in on one at a time.* Do your due diligence up front so if you get a response, you're ready to roll.

Both methods have their downsides. If you get a response from someone whose site you have not checked out and that site turns out to be a poor choice, you have wasted time and potentially irritated a webmaster. If you do all your checking up front, you might spend days finding your target sites and emailing them only to get zero responses.

The main thing we ask ourselves when evaluating a site is whether we'd trust it *and* click on whatever particular link we want to place. Can our link flow with the content? Does it make sense to the user? I'll tell you that I can most likely find a way to work a client's link into just about any content. That doesn't mean that I should, though. This is a difficult concept for some of our link builders, even today, and even with ones that have been doing this for years. Link building is such time-consuming work that when a webmaster is willing to work with you, sometimes you are desperate enough to try and shoehorn a link. With clients pressuring you, and potentially your employer pressuring you as well, it's important to remember that you really only want the good links.

In terms of metrics, I have to say that I'm not a big fan of them in general. I think that people rely too much on them. There are various sources, too, as it seems everyone has their favorite. They are obviously very helpful in many ways, especially to help narrow down potentially harmful links if you're analyzing a backlink profile. My problem is that for many people, and especially SEOs (no offense, folks), metrics trumps relevance. As we're buying links for clients and they're the ones at risk, I do abide by their guidelines on metrics, of course.

I can summarize what most clients want us to look at. They want a domain authority of at least 30 if they use Moz. They want their traffic to be from the targeted geographical area using Alexa. They want to see traffic increasing or being steady without major drops on SEMrush. Some use Majestic metrics. Some use only Ahrefs. Almost all of them pay quite a lot of attention to numbers.

OUTREACH

Outreach starts out fun and then you quickly realize that it becomes more and more difficult to have someone actually open and read your emails, let alone respond to them. Some people like a longish personalized email that shows you've really thought about the decision to contact the webmaster. Some people like a quick and dirty email that's straight to the point. I err on the side of brevity with my outreach.

When you're buying links, you certainly do not want to name your client in the initial email. If a client is trusting you to buy links for them, you need to do everything possible to keep them safe, and naming them outright, before you've gotten an interested reply, is inexcusable. You can mention the industry, of course—that's how we do it.

You're also fully intending to buy links, so go ahead and say it. If the webmaster sells links, then they'll let you know, and if they don't, they will usually let you know even quicker.

Some link buyers will say, "We want to buy a link," but many will use all sorts of other wording, such as:

- "We're fine with paying you for your time."
- "We can offer you a fee for your services."

No matter how you phrase it, if someone's willing to work with you, then they most likely know what you mean.

Here's a sample outreach email:

> Hi John!
>
> I am curious as to whether or not you would be interested in updating an old article on your site. My client is in the home design sector, and we could offer you a fee for your time. Let me know if we can work together!
>
> If you do not want to be contacted again, please let me know so I can add you to the noncontact database.
>
> Angie Nelson

Here's the neat thing about this type of link outreach: People who are willing to sell you a link usually do not care what email address you're using. You can use Gmail, you can use an alias domain, whatever. As I mentioned earlier, I do not think it's wise to buy links using a company email address as it's not been necessary from our experience.

Just remember to always include that opt-out line, and make sure you abide by it.

NEGOTIATION

This is the fun part. Much of the time this process is straightforward and fast. Webmaster says "Yes, I'll do that and send me the details." You send details. Webmaster notifies you that the link is live, and you pay them. Very easy.

However, some webmasters aren't that easy, and I respect them for it. I would encourage you to do the same. They are the experts on their audience after all. If they say "I don't think that would work for my audience," then by all means ask them what would work. In fact, if you want the most natural links possible, ask them to write the content and work your link in. I like to have it ready to go and supply them with it because it's easy, but if a webmaster wants to write out the placement, I'm usually in love.

You also will probably get webmasters asking questions like "Will this hurt my site? Is this illegal?" These are all questions we still get fairly often. I don't ever lie about this. Selling links could hurt you, so say it could. Always let them make that call.

Price haggling is the most common negotiation we encounter, so here is some advice: Tell them what your budget is and if they come back with an outrageous amount, simply repeat that it's out of your control and thank them for their time. Many, many times they'll agree to what you offer. I've had webmasters say $2,500 is the fee, so I've said sorry, I can only give you $100, and they will come back and say they will accept $100. If you have a maximum cost you can pay, never start negotiating at that amount. Always start low.

FOLLOW UP

The goal is to follow up until you're told to stop. Yes, it's annoying when it happens to you. However, we get a large amount of links by following up. If you follow up ten times and get no response, I'd assume it's not going to happen though.

Just last week I sent 30 emails for a project. Within 24 hours, I had five replies. Within 48 hours, I had ten replies. I followed up with the 20 who had not replied. Within 24 hours, I had five more replies. After waiting a few days, I followed up with the outstanding ones, and got five more replies. That means I sent 30 emails, and 20 webmasters responded just from two follow-up rounds.

It can be as simple as going into your sent items and resending with one line saying, "I just wanted to check with you to see if you had time to consider my offer." It can be as complex as writing another email to that same webmaster. I like to be as efficient as possible, but sometimes you may have an idea of how to get a response, so whatever works for you is the best way to do it.

CHECKING THE CODE

If there is one mistake that my team continues to make, it's not checking the code. It's so easy to just click the link and see that it's there and it goes to the right page, but you need to look at the link code to make sure it's done as you asked. You can use tools to highlight nofollowed links, but I don't trust tools. I trust code.

MONITORING THE LINKS

In my view, it's critical to monitor your paid links as, of course, you've paid for them! While I don't see it happen as often as I once did, some webmasters will remove or alter the link before the agreed-upon termination date. Many times it's for innocent reasons though, such as moving to a new site structure or removing a page where that link was. Sometimes the link will become nofollowed. From my experience, if you contact the webmaster, it's generally something that's easy to work out.

In the next chapter, we will continue to learn link-building lessons from a few of our highly esteemed peers.

Chapter 23

Link-Building Lessons from Our Peers

Now, for some field experience from six professionals using the link-building tools and methods discussed earlier. All these experts have worked in the link-building world for a long time, and their insight is valuable to anyone taking on link-building tasks, whether your company is large or small.

UNDERSTANDING ORPHANS AND SILOS

by Shari Thurow, Founder and SEO Director of
Omni Marketing Interactive (https://www.search-usability.com)

Suppose your website contains many content assets. The site has a blog with plenty of tips, guides, and best practices. The support section of the site has great sets of useful FAQs. The site might have an image gallery and/or a video library. The site even has a glossary of commonly used terms in your industry.

All your content assets have clear labels (titles, headings, subheadings, etc.) Both browsers and web search engines have easy access to content via a clear, consistent URL structure (web address). Social media icons are used judiciously so that it is easy to share content via your target audience's favorite social media sites.

In other words, you have prepared your website's link-worthy content to share on social media outlets, and you are ready to begin link outreach to your content assets.

However, you should review two specific items *before* you begin link outreach and social media distribution: orphans and silos. If you skip this extra step, then incoming links and social citations will not have the strongest impact on your site.

On a website, content assets should not be orphaned or siloed. A content orphan (or near orphan) is content that is only accessible via a small number of links. In addition, orphaned content usually does not link out to related, relevant content.

One example of orphaned content is a pop-up window. In Figure 23–1 glossary definitions are only available in individual pop-up windows:

This glossary format creates multiple content orphans. Furthermore, individual definitions are difficult to share. If a link to this definition were shared, for example, all users would see is the content in the pop-up window. They would not see global site navigation and contextual links to related content. In other words, this is not a good format for glossary content or any type of content asset.

Glossary content should be organized in one of the following ways:

- One full page (if your glossary has a small number of terms and definitions)
- Page per letter
- Page per definition (if your glossary has a very large number of terms and definitions)

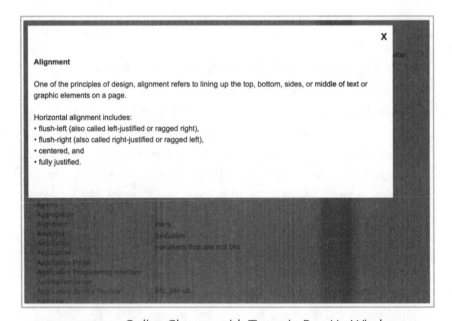

FIGURE 23–1. Online Glossary with Terms in Pop-Up Windows

When a glossary page or glossary pages are organized and formatted in this manner, the content orphans are eliminated. Linking to related terms within the glossary will also help eliminate orphans in a page-per-letter or a page-per-definition glossary.

Furthermore, items in the glossary can link to other relevant content within the site. For example, the glossary might contain a term with a concise, accurate definition. That definition might link to a blog article that contains more details about that term.

Linking related content assets will also eliminate another item that impedes findability: silos. What exactly is a silo? On a website, a silo is a repository of content that remains under one specific category and is isolated from the rest of the website. A real-world analogy is a kernel of corn located in a farm silo. The kernels of corn are protected and isolated from outside elements.

One common mistake with link development is siloing content assets, such as a blog or the FAQ section of a website. For example, if the only way to reach blog content is through the blog category page, then the blog content is siloed. If the website contains an additional link from the wayfinder site map to the blog content, the blog content is still mostly siloed. Even if links to blog content are put in an XML sitemap, the blog content is still mostly siloed. For an example of a blog post silo, see Figure 23-2.

Even if blog posts link to each other via various means (most popular, most recent, etc.), the content is still siloed. Reason? The blog content still falls under one main category: blog.

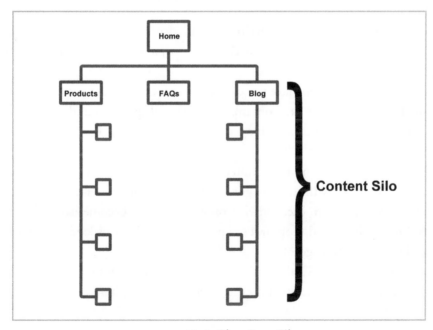

FIGURE 23-2. Blog Post Silo

Users expect a website to be categorized. Categorization in and of itself does not make content more difficult to find. In fact, according to the *Merriam-Webster* dictionary, a category is a division within a classification system. It is a category, a class, or a division of things regarded as having particular shared characteristics, such as sets of FAQs.

Problems arise when the content within a category or subcategory is isolated from other parts of the website. Another way to think of a silo (on a website) is an isolated pocket of content. Remember, categorization is not a link-building problem. Siloing is a link-building problem. The easiest way to unsilo content assets is to link relevant, contextual content to each other in multiple categories.

To unsilo blog articles, make sure the blog articles contain: a) sibling-sibling links, where related blog posts link to each other, and b) cousin-cousin links, where specific blog articles link to content in other categories, such as a product page or another content asset, such as a relevant FAQs page.

For example, suppose you have an ecommerce site with multiple products, like IKEA. Anyone who has shopped at IKEA knows that a lot of IKEA's furniture must be assembled. Maybe a buyer lost the instructions on how to assemble a piece of furniture. Or the assembly instructions in the box are in a language that the buyer does not understand. A blog writer could write an article with tips on how to assemble a specific piece of furniture, which would be very helpful for users. The blog author might provide direct links to each manual written in a different language. Furthermore, the blog writer should also link to the furniture's product page within the blog article. Likewise, the product page should link to the blog post that provides those tips.

Even better? Maybe users have frequent questions about that specific piece of IKEA furniture. If an ecommerce site contains a set helpful question and answers about a specific product, the product page, blog article, and the specific FAQs pages can all link to each other.

What ends up happening is a curated, contextual type of navigation evolves. Not only do related pages within a category link to each other, related content within different categories link to each other. Content does not become isolated under one category. The result? Silos disappear. For an example of what unsiloed blog articles look like, see Figure 23–3, on page 247.

So, whenever you create link-worthy content, make sure your content assets are easy to find. Remember to not isolate link-worthy content via orphans and silos.

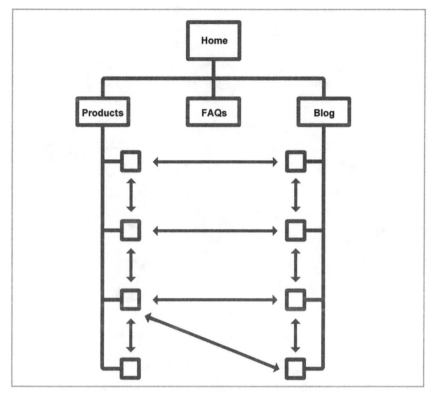

FIGURE 23–3. Unsiloed Blog Articles

INFOGRAPHICS, LINKS, AND LINKBAIT

by Bruce Clay, Founder of Bruce Clay Inc. (BCI, www.bruceclay.com) and Creator of the Award-Winning SEOToolSet® and its Acclaimed SEO Training Course

Back in the late 1990s, when we were all fighting to understand how to get websites indexed by the search engines, it became obvious that a map was needed. And as there were no maps that helped us with this, we decided to develop our own data-mapping diagram as seen in Figure 23–4, on page 248.

The first Search Engine Relationship Chart (SERC) took weeks to research and assemble. Once we had the data, it was a matter of deciding to publish our SERC. As the first industry infographic, we published it as a PDF. We posted information in the major email newsletters of the time, complete with the download link, and within no time, the PDF was downloaded more than 300,000 times. We were happy to have our chart on the wall of colleagues nationwide, and especially our brand. This was singularly the most

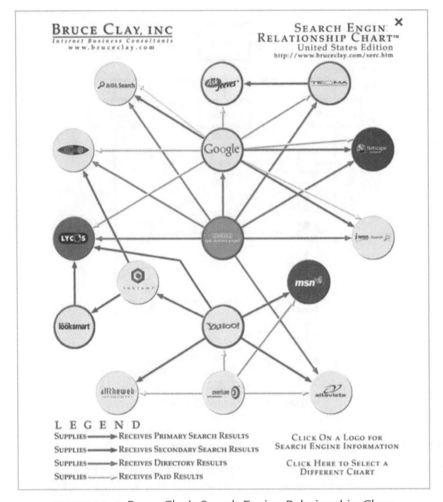

FIGURE 23–4. Bruce Clay's Search Engine Relationship Chart

successful branding and visibility program we have ever done. Now, with more than a score of follow-on versions, we are finding the attraction of the chart waning, but for 18 years, we certainly had a great run. The SERC was a landmark of every SEO office, and we are proud to have been the firm that developed and provided it for all these years.

DETECTING LINK MANIPULATION AND SPAM WITH DOMAIN AUTHORITY

by Russ Jones, Principal Search Scientist at Moz (https://moz.com)

Several years ago, while still an employee at Virante Inc. (now Hive Digital), I wrote a post on Moz outlining some simple methods for detecting backlink manipulation by comparing one's backlink profile to an ideal model based on Wikipedia. At the time, I was limited in the research I could perform because I was a consumer of the API, lacking access to deeper metrics, measurements, and methodologies to identify anomalies in backlink profiles. We used these techniques in spotting backlink manipulation with tools available online, but they were always handicapped by the limitations of consumer facing APIs. Moreover, they didn't scale. It is one thing to collect all the backlinks for a site, even a large site, and judge every individual link for source type, quality, anchor text, etc. Reports like these can be accessed from dozens of vendors if you are willing to wait a few hours for the report to complete. But how do you do this for 30 trillion links every single day?

Since the launch of Link Explorer and my residency here at Moz, I have had the luxury of far less filtered data, giving me a far deeper, clearer picture of the tools available to backlink index maintainers to identify and counter manipulation. While I in no way intend to say that all manipulation can be detected, I want to outline just some of the myriad surprising methodologies to detect spam.

The General Methodology

You don't need to be a data scientist or a math nerd to understand this simple practice for identifying link spam. While there certainly is a great deal of math used in the execution of measuring, testing, and building practical models, the general gist is plainly understandable.

The first step is to get a good random sample of links from the web, which you can read about here. But let's assume you have already finished that step. Then, for any property of those random links (domain authority, anchor text, etc.), you figure out what is normal or expected. Finally, you look for outliers and see if those correspond with something important, like sites that are manipulating the link graph or sites that are exceptionally good. Let's start with an easy example: link decay.

Link Decay and Link Spam

Link decay is the natural occurrence of links either dropping off the web or changing URLs. For example, if you get links after you send out a press release, you would expect some of those links to eventually disappear as the pages are archived or removed for being old. And if you were to get a link from a blog post, you might expect to have a homepage link on the blog until that post is pushed to the second or third page by new posts.

But what if you bought your links? What if you own a large number of domains and all the sites link to each other? What if you use a Private Blog Network? These links tend not to decay. Exercising control over your inbound links often means that you keep them from ever decaying. Thus, we can create a simple hypothesis: The link decay rate of sites manipulating the link graph will differ from sites with natural link profiles.

The methodology for testing this hypothesis is just as we discussed before. We first figure out what is natural. What does a random site's link decay rate look like? Well, we simply get a bunch of sites and record how fast links are deleted (we visit a page and see a link is gone) vs. their total number of links. We then can look for anomalies.

In this case of anomaly hunting, I'm going to make it really easy. No statistics, no math, just a quick look at what pops up when we first sort by lowest decay rate and then sort by highest domain authority to see who is at the tail-end of the spectrum. For an example of this, see Figure 23–5.

	A	B	C	D
1	URL	Links	Deleted Ratio	DA
2	http://ycpjkg.bngkb.eu/dokumenty-neobxodimye-dlya-c	9.254452947	0	63
3	http://007jiumei.lmpy.info/view-86.html	8.878079256	0	60
4	http://www.472sihu.com/nlpq/78440/index.html	8.473241304	0	56
5	http://whatupwally.com/ghyz/41930/index.html	8.473032296	0	56
6	http://www.dyjdljz.com/wnh/51735/index.html	8.470939807	0	56
7	http://fakd.net/ctn/80621/index.html	8.470730317	0	56
8	http://njlxjc.com/znq/26166/index.html	8.470101584	0	56
9	http://www.baibai4.com/lppj/49678/index.html	8.469682209	0	56
10	http://zzbuxiugang.com/qcf/33595/index.html	8.469052816	0	56
11	http://www.fangshuike.com/gzdg/78796/index.html	8.46884293	0	56
12	http://www.av78.net/ry/65820/index.html	8.468633001	0	56
13	http://cddajing.com/fkx/82313/index.html	8.468423027	0	56
14	http://www.941875.com/mn/11319/index.html	8.468423027	0	56
15	http://www.693301.com/rl/76116/index.html	8.468423027	0	56
16	http://www.arepdf.com/jl/09024/index.html	8.468423027	0	56
17	http://www.106627.com/ksxd/25819/index.html	8.468002947	0	56
18	http://www.hweibo.com/mhx/33100/index.html	8.468002947	0	56

FIGURE 23–5. Low Decay Rate, High Domain Authority

Success! Every example we see of a good domain authority (DA) score but zero link decay appears to be powered by a link network of some sort. This is the aha! moment of data science that is so fun. What is particularly interesting is we find spam on both ends of the distribution—that is to say, sites that have zero decay or near 100 percent decay rates both tend to be spammy. The first type tends to be part of a link network; the second part tends to spam their backlinks to sites others are spamming, so their links quickly shuffle off to other pages.

Of course, now we do the hard work of building a model that takes this into account and accurately reduces DA relative to the severity of the link spam. But you might be asking "These sites don't rank in Google, so why do they have decent DAs in the first place?"

Well, this is a common problem with training sets. DA is trained on sites that rank in Google so we can figure out who will rank above who. However, historically, we haven't (and no one to my knowledge in our industry has) taken into account random URLs that don't rank at all. This is something we solved for in the new DA model we launched in early March 2019, which represented a major improvement on the way we calculate DA.

Spam Score Distribution and Link Spam

One of the most exciting new additions to the upcoming Domain Authority 2.0 is the use of our Spam Score. Moz's Spam Score is a link-blind (we don't use links at all) metric that predicts the likelihood a domain will be indexed in Google. The higher the score, the worse the site.

Now, we could just ignore any links from sites with Spam Scores over 70 and call it a day, but it turns out there are fascinating patterns left behind by common link manipulation schemes waiting to be discovered by using this simple methodology of using a random sample of URLs to find out what a normal backlink profile looks like, and then see if there are anomalies in the way Spam Score is distributed among the backlinks to a site. Let me show you just one.

It turns out that acting natural is really hard to do. Even the best attempts often fall short, as did this particularly pernicious link spam network. This network had haunted me for two years because it included a directory of the top million sites, so if you were one of those sites, you could see anywhere from 200 to 600 followed links show up in your backlink profile. I called it The Globe network. It was easy to look at the network and see what they were doing, but could we spot it automatically so we could devalue other networks like it in the future? When we looked at the link profile of sites included in the network, the Spam Score distribution lit up like a Christmas tree (see Figure 23-6 to see the results).

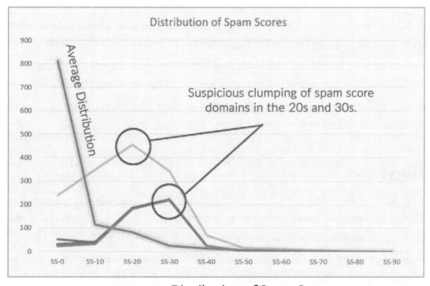

FIGURE 23–6. Distribution of Spam Scores

Most sites get the majority of their backlinks from low Spam Score domains and get fewer and fewer as the Spam Score of the domains go up. But this link network couldn't hide because we were able to detect the sites in their network as having quality issues using Spam Score. If we relied only on ignoring the bad Spam Score links, we would have never discovered this issue. Instead, we found a great classifier for finding sites that are likely to be penalized by Google for bad link-building practices.

DA Distribution and Link Spam

We can find similar patterns among sites with the distribution of inbound DA. It's common for businesses seeking to increase their rankings to set minimum quality standards on their outreach campaigns, often DA30 and above. An unfortunate outcome of this is that what remains are glaring examples of sites with manipulated link profiles.

Let me take a moment and be clear here. A manipulated link profile is not necessarily against Google's guidelines. If you do targeted PR outreach, it is reasonable to expect that such a distribution might occur without any attempt to manipulate the graph. However, the real question is whether Google wants sites that perform such outreach to perform better. If not, this glaring example of link manipulation is easy for Google to dampen, if not ignore altogether. View Figure 23–7, on page 253, to see examples of sites manipulating link graph.

A normal link graph for a site that is not targeting high link equity domains will have the majority of their links coming from DA0–10 sites, slightly fewer for DA10–20, and so on and so forth until there are almost no links from DA90+. This makes sense, as the web has far more low DA sites than high. But all the sites above have abnormal link distributions, which make it easy to detect and correct—at scale—link value.

Now, I want to be clear: These are not necessarily examples of violating Google's guidelines. However, they are manipulations of the link graph. It's up to you to determine whether you believe Google takes the time to differentiate between how the outreach was conducted that resulted in the abnormal link distribution.

What Doesn't Work

For every type of link manipulation detection method we discover, we scrap dozens more. Some of these are quite surprising. Let me write about just one of the many.

The first surprising example was the ratio of nofollow to follow links as seen in Figure 23–8, on page 254. It seems straightforward that comment, forum, and other types of spammers would end up accumulating lots of nofollowed links, thereby leaving a pattern that is easy to discern. Well, it turns out this is not true at all.

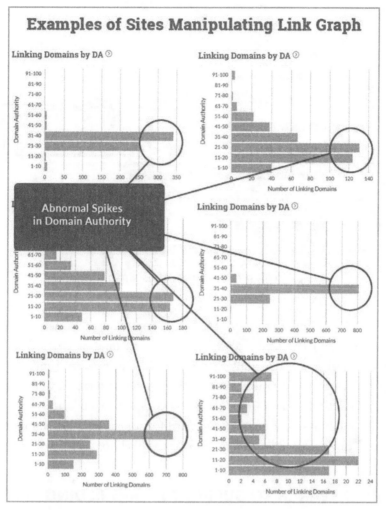

FIGURE 23–7. Examples of Sites Manipulating Link Graph

The ratio of nofollow to follow links turns out to be a poor indicator, as popular sites like Facebook often have a higher ratio than even pure comment spammers. This is likely due to the use of widgets and beacons, and the legitimate usage of popular sites like Facebook in comments across the web. Of course, this isn't always the case. There are some sites with 100 percent nofollow links and a high number of root-linking domains. These anomalies, like "Comment Spammer 1," can be detected quite easily, but as a general measurement the ratio does not serve as a good classifier for "spam or ham."

So What's Next?

Moz is continually traversing the link graph looking for ways to improve DA using everything from basic linear algebra to complex neural networks. The goal in mind

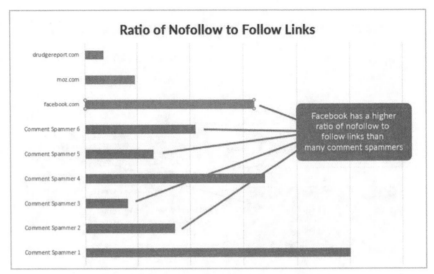

FIGURE 23–8. Ratio of Nofollow to Follow Links

is simple: We want to make the best DA metric ever. We want a metric that users can trust in the long run to root out spam just like Google (and help you determine when you or your competitors are pushing the limits) while at the same time maintaining or improving correlations with rankings. Of course, we have no expectation of rooting out all spam—no one can do that. But we can do a better job. Led by the incomparable Neil Martinsen-Burrell, the senior data scientist at Moz, our metric will stand alone in the industry as the canonical method for measuring the likelihood a site will rank in Google.

USING PAID SEARCH TO SUPPORT LINK-BUILDING EFFORTS

by Christine Churchill, President of Key Relevance (www.keyrelevance.com) and Search Engine Marketing Expert

Paid search can be used in a variety of ways to support link building. Here are some ideas to help you identify keywords and possible link partners using paid advertising.

Using Paid Search for Keyword Research

Pay-per-click advertising has long been a favorite way for search marketers to acquire real performance data on keywords. While keyword tools can provide lists of relevant keywords, the best way to really know which keywords perform best for your site is to test their performance in a paid search campaign. This requires a fair amount of effort to ensure that this is a legitimate test, in that in addition to coming up with the keywords, you would also need to develop effective ad copy and landing pages to support the test.

Paid search combined with conversion tracking gives the search marketer information on exactly which terms work best for the site. If you know certain terms are popular and—more important—convert well, you would want to target them both in your paid and organic optimization as well as your link-building efforts.

With Google now encrypting search for logged-on users, the information provided by a site's analytics data on organic queries will be limited. Webmasters looking at their analytics will no longer receive referring data on keywords used to bring users who were signed into Google when they clicked on a search results page. While Google claims that the number of users signed in is very small, many sites are reporting that their analytics are displaying "not provided" where their main keywords used to show. Because Google is encouraging users to log in, the trend to search while logged in will continue to increase, further limiting the availability of organic keyword data over time. Going forward, the best referring keyword data and keyword performance data will be from paid search.

Using Paid Search to Find Linking Partners

The best link partners are sites that are related to your site. Specifically the best link partner sites are sites that are complementary to your industry but not direct competitors. One way to identify complementary sites is to do keyword searches on terms related to your main terms and look for sites that show up in the search results that aren't competitors. For example, if you sold shoe accessories, you might want to be aware of sites selling women's shoes.

If you search on a term related to your main term, scan over the sites showing up in the paid listings. Often you see the big brands showing up in the organic top results and the top paid results, but if you look below the fold, you often find sites that are off your radar. These could be sites that are viable companies related to your business but are not competitors. A quick review of these sites would tell you if they sell complementary products but are not competition. If they are not competitors, these sites could be potential business and link partners.

Serious businesses are more likely to be found by analyzing the paid search advertisers because they have the resources to be paying to bring clients to their sites. As such, these will make better potential linking partners.

Look for Ads on Content Sites to Discover Link Partners

Here's another tip to help you find potential link partners. In this case, you aren't spending money on paid search, but rather looking for content sites that use Google AdSense or another paid search advertising network. AdSense is Google's program for publishers. Google allows them to put some code on pages of their site, which Google then uses to place relevant ads on the page. Publishers are paid by Google for the clickthroughs the ads receive.

Many content publishers' sites rank well for terms related to your business keywords. If you review the search results pages for content sites related to your business, you might find sites that are financed by AdSense ads. Webmasters of these sites have monetized their site and may be more open to developing a business relationship with your site.

Business deals can take a variety of shapes. If you have an affiliate program, they may want to become an affiliate. They may allow you to sponsor a section of their site, or they may even agree to place your ad on their site. Don't worry that the ad may be a nofollow link. It may be that this site turns out to be a great traffic site or a great converting site for you. If that is the case, the link is valuable to you whether it is a follow or not.

Other business relationship options might be offering them a guest blogging post, an interview, or a review of one of your products. Again, don't get wrapped around the nofollow issue. Links are part of a business relationship. Some of the best links you'll ever get from a business perspective will be nofollow links from a related site.

DIRECTORY LINKS: ARE THEY WORTH IT?

by Debra Mastaler, President of Alliance-Link.com and Keytooles.com
Link Building and Content Strategy Consultant and Coach

Ask ten link builders if directory links are worth the time and effort to secure, and you'll get ten different answers. I think they are and that they can be a viable part of your linking mix—provided you consider a number of key elements when using them.

If you've spent any time in the SEO industry, you know there are hundreds, if not thousands, of small directories online; most of these sites lack editorial guidelines and were created to host AdSense and network links. I think it's important to draw a distinction between these sites and the responsible, well-run directories that I, and most link builders I know, use.

What Is a Directory?

In short, a directory is a collection of websites categorized by subject and/or geographic location. Human reviewers determine what source will be added and maintain the directory and its structure. You're probably familiar with the following three directories. All have been online for a long time and have strong editorial guidelines:

- The World Wide Web Virtual Library or VLIB (1991)
- The Yahoo! Directory (1994)
- Best of the Web (1994)

Each employs human reviewers to look at the sites submitted and determine which category they should be placed in. This process of being scrutinized to determine acceptance is known as editorial review. It is why these and other directories are respected algorithmically by the search engines.

Is This a Good Directory?

If you come across a directory and want to add your site, ask yourself the following questions before handing over your submission fee:

- Does the directory have minimal to no AdSense on category pages? AdSense ads detract from your listing; I shy away from a directory that hosts ads on my category page.
- Does the directory support sitewide links? Directories created to support manipulative linking go against the search engine terms of service; I'd stay away from them.
- Does the directory have full contact information available or an About Us page? Look for a directory owned by a reputable company, one that will answer your questions and be available if you need help.
- Is your category page in the Google and Bing index, and are the pages of your category cached frequently? If the page your link will be added to is not in the search index, you'll see no benefit.

Directory Submission Tactics as a Business Model

If you owned a business on Main Street and wanted to promote it to the community, it's doubtful you'd use just one advertising method to get your message across. You'd probably begin with the basic, less expensive options, such as buying ads in the Yellow Pages, your local newspaper, and Valpak mailers. Eventually you'd move up and buy radio, TV, and sponsorship opportunities, which will help make you a dominant presence in your community.

This scattershot approach to building a credible reputation can be done online as well. I advocate using directory links in the first wave of linking as a way to jump-start your linking program. Granted, they're not algorithmic giants, but directory links will pass link popularity and add to your overall backlink profile.

FIVE TOP LINK-BUILDING TIPS
by Rand Fishkin, Founder of SparkToro (https://sparktoro.com) and Author

The following are specific tactics, all designed to generate high-quality inbound links (often accompanied by social media shares) that can potentially send traffic, increase search engine value, and are entirely white hat.

1. Build a "Top X Blogs/Sites/People" in Your Industry

Curating a list of great sites and/or people always gets attention from audiences seeking to learn more about the field. It also frequently earns tremendous links because those listed share their position (notoriety) or via temporal media like Twitter or Facebook, as well as in their bios or About pages (which often make their way to third-party sites too). The bigger and more respectable your brand grows, the more links and attention these lists can attract.

2. Create Content That Adds Value to Prominent Conversations

The web world is filled with content taking sides on virtually every issue in almost any topical arena. Participating in these "conversations" by adding an intelligent voice with valuable research, a well-thought-out opinion, and quality writing will often earn you a place in the debate, which yields links and social shares. Over time, if you stick to participating honestly and appropriately, you'll earn a following of your own and a place in the online media world around your topic. Just be careful not to get too caustic or emotional—the internet's discussions can get rough and not everyone plays nicely (which is another reason measured responses and clear heads can earn links from positive participation).

3. Collect and Publish Unique Information in a Link-Friendly Format (and Prime the Pump Beforehand)

Aggregated information is tough to come by, but it is often incredibly valuable and link-worthy. The problem is that someone needs to do the legwork to assemble the aggregated material—that's where you come in. Whether it's the opinions of major bloggers in a field, the statistics from visitor data, the various perspectives on how an event occurred, or polling data from a hard-to-find set of companies/professionals/individuals, your marketing acumen plus some sweat equity can bring in the numbers. Once you have the information, building a link-worthy collection of graphs, charts, presentations, video, or even bullet points in a well-executed article can result in terrific returns in links and social shares. You can earn additional value by leveraging those who contribute their data/responses to help spread the word—and most will, given the nudge—both while providing their information (often in a web survey) and after in a personal email.

4. Offer an Embeddable Tool/Widget with Unique Functionality

Flickr, Vimeo, Statcounter, AddThis, and SlideShare are all among the most linked-to sites on the web, thanks to their popular embeddable widgets. Twitter, LinkedIn, Etsy, and Facebook all do likewise, employing snippets of code that can be placed on any web page and display information or provide functionality that a site owner couldn't provide on their own. And any site can build an embeddable widget—the key is to find something that other sites will have an incentive to share, build the widget such that links point back to the relevant pages, and spread the word (often through internal product usage). Embeddable content is a great way to not only earn links, but control what they say as they're linking back.

5. Use Research Data in Commercial Content (and Inform the Researchers)

The web offers a wealth of research from academic, corporate, and government sources, but these are frequently buried in hard-to-navigate sites inside tough-to-follow documents. By exposing research content in a more marketable, user-friendly way (think graphics, illustrations, videos, even simple, easy-to-read blog posts), you can add tremendous value to your niche's understanding of a topic and earn great links in return. One of my favorite tactics here is to contact those responsible for the research, let them know of your plans to use it, and invite them to help share the work. Many universities and research sites are thrilled to see others using their data and will happily link to it once live.

FILTHY LINKING RICH AND GETTING RICHER!

by Mike Grehan, Chief Marketing Officer and Managing Director at Acronym (https://www.acronym.com)

As a kid, I once asked my father, "How do you become a multimillionaire?" He looked at me and said, "Easy! First you make a million . . ." and then he had a good laugh.

Come the latter part of the '60s, my father was a very wealthy man. As a serial entrepreneur, his interests in show business had netted him a fortune. He had opened his first nightclub in 1962, which was home to a local group called The Animals, whom he helped on their way to international stardom (the bass player of the band and his former business partner would go on to manage Jimi Hendrix).

He drove a Jensen Interceptor (very cool car at the time), wore the most "fab gear" (Beatle-speak for hip clothes), and hung around Las Vegas with his pals quite a lot (a little too much for my mother's liking, unfortunately!). He was at the peak of his career and a major influencer within his social group. Not bad for a guy who had to catapult himself from his early beginnings as a typewriter salesman.

It was some time later in life when my father and I were talking about wealth creation that he used the expression "the rich get richer." I'll come back to my dear departed Dad again, but stay with me right now, as this is going somewhere. And I'm afraid some of it may be pretty bleak reading if you have newly created, lowly indexed web pages, and you're desperately waiting for someone to link to them so that they stand a chance of ranking in a search engine with a static link-based algorithm.

I have to tell you, for the past few months, I've been absorbed in an entirely new world of research. Network science can be regarded as a branch of complexity theory. Complexity itself describes any number of different sciences, theories, and world views such as chaos theory, emergence, and network science. And it's fascinating. In fact, I'll go so far as to say, enthralling.

By trying to further increase my understanding of the real power of linkage data in search engine algorithms, I've become even more aware of how "the rich get richer" power law affects search engine results and the ecology of the web itself. The richer you are with links pointing back to your site, the richer you are likely to become in search marketing terms.

Are search engines giving a fair representation of what's available on the web? Not really. If pages were judged on the quality and the relevance for ranking, then there would be less search engine bias toward pages that are simply popular by "linkage voting." Unfortunately, quality is subjective, so finding a universally acceptable measurement or metric is not going to be easy.

If you're involved in the search marketing industry, particularly on the link-building side, then you'll know better than most that getting links for a large and more visible website is easier than getting links for a startup or a mom-and-pop-type outfit.

Now you may feel that you're about to read something obvious and decide to skip the rest here. But please stay with me a little longer.

I believe you may be very interested to know that the scale of the problem is rapidly getting greater with the bias of a static-based "link popularity" algorithm such as PageRank—largely the cause of the problem.

"Now wait a minute, Grehan," I hear you say. "Aren't you the biggest skeptic about PageRank and its role in Google search results?" And the answer is, "You bet I am." However, what I want to do with this feature article is to highlight how great the bias is for high-ranking pages, which are fundamentally ordered on link-based algorithms to attract more links. I believe (along with many in the research community) it's becoming necessary for search engines to seek a new paradigm. I think it is of benefit to the search marketing community to understand the implications of such concerns by search engines to move away from current methodology, as it will certainly have its impact on our industry.

When speaking on the subject of linking at conferences, seminars, and workshops, I always attempt to explain the different manner in which search engine marketers look at links on the web compared to the way search engines view the same data. Search engine marketers are concerned, basically, with a hyperlink from another page back to theirs. And generally speaking, the more the merrier!

However, search engines take a much more mathematical, philosophical, and analytical impression of the entire web (or more to the point, the fraction of it that they have captured). To search engines, web pages that are linked together are nodes in the web graph. By applying random graph theory to the web, they have viewed it as a type of static, equilibrium network with a classic, Poisson-type distribution of connections.

Even though graph theory has made great progress and been an important factor in the way that search engines have been able to plot crawling of the web and ranking of documents, we now know that the most important natural and artificial networks have a specific architecture based on a fat-tailed distribution of the number of connections of vertices that differs crucially from the classical random graphs studied by mathematicians. Because, as a rule, these networks are not static, but evolving objects.

It hasn't been long since physicists have started extensive empirical and theoretical research into networks that are organized this way. The main focus prior to this research was in neural and Boolean networks, where the arrangements of connections was secondary.

So now I hear you say, "Hey, Mike . . . Whoa! Stick with search engines and optimization and such. I'm a search engine marketer, not a physicist! Random graph theory, equilibrium network with a classic Poisson-type distribution, fat-tailed distribution, neural networks . . . I'm brain zonked already, and this is only the second page of your article."

Yup, I understand that. I've scrambled my own brain a few times recently. But it's important that you do know a little more about what's really going on in the research field so that I can provide a better analysis of what currently makes one web page more important than another and how that is likely to change.

Your business may depend greatly on being able to optimize for search engines. And that's only going to become harder and harder.

I'll tell you what I'll do, I'll back up a bit here and try and do a brief history of what I've been kind of "glossing over."

Let's have a slightly (and I do mean slightly) more in-depth look at network science and how it is mathematically, philosophically, and otherwise applied to search. As Russian physicist and genius Sergei Dorogovstev put it in his excellent text, *Evolution of Networks*, I feel it's "more important to be understood than to be perfectly rigorous." Although I have tried to eliminate the math as best as I can and stick to the principles, there are bound to be sections that reference formula. Therefore, brave reader, as I frequently do myself, don't be afraid to skim over some parts you don't understand to reach those that you do. Remember: Like you, I'm a search engine marketer—not a scientist.

The history behind social network concepts and graph theory applied to ranking algorithms is something that can help you understand a lot more about their complexities and why some of your best SEO endeavors may, already, not be working.

It may seem as if the web grows in a very unorganized and haphazard way. But that's not really the case. It's beginning to show powerful underlying regularities from the way in which web pages link together, to the patterns found in the way users browse.

And it's interesting to note that these regularities have been predicted on the basis of theoretical models from a field of physics, statistical mechanics, that few would have thought would apply to the web.

Among the chaos of activity and information on the web, scientists have analyzed data that has been collected by the internet archive and other sources, which has helped to uncover hidden patterns that hold many clues to what's really happening in cyberspace.

These patterns are being discovered all the more by the many researchers worldwide who are intrigued by the new science of networks. And the discoveries they make are both surprising and very, very interesting.

What is of most interest to us in our little search-marketing community is how quickly researchers have established that the distribution of pages and links per website follows a universal and lawful behavior. The simple truth of the matter is, few sites have enormous numbers of pages and many have few. And it follows that few sites have many links pointing to them, and many have few.

How is it that the web in its distribution follows some kind of known patterns, when there is no central planner of the web? There is no central body to suggest how it should grow and who should have links and who should not.

You need to look at the origins of network theory, which throw light on a number of social mechanisms that operate beyond the World Wide Web. These theories help to explain why the web has become a huge informational ecosystem that can be used to quantitatively measure and test theories of human behavior and social interaction.

Phrases such as "it's a small world" and "the rich get richer" and "well-connected" have worked their way into everyday vocabulary. It's interesting that such phrases have been the byproduct of a mixture of research in social network analysis, physics, mathematics, and computer science, all of which can (and do) apply to the algorithms used by the major search engines.

It's a Small World

In the 1960s, American psychologist Stanley Milgram was intrigued by the composition of the web of interpersonal connections that link people to a community. To inform himself more about this, he sent letters to a random selection of people living in Nebraska and Kansas, asking them, in turn, to forward the letters to a stockbroker in Boston. But he didn't give them the address of the stockbroker. Instead he asked them to forward the letter only to someone they knew personally and whom they thought may be "socially" closer to the stockbroker.

Most of the letters did, in fact, eventually make it to the stockbroker. But the much more startling fact was how quickly they did so. It wasn't a case of hundreds of mailings to reach the final target, but typically, just six or so. This true experiment has passed into folklore and is now famously known as "six degrees of separation," although it wasn't Milgram who named it so; that was from the 1993 play of the same name.

Popular culture played its part again when in 1997, a new game called "Six Degrees of Kevin Bacon" arrived on the scene. The game was invented by a couple of movie buffs who (for some reason of their own) had come to the conclusion that Kevin Bacon was the true center of the movie universe (it has been proved that he is actually *not* the most connected actor in Hollywood circles, but nevertheless . . .).

If you haven't heard of the game, here's how it works. The movie network consists of actors who are connected by virtue of the fact that they have acted together in one or more feature films. If you have acted in a movie with Kevin Bacon, then you have a Bacon number of one. (Bacon himself has a Bacon number of 0.) As Bacon has acted in more than 50 movies, he has acted with more than 1,150 other actors. It follows, therefore, that more than 1,150 actors have a Bacon number of one. Moving outward from Bacon, if you ever acted with an actor who had appeared with Bacon, then you have a Bacon number of two. And so on and so forth . . .

But the Kevin Bacon game is not the only one in town. It's actually based on "Erdos numbers," these being applied to the distance between mathematicians who wrote a paper with the great Paul Erdos (more detail on him in just a few paragraphs) and those who authored a paper with a person who authored a paper with Erdos, and so on and so forth. Much like the Kevin Bacon game, the smaller your "Erdos number," the higher the prestige you have within the mathematician community.

The existence of these short chains of acquaintance have been observed and documented by social network scientists for years.

Milgram's experiment with the Boston stockbroker raised a couple of interesting issues, one regarding the properties that networks must have to become small worlds. If you were to draw a network of people (nodes) and links between those nodes relating to who knows whom, it wouldn't be at all obvious that any two nodes would be separated by six links. This is because there is something peculiar about a social network that is reflected in its link structure.

The second issue concerns what the best strategies are for navigating such small-world graphs in a short number of steps. Think about the people in Milgram's experiment. They did not have detailed knowledge of the social network in which they were embedded, but they still managed to pass the messages in a fairly short number of links.

These issues have since been addressed by Duncan Watts and Steven Strogatz at Cornell University and Jon Kleinberg (in a small world way), also at Cornell. However, the conclusions and finding are vastly beyond the scope of this paper as an introduction and covered in more detail in my book.

Does the same small-world phenomenon exist between websites and web pages? A few years ago, Lada Adamic, of Palo Alto Research Center, undertook a study of the average number of links you would need to traverse to get from one site on the web to another. She discovered that, just as in the social sphere, one could pick two sites at random and get from one to the other within four clicks.

This phenomenon was again shown to exist for the number of links between any two pages on the web. Albert-Lazlo Barabasi, at Notre Dame University (more about Barabasi coming) discovered that, in the case of pages, the number is 19.

Getting Connected

Hungarian mathematician and genius Paul Erdos was the first to address the fundamental question pertaining to our understanding of an interconnected universe: How do networks form? His solutions laid the foundations of the theory of random networks. To explain: Suppose we take a collection of dots on a page and then just haphazardly wire them together—the result is what mathematicians refer to as a random graph.

OK, now imagine that you've been given the task of building roads to connect the towns of an undeveloped country. At this time, there are no roads at all, just 50 isolated towns scattered across the map. Because the construction guys are likely to misunderstand your plans and build roads linking the wrong towns and, of course, the country has so little money, you need to build as few roads as possible. The question is then: How many will be enough?

Mathematician and author Mark Buchanan, in his excellent book *Nexus*, explained it this way:

If finance wasn't a problem, then you'd simply order the construction guys to keep building until every last pair of towns were linked together. To link each of the 50 towns to all 49 others would take 1,225 roads. But what is the smallest number of roads you need to build to be reasonably sure that drivers can go between any two towns without ever leaving a road?

It's one of the most famous problems in graph theory and could be expressed in any number of ways: houses and telephone links, the power grid, etc. It's a very difficult problem to solve, and it took the considerable mind power of Erdos back in 1959.

In this particular problem, it turns out that the random placement of 98 roads is adequate to make sure that the towns are connected. Even if that seems like a lot of roads, it only represents 8 percent of the original figure of 1,225 roads.

Erdos discovered that, no matter how many points there might be, a small percentage of randomly placed links is always enough to tie the network together into a more or less completely connected whole. To put this into the internet perspective, the percentage required dwindles as the network gets bigger. For a network of 300 points, there are nearly 50,000 possible links that could run between them.

But if no more than 2 percent of these are in place, the network will be completely connected. For 1,000 points, the crucial factor is less than 1 percent. And for 10 million points, it is only 0.00000166.

So, does that mean that if people were linked more or less at random, the typical person would have to know only about 1 out of every 250 million for the entire population of the world to be linked into a social web?

The Rich Get Richer

I want to just skip forward very quickly here for a moment. By 1999, Hungarian physicist Albert-Lazlo Barabasi had become completely engrossed in network theory; in particular, its application to the web. He himself had been schooled in the Hungarian tradition of graph theory, including the Erdos model of random graphs.

His excellent work in the field has given great insight into networks as diverse as those that begin as cocktail parties right up to the growth of the national power grid. And his innovative work has shown that many networks in the real world have degree distributions that don't look anything like a Poisson distribution. Instead, they follow what is known as a power law.

Barabasi's body of work has transformed the study of links and nodes. He has discovered that all networks have a deep underlying order and operate according to simple but powerful rules.

Duncan J. Watts, one of the principal architects of network theory, has argued that the origin of the Poisson degree in a random graph—and its corresponding cutoff— lies with its most basic premise: Links between nodes come into existence entirely independently of one another.

This means that, in an egalitarian system, things average out over time. An individual node can be unlucky for a while, but eventually, it has to be on the receiving end of a new connection. And in the same way, no run of luck can go on forever, so if one node gets picked up more frequently than average for some period of time, eventually others will catch up.

But you know, real life is not that fair, unfortunately, particularly when it comes to matters of wealth and success. Let's just think about the growth of a social web, as posed earlier, from the mathematician's viewpoint.

Watts puts it this way. Imagine you have a hundred friends. And each one of those also has a hundred friends. This means that at one degree of separation you can connect to 100 people, and within two degrees, you can reach 100 times 100, which is 10,000 people. By three degrees, you are up to almost 1 million; by four, nearly a 100 million; and in five degrees, about 9 billion people. What this would mean is that if everyone in the world had 100 friends, then within six steps, you can easily connect yourself to the population of the entire planet.

But as he also points out, if you're at all socially inclined, you'll already have spotted the fatal flaw in the reasoning. A hundred friends is a lot to think about. So think about your ten best friends, then ask yourself who their ten best friends are. Chances are, you'll come up with many of the same people.

It's what's known as clustering. We tend to not have friends so much as we have groups of friends, based on shared interests, experience, and location, all of which overlap with other groups. And this is an almost universal feature, not just of social networks, but of networks in general.

It's this social network phenomenon that is the underlying cause of the rich getting richer. And this phenomenon has been with us for a long, long time. The great 20th-century sociologist Robert Merton dubbed it the "Matthew Effect" as a reference to a passage in the Bible, in which Matthew observes, "For unto everyone that hath shall be given, and he shall have abundance; but from him that hath not shall be taken away even that which he hath."

The Matthew Effect, when applied to networks, basically equates to well-connected nodes being more likely to attract new links, while poorly connected nodes are disproportionately likely to remain poor.

In fact, it has been proposed that "the rich get richer" effect drives the evolution of real networks. If one node has twice as many links as another node, then it is precisely twice as likely to receive a new link.

Let's return, for a moment, to Barabasi's introduction of power laws to bring us into a real-world example. The distribution of wealth in the U.S., for instance, resembles a power law. The 19th-century Parisian engineer Vilifredo Pareto was the first to notice this phenomenon, which subsequently became known as Pareto's Principle and demonstrated that it held true in every European country for which the relevant statistics existed.

The law shows that very many people possess very little wealth, while a very small minority are extremely wealthy. We tend to refer to Pareto's Principle more generally as the 80/20 Principle.

Perhaps the greatest discovery of the laws of network organization focuses on the idea of "hubs" and how they form. These are the centerpieces of networks, around which many links form.

Before we even apply it to the web and search, a strong case has been made by Barabasi (and subsequently by others) that the best way to combat AIDS, for instance, would be to concentrate on identifying and treating the hubs in sexual contact networks.

Information about the structure of the web is of great importance to search engines. The common observation is that one good web document tends to link to other good documents of similar content. Therefore, there will be groups of pages of similar content (and similar quality) that refer to each other. The quality of the pages is presumed to be guaranteed by the recommendations implicit in the links between them. However, as we shall discover, this is not necessarily a good metric overall for quality as many had first thought.

Lada Adamic (Xerox) tested her theories (mentioned earlier) built around an application to examine a repository of web pages crawled by Google. For any given search word, she brought back results to the queries that provided PageRank, text match, and link information for each page.

She then identified all the connected clusters and selected the largest one, as it would most likely contain links across sites other than just the common ones. What she discovered was that connected clusters spanning several sites tend to contain the main relevant pages and are rich in "hubs" (pages that contain links to many other good pages). It is then possible to find the center of the cluster by computing the number of links among all the members of the cluster.

This shows that, rather than presenting a list of documents that contain many sequential entries from the same site, a search engine, using the phenomenon of the "small world," can present just the center from each cluster. Users can then explore the rest of the cluster on their own.

Hyperlink-Based "Popularity" Algorithms

Maybe it was a small-world event in a scale-free network (pun) or simply a quirk of fate that Kleinberg, foremost computer scientist, found himself as a professor at Cornell University at just the same time as foremost physicist and sociologist Watts. Whatever it was, the information exchange between them in the study of networks has helped to transform the way that search engines relied almost solely on methods such as the vector space model that had pages "standing in isolation" to the two major hyperlink analysis algorithms: Hits and PageRank.

The application of network analysis and physics has given search engines fundamental principles to base ranking mechanisms on, among other things, clustering, interconnectivity, and popularity.

I don't need to tell you that the majority of web page accesses are referred by search engines; you already know this. Given the sheer quantity of information on the web, it's no wonder that search engines have become an indispensable tool.

An individual could never sift through the billions of pages online trying to find the ten best. So, that becomes the job of the search engine: to narrow it down to a smaller number of pages worth looking at.

This method of "topic distillation" to tackle the issue of the "abundance problem (i.e., too many relevant pages being returned for a query), with little indication as to which are the most important, or authoritative, is centered around PageRank and Hits.

These algorithms applied to the link structure of the web fundamentally suggest the higher number of quality links you have pointing back at you, the higher you should rank in the results. It's a popularity metric.

Of course, the fact that strong hubs form in networks such as the web, the utopian dream of a free and equally democratic internet that many have dreamed of, becomes somewhat nonsense. The basic ideas of how networks form and strengthen and dominate topological degrees give us an indication of what is bound to follow with a static hyperlink-based ranking algorithm.

I write a lot about hits/clever, which is a query-specific algorithm. Using this approach, hits builds a subgraph of the web that is relevant to the query, then uses link analysis to rank the pages of the subgraph. But [here] I just want to stick with PageRank, as it is this approach that causes the accelerating "rich get richer" problem that many search marketers struggle with.

PageRank is the most visible of the link-based algorithms due to its association with Google. It can be referred to more as a static ranking scheme. Using this method, all pages to be indexed are ordered once and for all in a best-to-worst rank, regardless of any query. When the query arrives, the index returns the best ten pages that satisfy the query at the top of the pile. Here, best is determined by the static ranking.

But this is also the creator of a very worrisome problem that affects new web pages with low linkage data, regardless of the quality of those pages. Quality and relevance are sometimes at odds with each other. And the ecology of the web may be suffering because of the way search engines are biased toward a page's popularity more than its quality. In short, "currently popular" pages are repeatedly being returned at the top of the results at the major search engines.

So, the "filthy linking rich" get richer and popular pages continue to hit the top spots. The law of "preferential attachment," as it is also known, wherein new links on the web are more likely to go to sites that already have many links, proves that the scheme is inherently biased against new and unknown pages.

When search engines constantly return popular pages at the top of the pile, more web users discover those pages, and more web users are likely to link to them. This, therefore, means that currently unpopular pages (as such) are not returned by search engines (regardless of quality), so they are discovered by very few web users. And this, of course, is unfortunate for both the publishers of web pages and the seekers of their information. (Not to mention web marketers!)

This has been a lengthy journey already, and we're still only scratching the surface. I want to finish by making you aware of an experiment that took place in the U.S.

First, the experiment suggested that by 2002, around 70 percent of all web searches online were being handled by Google. It also suggested that while Google considers more than 100 factors in its ranking algorithm, the core of it is based on PageRank. This is a "static" link popularity metric to represent importance or authority for ranking purposes.

It's important to understand that there is a distinction between the importance or quality of a page and the relevance of a page following a user query. The scientists suggest that the relevance is a quantity that relies heavily on the search issued by the user. But the importance or quality of a document could be computed at crawl time and could be seen as intrinsic to the document itself.

And the reason they are looking at this intrinsic quality is to find a new paradigm for ranking web pages that is not so heavily based on link popularity. The problem is that Google repeatedly returns popular pages at the top of the results and ignores newer pages that are not so densely connected. Therefore, it is inherently biased against "unknown" pages.

So, are the "rich getting richer" insofar as linkage is concerned at search engines? Yes, and it's a rapidly worsening factor. The experiment carried out covered data collected over a seven-month period. And from that experimental data, they observed that the top 20 percent of the pages with the highest number of incoming links obtained 70 percent of the new links after seven months, while the bottom 60 percent of the pages obtained virtually no incoming links at all during that period.

So, where's the good news, Mike? Well, there is a little consolation in that the "rich get richer" behavior varies in different categories. A new model has been developed that can be used to predict and analyze competition and diversity in different communities on the web.

I'll round up here where I started with my dear departed Dad. Just as he became a social bright light earning (and burning) lots of cash, so he attracted lots of new friends (links). But when the Betting and Gaming Act in the late '60s forced him to close many of his venues (something he hadn't seen coming), the cash reserves slipped away, and so did the friends.

Still, he left me with one excellent piece of advice. I said to him, "It's all right saying you become a multimillionaire by becoming a millionaire first, but how do you do that?"

He looked and smiled and said, "In my experience, I've discovered that looking for the million-dollar deal is very difficult. Getting a million dollars from one person is hard. However, getting one dollar from a million people is really not so difficult."

Like myself, my father was much more of an optimist than a physicist!

Chapter 24

Epilogue

The web moves quickly. During the time we've been writing this book, hundreds of updates have been made to Google's algorithm. You can find thousands of blog posts, articles, and columns about these and many other algorithmic updates just by doing a few Google searches for them. But beyond the changes that make their way into the SEO community's consciousness, it's important to remember the overall purpose of these changes in the first place: to improve the search results for end users and to root out spam and link schemes. And I applaud Google for it. For Google and other search engines, this means constantly evaluating and re-evaluating the hundreds of signals they use when examining content, links, and web pages.

As the engines get smarter, one of the unfortunate downsides is the amount of bad information that finds its way into the mainstream SEO community. Making decisions based on bad information can cost you dearly. After seeing so many companies waste large sums of money chasing poorly thought-out linking strategies, about a year ago I began a private strategy service called LinkMoses Private, which is a play on my industry nickname (I'm a notorious white hatter). LinkMoses Private is designed to teach you linking techniques that help with both click traffic and organic rankings today and for the long term. The goal of LinkMoses

Private is to help you improve and sculpt a more effective inbound link profile. This involves recognizing the wide variety of linking opportunities that are available to you, from social media to the deep web, if you know where to look and how to pursue them.

Resources

R ather than build a glossary from the terms in our book, we decided to list various SEO glossaries, as definitions vary. The following can help you better understand the world of link building.

LINK BUILDING AND SEO GLOSSARIES

https://www.linkbuildingwiki.com/glossary/

www.seobook.com/glossary/

https://moz.com/beginners-guide-to-seo/seo-glossary

https://www.seo-theory.com/seo-glossary/

https://www.sempo.org/?page=glossary

https://www.pageonepower.com/link-building-glossary/

https://www.searchenginewatch.com/static/glossary

https://www.kunocreative.com/blog/bid/66998/The-Inbound-Marketers-Link-Building-SEO-Glossary

About the Authors

ERIC WARD (1959–2017), aka LinkMoses, founded the web's first link-building and content-publicity service, NetPOST. Eric trail blazed the practice of link building by writing hundreds of articles, speaking at over 150 events, and lending his personal guidance and inspiration to up-and-comers. He developed linking strategies for PBS, Warner Brothers, The Discovery Channel, National Geographic, and TV Guide—not to mention Amazon, whose website he helped launch in 1995.

GARRETT FRENCH founded Citation Labs in 2011, and grew it into a 120-person operation specializing in enterprise-level link building. In 2016, he spun out another agency, ZipSprout, which delivers hyper-local links and event discovery. You can find him online at CitationLabs.com.

Index

A

Adamic, Lada, 264, 267
AdSense, 69, 255–257
affiliate links, 219–220
aggregated information, 258
aggregation, 68, 155–158
alias accounts, 235, 236–237
anchor text, 24
art-based assets, 216–217
asset relevance, 83
assets, 216–217, 219, 229–231
at-a-glance site quality, 84
audience research, 74–80
authority, 24
authority content, 20–21
authority of host name or URL, 82

B

backlink checker, 183–184, 185, 189
backlink manipulation, 248–254
backlink prospecting tools, 66–67
Barabasi, Albert-Lazlo, 264, 265–267
blogs, 17–18, 44–45, 79–80, 218
brainstorming opportunity types, 36–37
brand awareness, 220

brand building, 25–26
brand limitations, 203
brand mentions, 134–135
brand sponsorships, 196–198
broken link-building campaigns, 181–189
   about, 181
   broken-link outreach, 133–134, 186
   dead backlinks, pulling and qualifying, 185–186
   dead pages, reviewing, 183–184
   link equity salvage, 186–189
   outbound links, scraping, 182
   outbound links, verifying status, 182–183
   searching for links pages, 181–182
bulk backlink checker, 183–184, 185, 189
bulk outreach, 189, 191–194
business and marketing goals, 14
buying links, 233–242
   about, 233–235
   checking code, 242
   finding link partners, 238–340
   following up, 241